Books by J. Bryan, III

MERRY GENTLEMEN
(and One Lady)

MERRY GENTLEMEN
(and One Lady)

J. BRYAN, III

FOREWORD BY CASKIE STINNETT

Atheneum

NEW YORK

1986

The excerpt from Nunnally Johnson's letter to Frank Sullivan is from
The Letters of Nunnally Johnson, Alfred A. Knopf, Inc. Edited by Dorris
Johnson, copyright © 1981 by Dorris Johnson. Reprinted with permis-
sion.

Photos of Dorothy Parker and Arthur Samuels reprinted with permission
of UPI/Bettmann Newsphotos.

Library of Congress Cataloging-in-Publication Data

Bryan, J. (Joseph). 1904–
    Merry gentlemen and one lady.

    1. American wit and humor—History and criticism.
2. Authors, American—20th century—Biography.
3. Humorists, American—20th century—Biography.
4. Algonquin Round Table. 5. New Yorker (New York,
N.Y. : 1925) 6. New York (N.Y.)—Intellectual life.
I. Title.
PS438.B78   1985   817'.52'09 [B]   84–45610
ISBN 0–689–11533–4

To the memory
of these warm, witty, delightful
people—a small return for the
huge pleasure of their company

Think where man's glory most begins and ends
And say my glory was I had such friends.

YEATS

FOREWORD

By Caskie Stinnett

J. Bryan, III, the possessor of the most economic by-line in contemporary American literature since O. Henry, is in all other respects a genial and outgoing man whose natural taste is for the richer, riper qualities of life and whose manner conveys the spirit of one who knows how precious the passing moment is. The abbreviated signature is, I suspect, a cantrip since—as you will see as you read this book—his admiration for acts of this nature is limitless. A Virginian by birth and quite possibly by nature, he displays to the world an austerely chiseled countenance that conceals a mordant wit and a free-floating irreverence that is unsettling to those who have been betrayed into taking him at face value. He is a thinker, a sophisticate, an impressive storyteller, and a writer capable of putting a very special spin on the ball that sets him apart even in the rarefied company of the famous writers who inhabit the pages you are about to read.

Joe Bryan's literary domain recognizes no boundaries, its ken knows no compass. Over a period of a half century he has written biographies (of Admiral Halsey, P. T. Barnum, and the Windsors), verses that brought him a prize (from *Vanity Fair*), memoirs, travel articles, profiles, light essays, accounts of naval battles, newspaper editorials, theater criticism, book reviews, and—probably just to round things off—a short-short story. This wide-ranging work has been published in the leading magazines of the times: *The New Yorker, Holiday, The Saturday Evening Post, Reader's Digest, Esquire, Travel & Leisure, National Review, McCall's,* and other journals whose editors were attracted to the grace and wit of the Bryan style. Some of this writing appeared as books, some as journalistic dispatches, some as magazine articles; he has never found difficulty in accommodating his subjects to proper length. All tell the story at hand with no lost motion, no spinning of the wheels, no needless rhetorical flourishes.

I think that Joe Bryan is capable of putting down roots wherever he chances to be; he requires no extensive stay to get the feel of a place, to take bearings. The pieces in this book carry the reader from New York to Hollywood, with some side journeys to Outer Limbo and Hysteria. But what is most remarkable, of course, are the people one encounters, for Bryan has drawn for his readers a series of portraits of some of the keenest wits of our time, outrageous eccentrics whom he met with delight and writes about with glee. These were his friends—that group of writers connected one way or another with the Algonquin Round Table, and those drifting in and out of *The New Yorker* in its early days, plus a few others that he was drawn to, perhaps out of a dread of the commonplace.

There is nothing about these people—Benchley, Corey Ford, Marc Connelly, Dorothy Parker, et al.—that is alien to Joe Bryan's own spirit; in them he experiences an empathy and a sense of recognition. One suspects that he, too, is part Boswell, part Groucho Marx. Either that, or the implosion of comic genius and talent showered him with sparks and he became a cheerful casualty. Whatever the cause may be, the effect is pure good fortune; his friendship with the people he writes about permits him to send us dispatches from within the charmed circle. If there are lacunae in the text, if someone's favorite Benchley story does not appear, it doesn't really matter; there is enough here to adorn the subjects and to celebrate a view of life that, if not always reassuring, is almost always amusing.

I first met Joe Bryan many years ago when I was working on a magazine in New York, and had come to look forward to his contributions. There are certain writers—dismayingly few of them—whom editors cherish because of their understanding of the magazine and its needs, because of the originality of their proposals, and chiefly, of course, because of the unfailingly high quality of their writing. Joe Bryan was one of these. He had been lured to the magazine by my predecessor, but when I took over I went to great pains to see that he would sense no lack of warmth in the relationship, no decline of interest in his proposals and his contributions. Soon I found myself looking forward to his visits to the editorial office, and I would often hold him there, despite his restlessness, to talk, a talent that I soon grew to realize was as gratifying as the sureness of his writing style. His mind was a storehouse of fact and anecdote which accommodated instant retrieval, and his wit was warmed by an instinctual awareness of human frailty that struck me as being as much a part of a southern emotional economy as was his Virginia accent. Most of the pieces he wrote for the magazine were sophisticated essays, but all, one way or another, sought to puncture pomposity, to deflate the windy and the overblown, to separate the spurious from the real. There was a confidence in his manner, whether he was talking or writing; I never had the feeling that he was walking in the dark.

I live on a small island off the coast of Maine during all but the severe months of winter, and like all island dwellers I value guests more than most people. Sid Perelman, Marc Connelly, and some of the other people who appear in this book visited me there, but it was only recently that Joe Bryan arrived. For two days I sat on the sun deck and listened to him talk, getting up from time to time to top off his drink, and I don't think I have ever known two days of such total enthrallment. Dorothy Parker—the one lady in this book—once voiced the belief that wit has truth in it but that wise-cracking is simply calisthenics with words. It was wit that decorated Bryan's wisdom, and has caused me to yearn to have him back. Until he returns I will have to satisfy myself with this book. There is nothing I can say about *Merry Gentlemen (and One Lady)* that wasn't said much more gracefully by André Maurois: "Style is the hallmark of a temperament stamped upon the material at hand." Joe Bryan possesses style.

Knoxville, Tennessee
March 1985

ACKNOWLEDGMENTS

I am indebted to the Saratoga, New York, Public Library, which owns the copyright on Frank Sullivan's letters, for permission to quote from them.

To Finis Farr's sister, Mrs. Robert Dyer, for letting me draw on his letters and for lending me the photograph of him (taken by her son).

To Caskie Stinnett, for the deep massage he gives my shoulder in his foreword to this book; for letting me quote his two letters about Marc Connelly; and for the photograph of himself and Marc dancing (I expect you can call it that).

To Nunnally Johnson's widow, Dorris, for the use of his letters; for lending me the photograph of him with Lauren Bacall and Marilyn Monroe, and for letting me reprint portions of her accompanying letter.

To John Steinbeck's widow, Elaine, who owns the copyright on his letters, and to his agents, McIntosh and Otis, for permission to quote from them.

To Corey Ford's agents, Harold Ober Associates, for the same.

To the late Nat Benchley for correcting and amplifying what I had written about his father.

To George Bond's daughter Margo, for photographs.

To Hugh Troy's cousin Con, for giving me one of Hugh's "Sidewalk Superintendents" cards, and to Bill Sims and Howard Hunt for anecdotes about Hugh.

To John Falter's widow, now Mary Elizabeth Falter Jones, for permission to quote from his letter.

I am most grateful to them all.

CONTENTS

MERRY GENTLEMEN
(and One Lady)

ARTHUR H. SAMUELS

1888-1938

Artie, the Life of the Party

Mr. and Mrs. Arthur Samuels aboard ship, 1931
(UPI/BETTMANN NEWSPHOTOS)

I CAN remember how and when and where I met the subjects of all these sketches—all except one, the one who introduced me to many of the others. He was Arthur Samuels. I see him vividly, but I have no picture of our meeting. We both worked for Hearst (this was around 1934), though in different branches of that huge organization—Art was editor in chief of *House Beautiful*, I was managing editor of *Town and Country*. The offices of both magazines were in the same building, at 56th and Madison, so it's quite possible that my chief sent me upstairs to get Mr. Samuels's opinion on some question of policy, and we met then. No matter; it's not important; but Art Samuels quickly came to mean so much to me and my family that I wish I could make the record correct and complete.

He was forty-five then, sixteen years older than I, but he looked only thirty-five. Three things I noticed about him at once:

First, he was the cleanest, neatest person I'd ever seen. He was always freshly shaven; his suit was freshly pressed; the flower in his lapel was fresh; he never needed a haircut; his linen was crisp and spotless, his shoes polished.

Then, his grin, one that almost always turned into a fat, rich laugh that made him take off his glasses and wipe his eyes. I say *grin*, not *smile*, because *grin* carries an element of impishness. No, I'll change *impishness* to *deviltry*, for Samuels was New York's paramount and nonpareil needler, kidder, and tease. Alexander Woollcott once told me, "Being kidded by Art Samuels is like being tossed in a blanket—you never get a chance to catch your breath." How right Aleck was I found out soon and often and sometimes painfully.

The third thing I noticed may sound anticlimactic: it was his necktie, which was colored and striped like a coral snake. I knew it of old: it signified membership in Princeton's (and notably Scott Fitzgerald's) Cottage Club. So Samuels and I, above and beyond being Hearstlings, were also fellow Princetonians; he (it transpired) in the class of '09, I in '27. Moreover, both of us had been members of the musical comedy club, the Triangle. My only contribution to the shows was one unsingable lyric and a piece of another. But Art had played the piano in the club orchestra and had written songs *and* lyrics. Indeed, he had continued writing them after graduation—successfully, too. Schirmer had published two of his songs, and Harms two others, one of which, "Moonshine," Reinald Werrenrath had recorded for Victor. More than that, Art had collaborated on the score of a musical, *Poppy*, which starred the great W. C. Fields and ran on Broadway for over a year. Still more, he was married to a beautiful actress, Vivian Martin, who had starred on both stage (*Peter Pan, Officer 666*, etc.) and screen (*Molly Entangled, The Girl at Home*, etc.). This was the closest I had ever come to a celebrity in the world of entertainment—to *any* celebrity, in fact, since that intoxicating day in 1917 when I rode in the same elevator (Belvedere Hotel, Baltimore) with Jess Willard, the heavyweight champion boxer.

For all Art's talent, music was only a sideline, a hobby. His profession was journalism. He had been a special correspondent on the *Sun*, and then managing editor of *The New Yorker*, until he made the mistake of going to Europe on his vacation, and there received a cable from Harold Ross, the editor, firing him.* In 1931, Samuels became editor of *House and Field*, and a year later was put in charge of Hearst's *Harper's Bazaar*, where he stayed until 1934, when Hearst shifted him to *House Beautiful*. This was where I came in.

A single glance at Samuels and another at a copy of his magazine told you he was a perfectionist. Everything in his costume, from the knot of his tie to the hang, break, and depth of his trouser cuff, had to be exactly *so*. In his magazine, one typo, one inconsistent serial comma, one "river" in a block of print, gave the whole issue a C–minus and sentenced it to a pyre.

Alas for Samuels the gourmet and Samuels the oenophile! An issue of *House Beautiful* presently appeared with a plug in its shopping column for a new sort of ice bucket. A photo of the bucket accompanied the plug, and in the bucket was a bottle of Bordeaux, its shape and label not to be mistaken. *Bordeaux*! On *ice*! Samuels's rage was volcanic, his grief more poignant than the Twelve Apostles', his shame deeper than Hester Prynne's. Despite Aleck Woollcott's warning, I felt I knew Art well enough by then to dare an impertinence: I sent him a heavy, cracked, chipped beer stein, with a tag, "For your Ch. Beychevelle."

Like Aleck, Art was a master of the phony letter. (There was quite a run on phony letters in those days.) Aleck has told about the one he sent to Wanamaker's, in Philadelphia—rather, *pretended* he had sent—in response to Dottie Parker's request for a

---

* Ross would never fire anyone face to face; it was done either by message or through an unhappy, embarrassed subordinate.

credit reference. Samuels's specialty was the phony letter on the genuine letterhead. My wife and I once took him and Vivian to dinner at Lüchow's, where he introduced the headwaiter, Ernst Leute. A few days later I received a letter on Lüchow's stationery, expressing Ernst's pleasure at my acquaintance having made, and assuring me that all Mr. Samuels's friends he in highest esteem held. If ever I wanted a special table or a special dish, simply telephone him and Mr. Samuels's name mention. "But there was one small matter, Herr Bryan: in your so-happy evening with Herr and Frau Samuels, you have an item of $23 on the bill overlooked." Ernst would be obliged if I would attend to this at once. Perhaps I could bring the money down to 14th Street by taxi that afternoon?

I refuse to admit how close I came to not recognizing Samuels's wicked hand.

Our third child, Courty, was born in April 1936. By then we had come to love the Samuelses, and had learned how much the Samuelses loved children. They had none of their own, so this was an additional reason for asking Arthur to be one of Courty's godfathers. He beamed. His letter of acceptance, addressed to Courty himself, was a model of gentleness, tenderness, and affection. A void in his life (he wrote) had been filled—and filled perfectly. He looked forward to the christening, when he would have the joy of meeting his godson. His highest hope for Courty was that he had inherited a share of his mother's charm, good looks, and the sympathetic, responsive personality that Arthur so admired and which, frankly, he had found so irresistible. He had always felt close to her; now he felt closer than ever. In fact, confident that Courty was a man of the world, Arthur did not mind informing him—it would come out sooner or later anyhow—that their relationship was a good deal closer than that of godfather and godson. . . .

My wife and I never dared show the letter to any of our parents.

We put it away and gave it to Courty when he came of age.

Being fired from *The New Yorker* did not affect Arthur's happy relations with its founder and publisher, Raoul Fleischmann. Their friendship remained firm enough to survive the heavy strain to which Art's deviltry had once subjected it. Raoul and his wife, Ruth, were good hosts and they enjoyed entertaining at their house just outside Port Washington, Long Island. Their pride was a dozen dinner plates of Chinese export porcelain, magnificent pieces, which Ruth used as service plates on special occasions. Few guests failed to admire them, and their admiration often encouraged Raoul to tell how they had come into his possession.

Art had heard the account again and again. He knew it as well as he knew the pattern of the plates: gold edging, a dark blue stripe, and a heraldic scutcheon in the center. The morning before a dinner of the Fleischmanns', he happened to see a plate of roughly the same size, color, and pattern in the window of a cheap shop, and bought it. That night, he wore a double-breasted dinner jacket and tucked the plate into the waistband of his trousers. When the company went to the table, a surreptitious exchange for the real plate was easy and unnoticed. In a moment or two, as expected, Raoul was cued into his account. He had got no further than "It may interest you to know that this particular design—" when Samuels jumped to his feeting, shouting, "If I have to hear about this goddam china *once* more—" and picked up the cheap plate and slammed it into the fireplace.

Raoul went white. He stammered, "Art—! Art—!"

Samuels let a tense minute pass before he took the real plate from his waistband, grinning like a demon, flourished it in front of Raoul, and restored it to the table.

The summer of 1937, we had a beach cottage at Wainscott, Long Island. One of our neighbors was the delightful, mischievous Grace Hendrick. She had known and liked Samuels for years, and when we mentioned that he was spending the next weekend with us, she begged us to bring him to dinner on the Saturday, and for him to ring her when he arrived: "I'm going to have a problem that night," she explained, "and I'm hoping that Art can handle it for me. I won't say anything more. I don't want you implicated."

Her problem proved to be a pompous young man who tended to wrench the conversation around to his illustrious connections in Washington, and to expatiate upon them to the suffocation of everyone else present. (I have to call him something; "Mr. Winthrop" will do.) Sure enough, no sooner were we into the second course than Winthrop's fruity voice rolled down the table: "Cousin Charlotte was telling me in Washington only yesterday that—"

Samuels, bright-eyed, ingratiating, broke in: " 'Cousin Charlotte'? No, no. It would be too much of a coincidence . . ."

"I beg your pardon?"

"Oh, excuse me! My name is Samuels. My friends call me Artie, and I hope you will. And your name, sir? I didn't catch it."

The pompous man seemed to have difficulty believing his ears. This boor didn't know who *he* was? He disclosed his name with appropriate modesty and resumed, "Cousin Charlotte, as I was saying—"

But here was Samuels again, his face glowing with eagerness to be friends. "*I* have a Cousin Charlotte" he said proudly. "Do you suppose they could possibly—? Cousin Charlotte Schnartz, she is. Cousin Gus—her husband—has a little drugstore in Toledo—Toledo, Ohio, I mean—and I couldn't help thinking for a moment that they might be the same Charlotte, 'Charlotte' being such an unusual name, but then I remembered you said *your* Cousin Charlotte was in Washington, so I realized— Oh, I interrupted you, didn't I? Pardon! But you admit it would be strange"—making a gesture that embraced the whole table— "if Mr. Winston here and I turned out to be kin. Well, better luck next time, as I always say! Anyhow"—he beamed at the outraged gentleman and lifted his glass—"here's to us, Honorary Cousin!"

Samuels's act was so beautiful, from the fumbled name to the vulgar "Pardon!"—so innocent, with such a transparently sincere effort to be friendly, that only the most arrant snob could take offense. Well, this snob did, and matters weren't helped when he saw that Grace was laughing herself into hiccups.

Would you believe that this wretched, abandoned woman put Samuels up to his devilish tricks *again*, when he came to stay with us a month later? This time she had "chosen" a New York attorney, a partner in a haughty firm of private bankers. She never told us how he had offended her; his manner and appearance were sufficient offense. He was a feisty little man with lifts in his shoes; and his way of speech was abrasive enough to scour a grits pot. Most important, Grace said, he couldn't bear to be contradicted or corrected—and this was the area where she recommended that Samuels perform his acupuncture.

There was no trouble until halfway through dinner, when I heard the little man say, "But of course I couldn't expect you people to know anything about *that!*"

The look that Grace gave Samuels didn't actually ask, "What did I tell you?" It didn't need to. Nor did she actually add, "Quick, Arthur: the needle!" That wasn't necessary either. Samuels was ready to begin the operation.

He waited for a pause, then remarked, slowly and seriously, "Grace, I'd be interested to know if any of your other guests have read it. I mean, *You're Wrong About That.*"

"I'm wrong about *what?*" Grace asked. "*What* am I wrong about?"

Samuels patted her hand. "Not *you,* dear! It's the title of this book that everybody in town is discussing: *You're Wrong About That,* by Professor Wholecloth, Avery Wholecloth."

I thought he had gone too far with that name, but no one questioned it. He went on, "I was reading it coming out on the train this afternoon, and I can tell you it's a shocker! Wholecloth seems to be quite well-known and to have quite a rep—he's head of the psychology department at Northwestern—though frankly I've never heard of him myself." He looked around the table. "Perhaps one of you knows this extraordinary book?"

Somebody asked, "What's so extraordinary about it?"

"Well, his thesis is that a great many things we know to be true—at least, that we have always *believed* to be true—simply aren't so at all. I confess that some of them   "

Grace said, "Give us an example."

Samuels seemed to be searching his memory. "Let's see. . . . Yes, here's one. Do any of you gentlemen happen to be in law?"

The patsy snapped, "I'm an attorney. What about it?" The chip on his shoulder would have cut up into three cords of firewood.

Samuels said, "Well, sir, what would you say is the legal distinction between premeditation and malice aforethought?"

"Simple! Premeditation is—" I have forgotten his definition. I daresay it was correct even to the commas.

Samuels was all sympathy. "Just what *I* thought! But Professor Wholecloth"—now he put on a smirk that was part apologetic, part triumphant—"says we're *wrong* about that! He says that technically—"

"Wrong?" The little man repeated it in a strangled voice: "*Wrong?* Let me inform you, sir, that I am *not* wrong, whatever the opinion of your Blackstone from the boondocks!"

Samuels soothed him. "I'm sure you're not wrong, sir! *Sure* of it. Still, Wholecloth—I don't attempt to defend him, but he *does* cite an impressive number of authorities. If only I hadn't left his book on the train!" (The cunning rascal!)

Someone called, "Give us another."

"I'll try. Anybody here in the brokerage game?"

A man raised his hand.

Samuels addressed him: "In the transactions of the Exchange between 1930 and 1934, who profited more, the buyers or the sellers?"

Whatever the broker answered, Samuels quoted Wholecloth as saying he was "wrong about that." We had to understand (Samuels said) that he himself didn't "necessarily support Wholecloth's views"; he was "simply quoting"; but he had to admit that "the good professor" had "credentials that no fair-minded person could dismiss."

Next, somebody else was "wrong" about something else. Half the table was heating up now; the other half had twigged that it was a leg-pull and was enjoying it. Throughout, the feisty little attorney, like a minute gun, had continued to bark, "Damn it, I'm *not* wrong! I'm *right*! Damn it all—"

Grace saw that he was on the edge of an outburst and gave Samuels a knock-it-off signal: "Oh, dear, my poor confused head is spinning! Professor Holycross has turned everything upside down. I've had enough and I'm not wrong about *that*! Be an angel, Art, and trot over to the piano, and I'll send you a brandy."

Slowly the conversation became general.

Next morning, when the sun and surf had balmed bruised pride, Grace and Art admitted their guilt and were forgiven. It was premature in every respect. Samuels was an incorrigible recidivist, and no sooner had everybody trooped over to our house for lunch than— What happened was this: A high-nosed Boston lady (my wife and I didn't know her; one of our other guests had asked to bring her) bit off too many martinis and suddenly, unprovoked, attacked me for "the unspeakable oppression" to which we in Virginia were "still subjecting those helpless, lovable Negroes."

I could see that she was loaded and I was trying merely to slip her wild punches, when Samuels pulled up a chair. "I couldn't help overhearing your remarks, madam. I can't believe that you are conversant with the facts. Do you know Virginia well? . . .Ah, I thought not! I myself have often visited the Bryans on their ancestral plantation, and you have my word that the darkies there ["darkies"!] are sublimely happy. Banjos—fish fries—camp meetings—watermelons—possum—hoedowns—why, they live in a veritable Eden!"

I happened to know that Samuels had never been south of Baltimore in his life. I also knew—who better?—that the Bryans had no "ancestral plantation."

He pressed on, ignoring my scowl. "Oft have I—["Oft"! I ask you!] Oft have I seen Joe here's venerable body servant, old Uncle—er, Uncle Cab, break into a buck-and-wing out of sheer joy at the young master's return! . . .Dear old Unc' Cab! His skin was nearly as white as yours, madam—more of a yellow, really— but his heart was black."

The Boston lady frowned; something in that last sentence struck her as not quite right, but she was in no condition to puzzle it out. " 'Uncle Cab,' " she repeated. " 'Uncle Cab'. . . What a strange name!"

"An affectionate diminutive," Samuels explained. "Joe told me how he came by it. He was the grandson of a Massachusetts carpetbagger and a former slave woman. Right, Joe?"

I choked. I felt as if I were trying to swallow an overcoat button. I could only gasp, "Uh—"

"Thank you," Samuels said. "I thought I remembered correctly. His full name was Cabot Saltonstall, was it not? Yes, of course. Yes."

Much as I would prefer to forget it, another Sunday luncheon clamors for mention here. This one was not at my house—thank God!—so I had no responsibility for Samuels's behavior. Our hosts were Jack Baragwanath and his wife, Neysa McMein, who did those pastels of beautiful girls for the covers of *McCall's* and other magazines. Neysa was a blond goddess, calm and unflappable (I had thought) and far too wise (I had also thought) to allow Jack and Art, both of them notorious mischiefmakers, to sit at the same table. I was "wrong about that" on both counts. The other guests were the formidable lady novelist Mrs. Martha Mary Baker (I'll call her), my wife and myself, a couple whose name had slipped past me, and, to be sure, the detestable Samuels.

The Baragwanaths' house was at Sands Point, Long Island. The month was May, and the weather was sunny; so when Jack proposed that we have our cocktails on the terrace, with its view of Long Island Sound, Samuels was enthusiastic. "Come on, Neese!" he urged. "It's much too pretty for you to sit indoors tracing all day!"

Tracing! Another artist might have taken offense but Neysa just smiled. It may have been the last time she smiled that afternoon.

I'm not going to embroider this story. I'm going to get it over with as quickly as possible and move on to something less painful. Well, our second course was roast beef with thick gravy and mashed potatoes. Art and Jack helped themselves, but neither ate; they just puddled their potatoes and gravy. Neysa asked, "Are you two lissome ballerinas on a diet or something?"

Samuels smiled weakly. Absently, he let his fingers drop into the mudpie on his plate. "I'm sorry, Neese," he said. "I guess overwork brought it on. This headache—" In a gesture that implied both pain and exhaustion, he rubbed his mucky hands over his forehead and across his face, leaving—*ugh!* This was *Samuels!*—Samuels the fop, Samuels the immaculate dandy, the Samuels who would be mortified to discover a crumb of tobacco on his lip or a speck of dried shaving soap on his jaw!

Neysa cried, "Arthur!" She looked to her husband for help, but Jack couldn't speak: he could only dribble and bubble. He had crammed his mouth full—so full that a slobbered surplus of potatoes was sticking to his cheeks, and a rivulet of gravy was running down his chin.

Neysa managed to give the only possible order: "Leave the table, *both of you!*"

As they stood up, their expressions showed bewilderment and hurt: "What have *we* done?" Neysa added sharply, "*At once!*" and they slunk out, behind the screen to the pantry.

Mrs. Baker, I was to discover, had a royal way with a contretemps: it had never happened. She kept on eating, placidly, her eyes on her plate. The unidentified couple, obviously embarrassed, stared into the middle distance. I myself was using my napkin to disguise a laugh as a cough.

A *laugh?* Yes. Please don't tell me that there was nothing funny about this exhibition—that it was boorish, obscene, vulgar, and disgusting. It was all of those, I grant, but it was *funny*. I was there and I saw it. I also saw, a moment later, the two culprits stick their washed and wiped faces from behind the screen and announce, "If you *must* know, the game is called Fun With Food!"

Enough. It's time I turned (though reluctantly) from Samuels's deviltries and tried to bring this sketch into balance. To begin with, then, he was one of the kindest, most generous of men, a tireless comforter of the sad or lonely or needy. When Frank Sullivan, living alone in town, became ill and depressed, Samuels went to see him, stifled his protests, packed his bags, and hustled him over to his own comfortable apartment, where he and Vivian put him to bed, fed him, cosseted him, and surrounded him with merry companions. One weekend he and Vivian drove Sullivan out to our house in Manhasset. They hadn't alerted us, and we happened to be away. We knew that they had dropped in because we found a slip of paper in the lavatory, weighed down with a five-cent piece and inscribed, "For use of toilet. F. Sullivan."

Plainly, he was recovering his spirits—so much so that when a small pimple appeared on his forehead, Samuels did not hesitate to make the coarse diagnosis "a booze button," and to address and introduce him as "Spotty."

I left *Town and Country* early in 1937 to become an associate editor of *The Saturday Evening Post*. Arthur left *House Beautiful* that fall to become the executive producer at Station WOR. Six months later, in March 1938, he suddenly died. The last communication I had from him was a postcard, mailed in Düsseldorf. It showed a couple, helmeted and goggled, whizzing along on a motorcycle. Beneath the printed title, *Weekendsfahrt*, Arthur had written, "Yes, but a very quiet one."

APPENDIX I

Not for some time after Art's death did I ever wonder what his middle initial, *H*, stood for. When I found out, I could hardly believe it. Here was the perfect man-about-town, the embodiment of suavity and elegance, accustomed to such metropolitan attentions as "Your usual table, Mr. Samuels?" and "May we narrow the lapels an eighth of an inch, Mr. Samuels?" and "I have reminded the chef that you like it with a soupçon of tarragon, Mr. Samuels." This man, who had edited two of the most sophisticated magazines in America—this most urban of New Yorkers—had the most bucolic of middle names: Hiram.

If I had known that in time, and if Sullivan had, we wouldn't have failed to hail him, "Hey, rube!"

APPENDIX II

Raoul Fleischmann, the publisher of *The New Yorker,* was quiet and gentle, with a smile of singular sweetness. I repeat that when Art Samuels was fired, he and Raoul remained good friends. So did Raoul and I, when it was my turn to be handed the Black Spot. I liked Raoul and enjoyed him, and I was pleased when he proposed coming down to Philadelphia (I had moved to a suburb there when I joined the *Post*) to spend a night and play a round of golf at Pine Valley.

He came, we played, we had refreshments, and then—apropos nothing at all—Raoul remarked, "Did you ever wonder where the Fleischmann family fortune came from?"

No, I never had. I assumed it came from the yeast and gin with which the name was associated.

Raoul said, "Well, I'll tell you. We started as bakers. You've heard of 'a baker's dozen,' meaning thirteen? Yes? *Our* 'baker's dozen' was eleven."

ROBERT BENCHLEY

1889-1945

Bedlam Bob

Benchley at Leisure

I CAN date my meeting with Bob Benchley almost to the minute: about eleven o'clock on Saturday morning, November 14, 1936.

It was the day of the Yale-Princeton football game. A family I knew, Yale alumni to a man, had invited me, a lone Princetonian, to ride down to Princeton in their private railroad car. When I came aboard at Penn Station, the car was already so thick with blue feathers, blue armbands, and blue scarves and neckties and mufflers that I could hardly trample my way to the bar table, so I was happy to spy one other alien like myself: my friend John McClain, who had gone to Brown and Kenyon. John was sitting beside a man I didn't know, a man whose face was pale and damp, and who was holding a half-empty glass. Perhaps "holding" is the wrong word; "clutching" would be better; "restraining" would be best, because if he hadn't been restraining it, the glass would have leapt from his hand like a frog. The diagnosis was obvious: he was beating his wings in the grip of a pitiless and impacted hangover.

John introduced me: "Bob Benchley," and added, needlessly, "He's not well. Something he ate at breakfast, I expect."

Mr. Benchley denied it. "Couldn't have been! All I had was one aspirin, lightly grilled." He smiled wanly and subsided.

The train started. As it gathered speed, so did the betting and the drinking. Since Princeton was a slight favorite, I accepted the counsel of a few highballs and covered everything that was offered, chuckling to myself. Indeed, when business slackened, I revived it by giving odds that were irresistibly handsome. I was accommodating the last few Yalies when our train rattled out of the tunnel and into the Jersey sunshine. One beam struck the beveled edge of a window and threw prismatic colors—red, yellow, green, blue—onto Benchley's ankle.

It caught our eyes at once, but nobody spoke until McClain remarked casually, "They tell me if that stuff reaches the knee, the whole leg has to come off. Do you suppose it's contagious?"

"Oh, thank the Lord!" burst from Benchley. "I was afraid I was the only one who saw it!" I'll take my oath that his relief was genuine.

Never mind the game. The record shows that those lumpish Yale muckers—those Hark Ness monsters, those Yale fellows ill-met—defeated the slim, clear-eyed, clean-living Princeton lads, 26–23. I want to forget that and instead remember that this was the day I met one of the gods in my pantheon of humor. I had followed Robert Benchley's work in the old *Life* and *The New Yorker* since earliest times. I could recite long passages from his books. To me, he was the funniest writer alive—*American* writer (to take care of P. G. Wodehouse). And, as things turned out, one of the most unforgettable and delightful men I was ever to know.

* * *

A few months after our meeting, I started work on *The Saturday Evening Post*. The urge to write something about Benchley had already taken root in my mind and it grew steadily stronger as mutual friends—McClain, Art Samuels, Donald Ogden Stewart, and others—told me marvelous stories about his doings and sayings. At length I ventured to ask the *Post*'s editor in chief, Wesley Stout, if I might try my hand at a Benchley piece. Stout had reservations; he wouldn't give me a definite assignment, but neither did he turn me down flat. Brimming with perhaps foolish optimism, I began the research.

It was so much *fun*, with one delightful source handing me along to another—Marc Connelly to Aleck Woollcott to Neysa McMein—that I was loath to stop interviewing and get down to writing. My desk job was full-time: five and a half days a week and many of the nights; few hours and little energy were left for moonlighting. Because of this, it was nearly two years before I was able to write "The End."

What follows here is an expanded and thoroughly revised (with the generous help of the Benchleys' late elder son, Nat) versions of the two-parter, "Funny Man" (a title that I protested against in vain), that ran in the *Post* for September 22 and October 7, 1939. The illustrations by Gluyas Williams outshone the text.

*   *   *

Just beyond Grant's Tomb, almost hidden from the traffic on Riverside Drive, a fence encloses a pedestal and urn. The stone is pitted and the letters are faint:

ERECTED TO THE MEMORY OF AN AMIABLE CHILD

ST. CLAIRE POLLOCK

DIED 15 JULY 1797

IN THE FIFTH YEAR OF HIS AGE

Once a year, usually at dawn, Robert Benchley made a pilgrimage to the forlorn little grave. His companions read the inscription and commented on its pathos. Benchley did not respond. He was in tears, they were astonished to find, and more astonished when they realized that his tears were not for the Amiable Child, but for his own "wasted life," his "cowardice," his "weakness," his "failure."

Benchley was the most versatile humorist in America, and one of the most successful. Two months after he began his radio program, a national poll placed him sixth in personal popularity to Jack Benny, Edgar Bergen–Charlie McCarthy, Bing Crosby, Fred Allen, and Bob Hope, veterans all.

His movie series—*How to Sleep, How to Vote, An Evening Alone,* and so on—was the most profitable in the one-reel field, with the single exception of cartoons. In 1936, the Academy of Motion Picture Arts and Sciences awarded *How to Sleep* its trophy for the best short feature of the year.

His dramatic criticism in *The New Yorker* was gospel to theatergoers, and his humorous articles make up ten books that have sold a total of 120,000 copies. Stephen Leacock said of them: "None excel Robert Benchley in the ingenious technique of verbal humor. As a writer of nonsense for nonsense' sake, he is unsurpassed." Leacock might have made it, "As a writer and *practitioner*—" There was, for instance, the cable he sent back from Venice: STREETS HERE FULL OF WATER. ADVISE. (The last word is the master touch, the Benchley touch.) And another cable, sent from New York to Charles Brackett in Paris, at the end of May 1927, when the whole civilized world had been rejoicing for a week over Lindbergh's successful flight: LINDBERGH LEFT HERE EIGHT DAYS AGO. ANY NEWS? Brackett's magnificent reply was YOU MEAN EDDIE LINDBERGH?

Benchley was respected as a craftsman and idolized as a person. Not even a jailhouse cat had more friends. Headwaiters rushed up special tables for him, and taxi drivers fought for his patronage. He was one of the few celebrities whom gossip columnists never vilified (well, hardly ever; a *Daily News* columnist was a shocking exception).

Under the circumstances, his companions on the pilgrimage seem entitled to their first surmises: that he was either drunk or ill or, at the least, paying lip service to the tradition that all humorists are melancholy at heart. But Benchley was not given to histrionics. Besides, the catharsis was too violent to be other than genuine. Eventually his sincerity was accepted; in his own eyes he was a miserable man, feckless, doomed to frustration and failure. "Look at me: a clown, a comic, a cheap gagman! *There's* a career for you!"

"What did you want to be, Bob?"

"I wanted to be a social-service worker, and I wanted to write a history of the Queen Anne period."

That, too, was sincere. But it was only a minor contradiction in a character where anomaly was the norm, and inconsistency the standard.

The public expects all great wits to conform with Whistler's pattern of slim elegance. Benchley was an unstylish stout; his clothes looked as if they had just come out of a hot box. He hadn't even the expected air of hauteur. Instead, his "seamy lineaments" —as Alexander Woollcott spoke of them—exuded a bluster and a specious joviality reminiscent of W. C. Fields, but with the difference that Benchley's bluster never quite concealed the underlying apprehension. His expression was that of a man who knew that the Marines would land in time to give him a loaded cigar.

On his forty-ninth birthday, his elder son, Nathaniel, wired him: "Nice going!" It was a tribute to Benchley's scatheless flouting of every precept of health and hygiene. He treated his constitution as if it were a derby on the sidewalk. The only thought he gave it was when his increasing girth fretted him into buying a rowing machine; the day it was delivered, he shoved it under his bed— and left it. Dorothy Parker often inquired about "Caligula's galley," but Benchley had no comment. The pink of his physical condition was the pink of a ripe squash. Withal, he spent but one night in a hospital, in Hollywood. A mild case of flu sent him there, in the care of a young doctor who was eager to try the then new "wonder drugs," the sulfonamides. He gave Benchley two tablets, warning him, "We don't know everything about these drugs yet—there may be some minor side effects—but we're confident of their broad general value. Drink plenty of water. I'll see you later."

One of Benchley's visitors, his friend Charlie Butterworth, had heard it all. He bought a bottle of glue, cut open one of Benchley's pillows, and helped him stick the feathers down his back, from his shoulders to his knees. When the doctor returned, his patient was moaning feebly. "Those tablets—" he managed to gasp. "Doctor, they must have been—you don't suppose—"

The frightened doctor whipped back the sheets. . . .

This was the Benchley of popular renown, the merry-andrew, the wellspring of legends. But he saw himself in a gloomier role— not the master of high comedy, but the victim of low tragedy. King Lear lost a throne; Benchley lost a filling. Romeo broke his heart; Benchley broke his shoelace. They were annihilated; he was humiliated; and to his humiliations there was no end. His whole life was spent as a dupe of "the total depravity of inanimate things." One morning a knickknack would topple of its own accord and shatter on the floor; that night his bedroom slippers would crawl away and wheel around backward; next day a hinge would have turned inside out, he would have to pull a doorknob he had always pushed.

Inverse vision complicated the persecution. Benchley's eyes were like microscopes. Look at the raging ocean through a microscope, and you see a serene blur; look at a drop of water, and you see a seething horde of monstrosities. Benchley seldom concerned himself with the crises, the major duties and decisions of his life,

because he seldom recognized them as such; but the minute per-
plexities loomed so huge that he shrank from even attempting a
solution.

He gave an impromptu speech from the balcony of a Paris
hotel and held a crowd spellbound, but he would make half a
dozen round trips in an elevator before he could control his voice
and call out his floor. He saw a friend off to Europe and spon-
taneously sailed with him, without passport, money, or change of
clothes; but he would teeter on a curb for ten minutes, trying to
choose between this taxi and that. He telephoned from Hollywood to the ex-Kaiser at Doorn, on a sudden impulse to speak
German; but he would crumple sheet after sheet of note paper
before deciding whether to address an acquaintance as "Dear Mr.
Doe" or "Dear John."

His mind became a flea market of uncleared trifles, a dog
pound where mongrel problems interbred and multiplied. Because
he existed in this unique, continuous confusion, he tried to stan-
dardize himself by confusing everyone else. Banks and magazines
regarded him as Typhoid Mary's psychic twin, Bedlam Bob, the
chaos carrier. A check signed "Peter Rabbit Benchley" or "Rob
[picture of a horse]ert Bench[a funny face]ley" was part of his
cunning campaign. Some of his checks are collectors' items. A Mr.
Hetzler, who supervised his account, had one framed and displayed in his office. The endorsement ran, "Dear Bankers Trust
Company: Well, here we are in picturesque old Munich! Love
to Aunt Julia, and how about Happy Hetzler, the old Hetzler?
Yours in Zeta Psi, Don Stewart and I love you, Bob Benchley."

The New Yorker stopped being surprised when his weekly
column was wired in from Albany or delivered by messenger
from Philadelphia. A master procrastinator, his business motto,
plain above his desk, was "The Work Can Wait." It was the sign-
post to a maze of evasions. When an editor telephoned him for a
promised piece of copy, reminding him that it was long overdue,

Benchley was indignation itself: "What? Hasn't that boy got there *yet?* I sent him off an hour ago—more like an hour and a half! If he doesn't arrive in fifteen minutes, call me back." His telephone had a cutoff switch.

Editors have had their revenge, even though accidentally. Arthur Samuels once told Benchley the story of a Mr. Mandelbaum and his family, picnicking in a grassy dell on Long Island. The rest is familiar: an angry gentleman rushes up, brandishing a putter, and asks what they think they're doing.

"Picnicking," said Mr. Mandelbaum pleasantly. "Have some egg?"

The gentleman choked. "I am Thomas Lamont [as Samuels happened to tell it], president of this golf club, and I demand that you get off this green immediately!"

"Well," observed Mr. Mandelbaum, "this is a hell of a way to get new members!"

Next day Benchley's phone rang. "Mr. Benchley? This is Thomas Lamont—"

Benchley laughed. "Well, Samuels, it's a hell of a way to get new members!"

"Mr. Benchley," the voice said patiently, "this is Thomas Lamont. My family and I have just come back from a Caribbean cruise. We took a number of your books along and we enjoyed them so much, I wonder if you would autograph them for us?"

Another person might have babbled something tedious and implausible, but not Benchley. The futility of explanation was taught him in France, when he tried to mail a package home. The official read the address aloud: "Boston, Massachusetts, U.S.A.," and looked up the postage in one of his registers. "Boston, Georgia," he murmured, as his finger moved down the list, "Boston, Indiana; Boston, Kentucky . . . Boston, Massachusetts, *n'existe pas!*" He slammed the book with intransigent finality and beckoned to the next customer.

Weddings were Benchley's special bane. He never managed to get through one unscarred by mischance. At his own, he absently supplied a single bouquet for the two bridesmaids. At Jock Whitney's, where he was best man, his only opportunity to shave came on the embankment at the North Philadelphia railway station. At Don Stewart's ushers' dinner, he mistook a cellar door for the door to a telephone booth and tumbled down the stairs, fracturing his kneecap.

The most solemn occasions trailed off into these anticlimaxes. When a friend asked him to appear in court as a character witness, Benchley spent hours selecting the costume most likely to impress the jury with his solid worth. He finally decided on a severe blue suit, black shoes, and stiff collar. As he took his place, an attorney whispered, "Your necktie—er—" He had forgotten to put one on.

He was leaving the staid Century Association one night when he saw his name on the bulletin board. Furious, he rushed to the club office and shouted, "I've always paid my dues right on the nail and I don't intend—"

"Mr. Benchley, if—"

"—being posted on account of some stupid clerical error! What's more—"

The manager got a word in at last: "If you'll look at the board again, Mr. Benchley, you'll see that your name is not there for delinquency, but as a new member of the nominating committee."

After weeks of house hunting in Hollywood, he discovered an ideal apartment, comfortable, convenient, and modest in rental. He was so overjoyed that, back for a last night at his expensive hotel, he telephoned a friend in London to share the news. Just as the connection was made, he fell asleep, and his forty winks ticked away at so many dollars per wink that he awoke to find himself in hock to the hotel. He couldn't leave until his bill was paid, and he couldn't work to pay the bill for worrying about it.

His native Worcester, Massachusetts, made him an honorary fire chief in 1937 and presented him with a helmet. It was his proudest possession. He was wearing it at his typewriter one evening in his New York apartment when a visitor dropped in.

"The old smoke eater himself, eh? Did you save the chee-ild?"

"Sure," said Benchley. "You know me: Dauntless Bob. I swarmed up the ladder and—"

"Up? You mean *down*, don't you?"

It took a moment to straighten things out. The visitor had naturally assumed that Benchley was fresh from fighting the fire that had just destroyed a suite two floors below.

Each day added its tittle to the evidence that he was misfortune's fool. Half of his mind recoiled from accepting it as a fact, but the other half rejoiced. It recognized in these experiences the raw material of humor, and it taught him to use the catalyst of his genius. Like cross-eyed Ben Turpin, he made capital of a handicap. A Benchley short is simply the refinement of a Benchley humiliation. It is commotion recollected in tranquillity. Yesterday's tragic ineffectuality has become today's comic effect.

Roy Rowland, his director, said that he could shoot a passable picture simply by following Benchley around and eavesdropping with a camera. They had no gagmen, no file of jokes, almost no rehearsals. Benchley didn't have to memorize his lines because he didn't write any; he made them up as he went. If he fumbled, Rowland told him, "Get that *worried* look, Bob!" and Benchley worked from effect to cause. His imagination supplied a phrase or a bit of business, his talent for mimicry conveyed it, and the flow resumed.

When they made *An Evening Alone*, the first scene was taken on a Tuesday morning, the last on that Thursday afternoon. He once ripped off three shorts between Monday and Saturday, although he played a dual role in one of them and had to make forty complete alternations of costume. He established his speed record with *The Love Life of the Newt*; it look ten hours.

When he first went to work for M-G-M, someone discovered that he never used his office. Another was assigned him, larger and more luxurious. Benchley still stayed away. Finally he was prevailed upon just to drop in and look it over. He professed to be delighted. That afternoon he returned with an armful of charts, graphs, maps, and blueprints, hung them on the walls, stuck them full of varicolored pins, and never set foot there again. He worked at home because an office represented discipline and was therefore intolerable—the explanation is that simple. So is the explanation of his insisting, in his contract, that he receive no personal publicity whatever. He regarded himself as a writer, not as an entertainer. More important, he was modest to the point of self-abasement.

A friend of his once remarked to Marc Connelly that Benchley didn't consider himself a success on the radio.

"What does he know about it?" Connelly asked. "As long as I've known that guy, he's never had a good word to say for Benchley."

Independent, modest, or plain perverse, he was the outstanding no-man in Hollywood, utterly indifferent to its products, personnel, and conventions. He made no bones about his reason for working there: it paid him more than he could earn anywhere else. He kept a packed suitcase ready for instant flight to New York the moment he felt that another day in Hollywood would drive him up the wall. A Renaissance hacienda with a barbecue pit, rifle range, and private zoo was considered an indispensable index to his salary bracket, but Benchley lived on the wrong side of the social tracks in an apartment that had only one entrance. His friends became used to seeing icemen and grocery boys saunter through his living room. The one jarring note in this simple strain was his butler-cook-chauffeur (Benchley never learned to drive a car), a Viennese whom he engaged on the strength of his having played the role of Judas Iscariot in Reinhardt's production of *The Miracle*.

Although Benchley was popular and gregarious, he took no part in the glitter set. His conception of hell's half-acre was a swarm of Hollywood dreamers prattling about the movies as a "medium of artistic expression"; he himself ranked them back of tattooing. The only movies he ever saw of his free will were his own shorts and, more rarely, a feature picture in which he had been cast: even then he went only to make sure he didn't repeat himself.

The wedding that was responsible for his fractured kneecap was also responsible for his first Hollywood job. It came through another member of the wedding party, Walter Wanger, then a power at Paramount. This was in the summer of 1926, and Wanger suggested that since Benchley's duties as theater critic didn't resume until fall, he might like to try a short hitch in Hollywood. (His agent was Myron Selznick. Their contract, in which each was "the party of the first part," simply said, "I agree," over their signatures.)

Benchley, who hadn't read a dozen mystery stories in his life, found that he was expected to cook up the plot of a murder on a houseboat. He managed to fake it well enough to be offered another job the following summer. He took that too. And he might have continued as a plot carpenter and handyman if Tom Chalmers, of Fox, hadn't already resolved that he should act in the movies as well as write them. Benchley dodged for a year and a half before Chalmers finally ran him to earth. Too exhausted to raise fresh objections, he dragged out a standby speech, "The Treasurer's Report," and recited it at the Astoria studio one day in January 1928. That night he sailed for Europe.

Nobody was sanguine about the prospects. Benchley was a

novice in front of a camera, and this was the first all-talking motion picture ever made. But as soon as Chalmers saw the rushes, he knew what he had. Benchley was three days at sea when he received a radiogram: COME BACK AND MAKE SOME MORE. TOM.

The series eventually added up to forty-five. But for Chalmers's pertinacity, it might never have started. But for someone's pertinacity, time after time, Benchley himself might never have started. He fought off radio for five years, and contracted to broadcast only after months of refusing to answer a tobacco manufacturer's importunities. When they wired him, "What do you smoke?" he answered, "Marijuana." Someone had to lure him or boot him along every step of his career. He was less a master of his fate than a stowaway aboard it. The fact that each change turned out to his advantage did not console him. "If they had just let me alone," he complained, "I might have been fire chief of Worcester, instead of only honorary fire chief."

He was born there on September 15, 1889. The Benchleys were Welsh, his mother Scotch-Irish, but both families were typical New England—plain, severe, and devout. His brother, Edmund, thirteen years older, was finishing his last year at West Point when war was declared against Spain. The class was graduated prematurely and ordered to Cuba. Edmund was killed in his first engagement, at San Juan Hill.

Robert went to Phillips Exeter Academy and on to Harvard. He had none of the background or qualities that make for immediate celebrity around the Harvard Yard. His family was not rich or fashionable. He did not enjoy a prep-school reputation as an athlete or scholar. He was not a rakehell or a picturesque eccentric. His face was orthodox, and his clothes were nondescript. In short, he was merely Benchley, Robert Charles, '12—shy, slight, and rather bewildered.

His favorite recreation was a good walk with a friend who

could discuss Thoreau or Carlyle. On rainy afternoons he pulled chest weights in the gym and trotted around the track. After tea he practiced on his mandolin. After dinner he studied and read until midnight. Next to last, he wrote up his diary and expense account, then looked through a dictionary for half an hour, memorizing definitions. He never drank, smoked, or gambled during his whole college life; his budget did not allow it, and he did not enjoy it. Daily chapel was voluntary, but he attended often. Occasionally he ushered at Sunday chapel. He joined Phillips Brooks House—the university YMCA—and headed a boys' club. Twice he went to Chautauqua meetings.

An undergraduate body has little appetite for youths apparently so insipid. It labels them "christers" and regards them with distaste when it regards them at all. But it began to appear that Benchley, christer or not, had a certain humor, a certain merry madness, that his classmates liked.

With an umbrella as a pointer and a napkin as a screen, Professor Benchley, the celebrated economist, gave an illustrated lecture on the woolen-mitten industry: "Our first slide shows that in 1904, it took 1487 man-hours to produce 1905, which, in turn, required 3586 man-hours to hold its own. This made 3,000,000 foot-pounds of energy, a foot-pound being the number of feet in a pound. This is, of course, all per capita . . . Next slide, please! . . . I'm afraid my assistant has it in upside down . . . There! That's better!"

Speeches by Senator Benchley, the Reverend Mr. Benchley, and Captain Benchley, daring leader of the Benchley-Gleeber Expedition, were cut from the same crazy quilt. Word of them spread; so did Benchley's popularity. When the forgotten freshman had become a social senior, he read this headline in the New York *Herald*:

ROBERT C. BENCHLEY MOST ACTIVE
MAN IN ORGANIZATION LIFE
OF UNIVERSITY

The story ran: "—holds the distinction of being the champion club member of the university, not alone for this year but for the last half score of years." He starred in the Hasty Pudding Club's annual production, but what pleased him most was being made president of Harvard's comic magazine, the *Lampoon*. He had been elected to its staff as an artist, not as a writer. His drawings were easy to identify; every face in them looked like his own. The first that the *Lampoon* published showed two scrubwomen near a garbage can; one of them was asking, "Ain't it offal, Mable?" The second showed Siamese twins, with the title "A-Men."

Benchley was proud to see his work in print, but hardly thrilled. It was not as if this were his professional debut. As far back as 1903, when he was fourteen, his bold grouping of a Pilgrim Father, a blunderbuss, and a turkey, to symbolize the Spirit of November, had won a citation from the St. Nicholas League.

Despite all his activities and despite the profligate indolence of his statement "I took the 'classical course,' which meant that I had no classes on Fridays and none before eleven in the morning," he managed to obtain an excellent, if random, education. When the fad for intellectual parlor games flourished in the 1930s, Benchley easily held his own against Herbert Bayard Swope, the polymath former editor of the *World*. He couldn't direct his education toward a definite goal because he couldn't choose one. He hovered over French for a while, with the idea that he might teach it at Groton, but finally alighted on international law, in preparation for a diplomatic career.

Only his irrepressible perversity saved the State Department from this outrage. An attack of grippe hit him just before his final exam in the course, and he sat down to it with a temperature of 103°. Worse, its key question concerned the Newfoundland Fisheries Case, about which he knew nothing whatsoever. His only hope was to "take a long shot" (according to his diary) and discuss the case from the viewpoint of a fish. His professor was not amused; he gave Benchley a resounding F. (There had been a coolness of the same sort at Exeter, when he was required to write an exposition of how to do something practical. His paper—luridly illustrated by the author—was entitled "How to Embalm a Corpse.")

Graduation found him still at loose ends. His only resolution was negative, but it was firm: "I'm not going to be a funny man all my life." A photograph taken that summer shows his earnestness. He might be posing for the stock cartoon of a fledgling graduate, ready to tilt at the world with his furled diploma as a lance—not the world of material success, but the world of privilege and inequality.

Meanwhile there was the question of finding a charger. He tried seven of them in the following nine years and, like Stephen Leacock's Lord Ronald, "he rode madly off in all directions."

His first job was as secretary to the director of the Boston Museum of Fine Arts, translating French catalogues. He was fired within a month. His next was with the Curtis Publishing Company, in the New York office of its advertising department. Richard Walsh, one of the executives, and a former editor of the *Lampoon*, remembered a speech of Benchley's at a *Lampoon* dinner and hired him on the strength of it. The job required him to put out a Curtis house organ and do general promotion work. When he came to edit a survey that began, "The automobile industry has three phases: its past, its present and its future. It is now emerging from its past and entering its future," he wrote on the margin "Great thoughts of great men" and put it on Walsh's desk.

If Walsh had treated this irreverence as it deserved, both would have profited. The office would have settled back into its routine, and Benchley would have struck his true line that much sooner. But Walsh believed that Benchley with tongue in cheek was abler than most of the sanctified. The trouble was, Benchley could not keep his tongue in his cheek. The announcement of a forthcoming staff dinner in Philadelphia led him to believe that it was time for another speech. He knew that Curtis had recently opened a branch office on the Pacific Coast and was eager to ingratiate itself with a certain San Francisco advertising agency. He also knew that none of his associates had ever met the agency's president, a Mr. Constantine. So, as "Mr. Constantine," magnificent in a red beard, he sat at the speakers' table.

Walsh and the toastmaster were in on the plot, but no one else. Not even Cyrus H. K. Curtis himself, who sat on Benchley's right.

"I've just returned from Denver," Mr. Curtis began. "A remarkable city, Mr. Constantine. Are you familiar with it?"

"Denver, sir? Why, my brother lives there!"

"Indeed? May I ask his business?"

"Burlap," said Benchley firmly. "He's in the burlap game."

Walsh would have been warned right then that hell was going to pop. He would have exposed Benchley at once or canceled the speech. But Walsh was at another table, and the toastmaster could think of no other way to break up the dangerous conversation than by introducing their distinguished guest.

"Mr. Constantine" opened with some perfunctory compliments to the Curtis organization and, on behalf of the Golden West, extended a welcome to its new branch. For their own sake, however, he wished to add a few words of advice: Don't think they were going to get away with the same stuff out there that they'd been pulling here in the East! Not by a long chalk! For instance—

Benchley knew just enough about the advertising department to flick its sore spots. The toastmaster signaled him to tone it down, but when Benchley began a speech, he began shooting the rapids. There was no turning back:

"I'm not representing only *my* agency. I'm representing the whole agency field. For years now, you fellows have been running over us roughshod, and we're not going to stand for it any more! You give us a fair rattle and roll, and we'll shoot square with you, but keep on this way, and we'll throw our business where it's appreciated. That statement is signed 'John J. Constantine,' and you can paste it in your hat!"

He glared around him, then grinned, ripped off his beard, chanted, "Heaven will protect the working girl," and sat down amid tumultuous silence.

The conventions of business fiction demanded that Benchley be fired for his impertinence or promoted for his frankness. Legend favors the former; both are false in fact. He lingered on for several weeks—whenever Mr. Curtis encountered him thereafter, he addressed him punctiliously as "Mr. Constantine"—until Walsh persuaded him that his peculiar talents were being wasted in the job. He resigned in the spring of 1914: "Curtis stayed in Philadelphia in its small way, and I went elsewhere."

"Elsewhere" was back to Boston, disheartened and in desperate search of a respite from the long pull devil, pull baker that his conscience had been undergoing. He found it when the Harvard Appointments Office placed him with the Russell Paper Company as a social-service worker, charged with organizing clambakes and bowling matches for employees of the company's five mills. At peace at last, he married Gertrude Darling, in June 1914. They had met at grammar school in Worcester. "I was eight," Benchley said, "and my life had been a shambles until then. You know, wild oats and all."

Their first child was born in November 1915. While Benchley was waiting for the obstetrician's report, he read *The Saturday Evening Post* for November 13. His wife kept it, with the play-by-play notes he scribbled through one of the stories (its title was, inappropriately enough, "A Disappearing Bridegroom"):

Decided to begin this at 12:15.

12:27. GAME CALLED. Nurse (a new one) comes in and asks my name. "Benchley." Well, Miss Erbstadt just telephoned down & said the baby has just arrived and they are both all right. She said she didn't know whether it was a boy "or what it was!" "Both all right" is more to the point. [Here a wild scrawl labeled: "relieved tension!"]

12:32. Another nurse says she thinks she said a boy, but not sure. It ought to be fairly easy to ascertain before long.

12:35. A Boy! and love from the Wife! Yea! Nurse tried to tell me twins, but I was a sly dog and didn't bite.

They named him Nathaniel.* He was a week old when Benchley was fired again: "Mr. Richard Russell, my boss, took me aside and said that the directors felt that the boys had had enough class."

Earl Derr Biggers, the creator of Charlie Chan, was then writing for the Boston *Traveler*. He was a friend of Benchley's and also of F.P.A.—Franklin Pierce Adams—who conducted the famous column "The Conning Tower" for the New York *Tribune*. Biggers wrote Adams, Adams came to see Benchley, and Benchley was told to report to the *Tribune* office on New Year's Day. His salary would be forty dollars a week.

He had published nothing since his graduation. The prospect of returning to New York and making a career of writing filled him with enthusiasm. To his distress, he was assigned to compiling obituaries, but his chance came in a few months. Adams was made editor of the *Tribune*'s Sunday supplement and took Benchley along at a raise of $2.50 to do a weekly humorous arti-

* Mr. and Mrs. Nathaniel Benchley's son Peter would be the best-selling author of *Jaws* and *The Deep*.

cle. For the first time since his *Lampoon* days, he was encouraged to follow his natural inclination.

The staff of the supplement included Irwin Edman, later of Columbia's philosophy department. Edman was a sensitive, sympathetic young man, so Benchley and Adams staged a periodic scene for his benefit. It began with Benchley coming in late.

"Bankers' hours!" Adams observed to the ceiling. "The sooner some playboys I could name get it into their heads that this is a newspaper office and not a lah-di-dah club—"

Benchley flared up. "If you've got anything to say to me, Adams, say it to my face!"

"You're damn right I've got something to say to you, Benchley! Go to the cashier and get your money!"

Here tenderhearted Edman always interceded. He took Adams aside and begged him to give the lad another chance. "He doesn't mean what he's saying. Besides, he's got a wife and baby."

Adams consented to forget the offense this once. He strode over to Benchley's desk and gruffly offered his hand. "Sorry, old man. I was hasty."

Benchley was no less magnanimous. "This is very handsome of you, old man. The fault is mine. I provoked you."

Next morning he was late again. As he came in, Adams shouted, "Don't take off your coat! Is this your idea of ten o'clock? You're fired!"

"You can't fire me!" Benchley shouted back. "I've already quit!"

Once again Edman would intercede. Once again Adams would let himself be persuaded against his better judgment. And, the following week, the scene would be rehearsed once again.

It was a happy year. Benchley was meeting convivial people, he liked his work, and his weekly articles were steadily strengthening his reputation as a humorist. So were his new friends. They arranged for him to address smokers and banquets, and saw that he was paid for it.

One of his speeches was at a banquet of the Navy League, in Boston. He was introduced as Josephus Daniels's chief assistant, a last-minute substitute for the Secretary. His subject was "Prohibition and the Navy."

"Grape juice," said Benchley, "is only our opening gun. Before we're through, we will have driven even the *memory* of vile spirits from our jolly jack-tars."

The more choleric sea dogs choked on their Madeira, but Benchley continued, "We are already making plans to have tea—choice of milk or lemon—and cakes—choice of cookies or ladyfingers— served on the mizzen hatch at ten bells p.m. Perhaps I should explain that this is navy parlance for twenty minutes past four."

Somebody guffawed. The barometer rose. Derringers were uncocked. The speech proceeded.

But as 1916 wore into '17, the *Tribune*'s jingo policy drove all humor out of Benchley's head. His hatred for war was violent. It was the one text that could utterly upset his critical balance. Any book or play, no matter how inept, that condemned war won his most fervent praise. That April, leaving no word at his office, he went to Charlestown, Massachusetts, and from there retraced a part of Paul Revere's route to Lexington, stopping at intervals to ask this question: "How do you feel about our going into the war?"

The replies were almost identically incredulous: "You mean the war in *Europe?*"

He bolted back and wrote his story at white heat. The supplement published it. He was fired the day it appeared.

Adams got him a temporary job as press agent for William A. Brady and Grace George, "but neither of them ever knew it." His next two years were desolate. He was not drafted because of his dependent family. The only service he saw was as publicity secretary to the Aircraft Board in Washington—rather, as *un*-publicity secretary; his duty was to keep news of airplane manufacture out of the press.

In April 1918, a new managing editor of the *Tribune* took him back to run the rotogravure section, but it didn't work out: "I passed the boy carrying my discharge just as I was taking my resignation to the front office." He spent the rest of the year in the publicity department of the Liberty Loan Committee.

Meanwhile he had been landing occasional articles in *Vanity Fair.* Its editor, Frank Crowninshield, liked their freshness and originality. In April 1919, he hired Benchley as managing editor, at a hundred dollars a week.

That didn't work out, either. But it was at *Vanity Fair* that he first met two other newcomers, Robert E. Sherwood and Mrs. Dorothy Parker. All that the meeting lacked was thunder, lightning, and a bubbling caldron.

When Benchley finished at Harvard in 1912, he looked like the stock cartoon of a young graduate. When he began at *Vanity Fair* in 1919, he looked like the stock cartoon of Mr. Average Taxpayer. Here it was spring, but those lumps bulging under his socks could mean only long woolen drawers. A heavy dew was enough to bring him out in overshoes. He caught the 8:04 from Scarsdale every weekday morning and went home on the 5:37, usually laden with brown-paper parcels. If he bought a newspaper or a stamp, he entered the cost in his expense book. He was the leader of a boys' club—the Seagulls A. C.—in an East Side settlement house, and was an active member of the Society for the Improvement of Urban Conditions Among Negroes. He still did not drink, smoke, or gamble, and when Dorothy Parker mentioned that she had been to a cocktail party, he was aghast.

"Mark my words," he warned her—and these were his exact words—"alcohol will coarsen you!"

The staff of *Vanity Fair* could conceive no reason why Crowninshield had picked this stick-in-the-mud as managing editor. Nor could Benchley conceive why he had been saddled with such a photograph editor as Bob Sherwood. It would have taken a crystal ball as vast as the dome of the Capitol to see in Sherwood the future author of two Pulitzer Prize–winning plays, *Idiot's Delight* and *Abe Lincoln in Illinois*. Benchley knew only that he had been on the board of the *Lampoon*, but had resigned from his class to enlist in the Canadian Black Watch, and had been gassed. He was preternaturally tall and thin, wore a rakish straw hat, and was suspected of frequenting Broadway cabarets. When he disclosed that he was the "Robert Sherry" who had published two popular songs—one beginning

> Roses flower in Lancashire,
> In my bower in Lancashire,

and the other,

> Reuben, Reuben,
> Where have you been?

Benchley took alarmed counsel with his drama critic, Mrs. Parker, who was as tiny and wistful as Sherwood seemed ogreish. She had recently been transferred to *Vanity Fair* from *Vogue*, where her wit had been exercised on coining for fashion illustrations such titles as "Right DRESS!—for Milady's motor jaunt." Alexander Woollcott later described her as "a blend of Little Nell and Lady Macbeth," but in 1919 she had written none of the verses or short stories that now make up eight books; and she had yet to fire one of those shots heard round the world—"That woman speaks eighteen languages, but can't say 'No' in any of them."

Mrs. Parker, too, was abashed by Sherwood; though Benchley

himself, in her finicky opinion, was something less than winsome. He was not at all the kind of person that his hilarious pieces in the Sunday *Trib* had led her to expect, but at least he was a known quantity, whereas that wild-looking young Sherwood was still an X. She and Benchley began having an occasional lunch together. One day they were surprised to find Sherwood waiting for them. "Look here," he said awkwardly. "Would you mind if I walked with you? And—uh—would you mind—uh—if I walked *between* you?"

His explanation came presently. A troupe of midgets playing at the Hippodrome down the block had discovered that he passed them every day at the same time. For a week, now, they had been lying in ambush for him, and as soon as his six-feet-six appeared, a pair of the smallest had flanked him and paced him to his restaurant, shouting, "Hey, Legs! How's the weather up there?" and when they crossed under the Sixth Avenue El, "Low bridge, Legs!"

His bodyguards invited him to lunch. Later, Mrs. Parker came to Benchley's office. "I was wrong," she said. "He's not tough. He's just as scared of us as we are of him. I think he's nice."

"I think he's one of the nicest guys I ever saw," said Benchley.

The three of them mixed as perfectly, as inseparably, and as explosively as saltpeter, sulphur, and charcoal. Although they were bringing a new wit and alertness to *Vanity Fair*, the office efficiency expert, Mr. Wurzburg, presently found himself wondering if these qualities were not being attained at the sacrifice of others even more valuable—discipline, for instance.

There was the time Wurzburg posted a notice forbidding employees to speculate about one another's salaries. Immediately, Benchley, Parker, and Sherwood splashed "$27.50 per" on huge placards and wore them about their necks. There was also the time that Wurzburg instructed the staff to report at eight thirty in the morning instead of the usual nine o'clock. Purposely late the very next day, Benchley was asked for an explanation. He was happy to give it. On a slip of paper hardly larger than a playing card, he wrote, "I would have been in plenty of time—early, in fact—but as I was passing the Hippodrome, a man rushed up to me and shouted, 'The lions have escaped! Help us!' Nobody with a drop of red blood in his veins could have disregarded such an appeal. With a prayer for the women and children who might be torn to pieces in front of my very eyes, I flung off my coat and joined the pursuit . . ." It led to the bottom of the paper, around the margin, over to the back, and around and around again—hundreds and hundreds of words in his minuscule handwriting.

Seven months of this impertinence was all that Wurzburg could endure. On his complaint, Crowninshield fired Sherwood as the ringleader, and warned Benchley and Mrs. Parker that they were on probation. It lasted only a few days, until the morning that the same mail brought two letters to Crowninshield's desk.

The first was from Florenz Ziegfeld, producer of *Caesar's Wife.* He quoted from Mrs. Parker's recent review: "Miss Burke plays her lighter scenes rather as if she were giving an impersonation of Eva Tanguay." Mr. Ziegfeld wanted it understood that he was not swayed by the fact that Miss Burke happened to be his wife, but this sort of thing was bad for the whole American theater. The second letter was from David Belasco, producer of *The Son-Daughter.* He too quoted from a review by Mrs. Parker: "Last season, in the exuberance of youth, I used to think that no play along the lines of *East Is West* could possibly be worse; that was before the dying year brought *The Son-Daughter.*" Mr. Belasco, too, wanted some things understood.

All in all, it was a case, in Saki's phrase, of "cows buzzing round a gadfly." Crowninshield concluded that the greatest good of the greatest number would be served if *Vanity Fair* engaged a more amiable critic. He informed Benchley that Mrs. Parker was being given two weeks' notice.

Benchley's only income was his salary, and he now had two

sons, the younger—Robert Charles, Jr.—only four months old, but he told Crowninshield that his conscience would not let him work for a magazine that refused to support its critics' honest opinions. *Vanity Fair* saw the last of him and Mrs. Parker in January 1920.

They took an office in the Metropolitan Opera House, a triangular room with space enough for a table, two chairs, and two typewriters. The only other furniture was a gigantic mirror. Since the room seemed to lack the personal touch, they soaped on the mirror, "Today's Special: Yankee Pot Roast, 45¢," hung up a pennant with the word "Spain," and had a sign painter letter their door:

UTICA DROP FORGE & TOOL CO.

ROBERT BENCHLEY, PRESIDENT

DOROTHY PARKER, PRESIDENT

Their last preparation was to obtain a cable address: PARKBENCH. The firm of Parker & Benchley was ready for business.

Business proved slow. *Ainslee's* magazine hired Mrs. Parker as drama critic, and Benchley got a part-time job doing book reviews for the *World*. He did occasional light articles as well, but he had little luck placing them. *Life*, in particular, would buy nothing that he contributed. And then, out of the blue, *Life** invited him to become its drama critic, at a salary of $250 a week.

Benchley thought what the money would mean to his family and what fun it would be to work again with Sherwood, now *Life's* movie critic. And he refused. The salary was plenty, he said, and he liked the theater; that wasn't it. The trouble was, he knew nothing at all about reviewing plays, and, in fairness to the readers, his conscience . . . *Life* proposed that he try the job for a week and see how it went. No? Well, how about coming over to the place and just looking around? They showed him the critic's of-

---

* This was the old *Life*, a humorous magazine, not Luce's pictorial.

fice, pushed him in, and locked the door. He was on the staff for
eight years.

Many of the writers and critics in those days used to lunch together at the Algonquin Hotel. Presently somebody in the group
suggested it might be fun to put on a show one Sunday night, and
give the actors a chance to do the criticizing. They sketched out a
program. Did anybody have any other ideas?

"Listen," Marc Connelly said, "do you know this fellow Benchley over at *Life*? Well, one day last summer . . ."

He and Benchley had finished lunch at Delmonico's, on Fifth
Avenue, and were standing at a balcony window when a crowded
open-deck bus stopped below them. Connelly looked down at the
bus and then looked at Benchley. "People!" he suddenly shouted.
Passengers and passersby stared up at them. "People!" Connelly
shouted again. "Your new prince!" He bowed toward Benchley
and withdrew. Far from being abashed, gracious Prince Robert
addressed his subjects in fluent German. He told them he was
aware that the thought of a foreign-born monarch was abhorrent
to many in this so great democracy, but they need no alarm have.
He would America's so precious heritage unsullied preserve.

Connelly continued, "He spoke for a full two minutes, absolutely deadpan! Do you suppose we could get him to do an act
like that for us?"

The show was called *No, Sirree!* after the current hit *Chauve-
Souris*. Opening—and closing—night was April 30, 1922. There
were no tickets; a fastidious committee issued invitations. The
cast was all-star, but except for Helen Hayes, Tallulah Bankhead,
and a few others, they were stars far from their usual courses. A
program note said simply and truthfully, "Offstage music by J.
Heifetz."

Benchley's skit was not billed. He was a stranger to most of the
audience when he walked on stage all alone and said, rather hesi-
tantly, "I shall take but a very few moments of your time this

evening, for I realize that you would much rather be listening to this interesting entertainment than to a dry financial statement—"

Many agreed. They left their seats and wandered up the aisles.

Benchley persevered: "—but I am reminded of a story—which you have probably all of you heard. It seems there were two Irishmen walking down the street when they came to a—oh, I should have said in the first place that the parrot which was hanging out in front of the store—or rather belonging to one of these two fellows—the first Irishman, that is—was—well, anyway, this parrot—"

It was that immortal mishmash of nonsense and ineptitude, "The Treasurer's Report."

F.P.A. heard him and wrote in his *Diary of Our Own Mr. Pepys,* "In the evening to a harlequinade, and laughed harder at R. Benchley's drolleries than ever I have at aught else." Irving Berlin heard him and signed him for the new *Music Box Revue.* He delivered the speech there for the nine months' run of the show and afterward for ten weeks in vaudeville. He used it as the title and set piece of a book which went into twelve editions and was translated into Swedish. It even achieved historical importance, as the first all-talking picture ever made. For the record, there are 1,185 words in "The Treasurer's Report"; it took eight and a half minutes to recite, and Benchley composed it in a taxi on his way to the first rehearsal.

Years afterward he said of that night, "My whole life changed its course." This is not true. The speech gave tremendous impetus to his career, but the course of his life did not change. What changed was his attitude toward it.

The Benchley who made his bow at *No, Sirree!* that April was substantially the same Benchley who had dismayed *Vanity Fair* three Aprils before. The shell of his New England rectitude had been chipped only once, and then minutely, but he remembered the date: July 2, 1921. Sherwood, Mrs. Parker, and the Scott Fitzgeralds were celebrating Dempsey's victory over Carpentier; Benchley joined them; and presently they teased him into taking his first alcoholic drink, an orange blossom cocktail.

They waited for his verdict. "I hope," he said grimly, "I hope this place is closed by the police!"

His salary from *Life* was ample to keep his family in comfort, but it allowed few luxuries. The extra $500 a week that Irving Berlin now paid him was far more than he had ever earned before. He didn't know what to do with it. Timidly at first, he took an occasional taxi instead of a bus. As he gained confidence, he bought some books, some clothes, some presents. Still the surplus piled up. He began spending desperately. The trick came with practice. His fielding average on restaurant checks was 1.000 for the season. His friends, even strangers, found that their own bank notes had as well have borne the likeness of Jefferson Davis.

No sucker ever has to hire a brass band on Broadway. The Music Box suddenly became a jinx theater; disaster struck backstage like a bomb. Platoons of weak brothers needed a hundred dollars apiece to leave town and make a fresh start. Brigades of aged fathers were wiped out of business by forest fires, monsoons, and meteors. Grief-stricken mothers tottered down flights of steps and fractured their hips. And generous Mr. Benchley was honored at being allowed to help "tide them over." In his expense book, entries under "Miscellaneous" became larger and larger. In his diary, entries of any sort became fewer and fewer. Soon there were none at all. There were none ever again.

The splurge lasted for a year. When it was over, Benchley had to ask *Life* for a month's salary in advance. But he had made two important discoveries. The first was that he didn't regret a penny or a moment he had spent; except for those perfunctory annual skirmishes at the grave of the Amiable Child, the long war of attrition between his character and his conscience was finished forever. The second was that whether he was flush or flat, people liked him.

His later biography could be written in terms of the friendships he formed at this time, perhaps under the title *Rob and His Friends*. The closest was Donald Ogden Stewart. Their friendship was not the sort that slowly budded and slowly flowered. It reached full bloom at the moment they met, one night in New York when they happened to leave a restaurant at the same time. The rain was heavy; no taxis were in sight. Just then a man carrying an umbrella passed by. Stewart stepped forward and took his arm with, "Yale Club, please!" Benchley took Stewart's arm and asked, "Can you drop me off at my place? It's on the way." Both laughed, and they didn't stop laughing at each other's nonsense for the rest of their lives together.

Benchley's dislocated logic, his trick of seeming to view everything Through the Looking Glass, was better suited to the uses of modern fiction than were some of his other characteristics. Outstanding among them was a courtesy so impervious that not even the most stupefying bore or pestilential drunk could breach it. F.P.A. wrote that Benchley "has one gift possessed by few humorists. In fact, possessed by few human beings. He is not only a wonderful listener but a flattering one. It doesn't matter what your yarn happens to be, how old or how shopworn. Benchley will burst into laughter and you will go away from him thinking that you must be a witty dog."

What Benchley himself thought after the bore had gone nobody ever knew. They knew only that he never made an unkind remark. Review the whole canon of his quips, and—an even rarer distinction among humorists—there is none with the dullest barb or faintest tincture of malice. Not his patience but his sense of justice had to be violated for him to take action.

He was a vigorous and heedless champion of persecuted minorities. When the desk clerk at a Hollywood hotel refused to let him receive the manager of a black orchestra in his room, he packed up and left at once. When theater critics were being accused during the Depression of "taking the bread out of actors' mouths," Benchley was worried only because it might transpire that he, on the contrary, had already turned over to Actors Equity the royalties from his books, amounting to some fifty dollars a week. He resigned from the Harvard Club of New York the moment he learned that a candidate for membership had been rejected on no other grounds than that he had written a book about Socialism. And when an executive at *Life* became so zealous in behalf of the Cathedral of St. John the Divine that he exhorted all employees to contribute 10 percent of their salaries to the construction fund, Benchley exhorted them to do no such thing. He risked his own job rather than have some twenty-dollar-a-week stenographer feel that she had to buy security for hers.

Sherwood became editor in chief of *Life* in 1924, at a time when its circulation had fallen and was still slipping. One of Benchley's most successful innovations on the *Lampoon* had been a burlesque issue of *Life*. Why not adapt the idea to *Life* itself? He and Sherwood settled on a mass burlesque of a dozen prominent magazines, featuring a business story by Stephen Leacock, in the manner of *The Saturday Evening Post*. A letter from the editor of the *Post*, George Horace Lorimer, was among the thousands they received; Lorimer said the story had so delighted him, he wished he had had a chance to buy it.

Life's readers begged for more, and Sherwood and Benchley gave it to them. Their second burlesque was of Sunday newspapers; their third, of tabloids. They wrote most of the stories, captions, and advertisements themselves. Benchley even posed for a photo of an ax butcher, with Mrs. Parker as the murdered paramour. Circulation bounced from the bottom to an all-time high.

The ramifications of "The Treasurer's Report" did not interfere with Benchley's regular job as *Life*'s drama critic. Both the Music Box and vaudeville obligingly scheduled his act so early that he missed only the opening lines of the show he had to review. In his movie shorts, Benchley is an extraordinary man in ordinary situations; as a critic, he was an ordinary man in extraordinary situations. Even after nineteen years of professional theatergoing, each show was still his first, and he was rapt with excitement over its promise. He once said that his favorite sport was "doing nothing at all, but next to that I like the ten minutes at the theater before the curtain goes up. I always feel like I did when I was a kid around Christmastime."

If he enjoyed a show, the cast never had to wait for his review. Brooks Atkinson, of the *Times*, said, "Mr. Benchley explodes like a dynamite pit"; John Anderson, of the *Journal-American*, spoke of his "frank and satisfying bellow." His enthusiasm poured from his typewriter unabated and unembellished. A drama did not remind him of Wedekind's *Frühlings Erwachen*; he was a Worcester boy telling Worcester people what he had seen—and telling them with taste and judgment. Professor Charles Townsend Copeland, of Harvard's English department—the famous "Copey"—said, "Watch him. Read him. He is the most diabolically skillful critic of our time!"

If he didn't enjoy the show, he sneaked away in sorrow. One of the memorable lines in *The Squall* was delivered by a lush, tropical half-caste: "Me Nubi. Me good girl. Me stay."

Benchley whispered, "Me Bobby. Me bad boy. Me go," and went. Even so, the tone of his review was distress, not disgust.

And yet a play so shoddy that the critics panned it with one voice was responsible for attracting to his column readers who had never followed it before. The play was *Abie's Irish Rose*. Benchley's original review dismissed it as twaddle, but unhappily for him, the dismissal could not be permanent. In addition to reviews of new plays, his department was committed to carrying summaries of previous reviews, rewritten weekly. And *Abie's Irish Rose* ran for six years.

As week succeeded week, Benchley's desperate paraphrases became first a professional, then a public joke. People bought *Life* simply to watch him writhe and squirm. The cast of the show was particularly gleeful. On the first anniversary of their run, they sent him a birthday cake; on the fourth, they invited him to speak. By this time he had exhausted even such evasions as "Will the Marines never come?" and had appealed to his readers for help. The prize he offered was won by Harpo Marx, with "No worse than a bad cold."

Benchley resigned from *Life* in 1929 to become drama critic of *The New Yorker*. Over the name "Guy Fawkes," he also contributed criticisms of the New York press.

During his last years, he spent half his time in Hollywood and the other half—the Broadway season—in New York. His family headquarters continued to be in Scarsdale, but for nights when he had to see a play, he also kept an apartment in town—two rooms in the Royalton Hotel, on West 44th Street, so close to the Hippodrome that he complained of being kept awake by the grunts of the wrestlers. The gloom and clutter suggested the basement of a theatrical warehouse. Around the clock and the calendar, his windows were closed and the blinds drawn. The furniture seemed to have been deployed by a designer of tank traps. Not even Red Grange could have swiveled across the living room without sustaining an ugly bruise. Every square inch of the walls was hidden behind photographs, drawings, thousands of books and curious signs. One of them read "We All Speak English"; another, "MR. Benchley, please!"

"I have no idea what this one means," he confessed. "None of my friends has an idea. F.P.A. gave it to me and *he* has no idea. You can see it's very deep."

Bead portieres hung in the doorway, and each chair had its anti-macassar. Stacks of newspapers and magazines slouched under the desks and tables. The top of one bookcase was reserved for pictures of Queen Victoria. For fear that a chambermaid might try to dust there, Benchley filled in the gaps with a china menagerie and a collection of miniature penguins. A cello stood in one corner, a stuffed, two-headed calf in another. Some discerning friend presented it, in the belief that if there was any decor where a stuffed, two-headed calf would not seem outré, this was unquestionably it.

Ernest Hemingway once said, "If these rooms were destroyed, I would not come back to New York." Benchley commented, "He lends an air of virility to my dainty apartment which I sorely miss after he has gone and the furniture has been repaired."

Two secretaries picked their way through this fusty lair to rouse the master at noon. When he first engaged them, they reported sharp at nine, but he put a stop to such nonsense by getting up, dressing, and stalking out in reproachful silence. He met his first secretary, Charles MacGregor, in a bar. MacGregor was clutching a withered bouquet so tenderly that Benchley asked for an explanation.

"It's for my shirt," MacGregor said.

"Your what?"

"My shirt, my favorite blue one. It's sleeve got torn, so I took it to the shirt hospital—got it a private room, too. I couldn't have it in the ward with waiters' dickeys and things like that, you know."

"Certainly not!" said Benchley sympathetically. "How's it coming along?"

"Fine, thanks! They had to take twenty-one stitches, but you never saw a braver patient."

"Look," said Bentley. "How'd you like to work for me?"

As a former naval officer, MacGregor found it hard to reconcile himself to his employer's disorderly schedule. He used to

pace the room muttering, "Noon, and not a lathe turning!" Benchley tried to deflect this briskness by proposing that he occupy his
mornings with a hobby. MacGregor was enthusiastic; his hobby,
he said, would be a frog farm in the bathtub. It took all of Benchley's tact to persuade him to collect rare books instead. "The Mac-
Gregor Memorial Library," as it came to be known, included
Secrets of Meat Curing and Sausage Making; *Forty Thousand Sub-
lime and Beautiful Thoughts*; *Making Money from Hens*; *Are
Mediums Really Witches?*; *Practical Railway Painting and Lac-
quering*; *Love's Law*; *The Culture and Diseases of the Sweet Potato*; *Astro-Bubbles*; and *A Manual for Small Museums*.

Benchley's own library was heavily weighted with books about
the early eighteenth century, collected against the day when he
would leave off his potboiling, as he thought of it, and settle down
to the work of his heart, a history of Queen Anne's reign. His
friends were puzzled when he announced his project; they suspected that he was being misled by the fact that the queen had
once supported a bill forbidding "occasional conformity." But
Benchley was serious; his plan was to write the history as one
would a play: describe the settings and characters, and have the
plot unfold by means of dialogue and stage directions. In preparation, he read and cross-indexed more than a hundred books on
the period. But when the ugly moment came at last and he wrote
"page 1" on a sheet of unblemished paper, there he stuck. The
plan that had seemed so radiant in contemplation, he now saw as
utterly unfeasible. He tried to salvage something from his research by narrowing his field to the humorists of the reign, but
this too foundered when he was forced to conclude that none of
them was really very funny. "So much for Queen Anne," he said
in relief.

When Harvard's class of 1912 held its twenty-fifth reunion,
Benchley wrote the class report, "Sobering Statistics":

In twenty-five years, we have produced only one Bishop of Albania, or, at any rate, only one Bishop of Albania who later became Prime Minister.

Only one member of the class has caught a giant panda.

We have only one weather man who advocates the "frontal method" (two dimensions). These are simple Weather Bureau terms, I trust.

Of all the "banana-knockers" in Eua, Nukualofa, Tonga Islands, only one is a Harvard 1912 man.

If I were a calamity howler, I could show that 72 percent haven't got three million dollars to their name, 91 percent can't juggle, and that we haven't had a single President of the United States.

Probably it grieved him even more to realize that his own name still appeared in the class records as "humorist" rather than as "historian," but no one could say for certain, not even Benchley. In his annual throes at the grave of the Amiable Child, he convinced himself that his life had been squandered; and his tears diluted the remonstrances of his friends until they took him at his word.

If later they relapsed into skepticism, Benchley could not fairly blame them. One year, they had hardly assuaged his sobs and straightened his tie before he was scribbling on the back of an envelope. Someone saw it as he slipped it under the door of Grant's Tomb, near by. The message read: "Please leave 2 quarts Grade A and 1 pint whipping cream. U. S. G."

APPENDIX I

Men seldom have names that seem to fit their personalities or their professions. Offhand I can think of only four: the late great archaeologist Flinders Petrie; the late great horseman and all-around amateur athlete Foxhall Keene; the late football coach of the U. S. Naval Academy, Slade Cutter; and the late great Robert Charles Benchley—his two given names commonplace, his family name weakly trailing off, exactly as Benchley pictured himself. He must have loved his family name, because his books are packed with others of the same pattern and cadence: Weevis, Beasley, Bemiss, Meeker, all trochees, and each attached to someone colorless, irresolute, ineffectual. But note this: whereas his first two books, *Of All Things* (1921) and *Love Conquers All* (1922), were signed "Robert C. Benchley," the next, *Pluck and Luck* (1925), and all that followed were signed simply "Robert Benchley." I never knew the reason for the change until his son Nat explained it to me:

Around 1923–24, Bob met Neysa McMein, the charming and persuasive artist. One day when he was feeling particularly dis-couraged about his work, she told him that during the first few years of her own career, when she was painting under her original name, Marjorie Moran McMein, she had so little success that she considered quitting. In desperation, she consulted a numerologist, who advised her to scrap "Marjorie Moran" in favor of the more provocative "Neysa." She did, and her career took off at once. Perhaps, she suggested, if Bob . . .? That's how "Charles" came to be abandoned. Certainly Benchley's career took off too, though not everyone would give sole credit to numerology.

APPENDIX II

I have all his books—at least, all that were published before World War II. Better yet, I have them inscribed by both the author and the illustrator, Gluyas Williams. When you asked Benchley for an inscription, you didn't get any paltry, grudging "With best wishes"; you got an *inscription*—something like this (in my copy of *Pluck and Luck*):

Late Period (Manic-Depressive) 1868–1875

12, Schnellgasse
Dresden, July 9, 1878

Dear Joe:

You are doubtless surprised at the above address, but we came here suddenly from Bonn directly George left Augsburg-Hochlese.

The sad, heroic acceptance (*sans arrière pensée*) seems to me to be the great tragic wind that blows through the *Iliad*, and comes out especially strong in Achilles. —And how are you and Bessie?

I think that, on the whole, I like Renan—*bien qu'il soit d'une laideur vraiment repoussante*. His wife is a plain and excellent person, niece of Ary Scheffer.[1]

Tomorrow we move on to Bridgeport, our winter quarters,

Yrs aff'ct'ly,
Bob Benchley

[1] Niece of Ary Scheffer.

APPENDIX III

In the summer of 1941, the *Post* sent me to Hollywood on an assignment. When I registered at my hotel, a telegram was waiting: MEET ME CHASENS SEVEN O'CLOCK TONIGHT STOP WILL BRING GIRL FOR YOU. BOB.

Bob was there. I remember how my stomach surged when he told me that the strange, muddy drink in front of him was vodka shaken up with chocolate ice cream; but I was soon diverted by the entrance of a dazzlingly beautiful Chinese girl. Bob introduced us. "This is Miss Ching Lee," he said. "I invited her for you because you're from Virginia, and everybody from Virginia is related to the Lees."

That was the last time I ever saw him. The war took me out of the country, and before I was discharged, Bob had died. The date was November 21, 1945, in New York City. A few weeks earlier, a friend had asked him about his health. Benchley said, laughing, "Except for an occasional heart attack, I feel as young as I ever did." The cause of death was a cerebral hemorrhage, complicated by portal cirrhosis of the liver. The man who, having choked down his first alcoholic drink, hoped that "this place is closed by the police," had closed a good many places himself, night after night, in the twenty-four years since then. One such place, the 21 Club, put a bronze plaque over his favorite table, in recognition of his loyal patronage:

ROBERT BENCHLEY

HIS CORNER

1889 – 1945

Some friends of his in Pasadena might have put a similar tablet over their bar, where Benchley had spent many, many happy hours. One evening there, after he had sipped an aperitif martini or so, he was surprised to have the butler bring him a glass of champagne.

"I was drinking martinis," Benchley protested.

"Yes, sir, you certainly were," the butler agreed, "but that was *before* dinner." (Benchley's formula for the martini was "Gin, and just enough vermouth to take away that nasty, watery look.")

Long after his death, I had a letter from his old friend Paul Hollister, a classmate at Harvard and his co-star in the Hasty Pudding show. Paul wrote that on rereading my piece in the *Post*, he realized for the first time that I had neglected a unique and important aspect of the Benchley humor: the way he amused *himself*, not caring a whit whether he had an audience or not. For example, Corey Ford had seen him striking a match and "trying to set fire" to the cornerstone of a New York bank, "furtively," because of the cop a few feet away. And Frank Sullivan had seen him "arguing" with a horse that was standing near the curb and fretfully nodding its head. Benchley would make a point and pound his fist into his other hand, and the horse would nod, and Benchley would make another point . . .

Paul's letter ended,

Our workplaces in New York were handy to each other, and Benchley and I sometimes lunched together at the Harvard Club nearby. Afterwards, we had a ritual for parting. We'd go outside and take a position in the middle of the busy front steps, then:

H. Tell you what you do—
B. I'll take it up with my people, and you—
H. Yep, I'll see my people, and—

B. We'll get together again and go over the last few
points.

Both (beaming). Well, I really think we got somewhere
today, don't you?

Bob certainly got somewhere, bless him!

Indeed he did!—and in so few years: he was only fifty-six when
he died. He is buried on Nantucket Island, where his family had
spent many summers, and his widow is buried beside him. A low
privet hedge shelters their plot; the inscription on the gravestone
reads:

—ROBERT BENCHLEY

1889–1945

GERTRUDE D. BENCHLEY

1889–1980

The dash in front of his name was the happy inspiration of his son
Nat; it represents his old by-line in *The New Yorker*. When its
editor, Harold Ross, was told about the dash, his eyes filled with
tears.

MARC CONNELLY
1890-1980

De Fish Fryer

Marc Connelly (in sombrero) and Caskie Stinnett.
Connelly's shoes were of green suede.

MARC Connelly wrote in my copy of his autobiography, *Voices Offstage*, "To Joseph Bryan, III, whose friendship and the purchase of this book have made me richer."

I was flattered. I never knew Marc well enough to claim more than an acquaintanceship. The few times I saw him were mostly at Dutch Treat luncheons and shows. My knowledge of him came secondhand, through Frank Sullivan, Art Samuels, and George Kaufman, who usually had some quip of his to pass along, or a letter to show around. George told me he saw Marc coming out of a Heifetz concert and asked if he had enjoyed it. Marc shrugged. "It was all right, I suppose, if you happen to like absolutely superb performances." Sullivan carried a postcard of Marc's in his pocket for weeks, bringing it out for everyone to enjoy. It said, "Guess who I just had a drink with at the Players? Corey Ford. Give up?"

Marc wrote a number of highly successful plays, of course,

some alone, like *The Wisdom Tooth*, and several in collaboration with Kaufman, among them *Dulcy, Beggar on Horseback*, and *Merton of the Movies*. But the top of the Marc (as I'm afraid I'll have to call it) is *The Green Pastures*, his adaptation of Roark Bradford's stories about the Old Testament, as seen through the eyes of country Negroes in the South. Otto Kahn advanced Marc five thousand dollars to carry him over the period of writing the script, and the play was such an instant, smash success that Marc could have paid off the loan before the last-act curtain came down. As the "green pastures" psalm promised, his soul was restored; his head was anointed with oil; his cup ran over.

Any collection of immortal lines from the American theater, such as "That's all there is; there isn't any more" and "Why don't you come up some time and see me?" (this is the correct version, by the way), will have to include two from *The Green Pastures*: "Let de fish fry proceed," and the line that Brooks Atkinson called "the greatest entrance cue in modern drama," when the Angel Gabriel shouts, "Gangway: Gangway for de Lawd God Jehovah!" Put them all together, and they spelled a Pulitzer Prize.

Inevitably Marc went to Hollywood. Afterwards, he had little to say about his indenture. One of the few tales he brought back was about the morning he and Benchley, sauntering along Sunset Boulevard, saw a woebegone old horse in a van parked at the curb. They asked the driver where he was going.

"I'm taking him to the knacker's, the glue factory."

"What do you want for him?"

"Say fifteen bucks."

"We'll give you twenty if you'll deliver him and us to this address in Bel Air."

It was Charlie Butterworth's. There, they led the horse past the dismayed servant who opened the door and into the library, where Butterworth was sitting. He peered at the horse, then at Benchley and Connelly.

"Gee, fellows," he said, "you've been reading my mind!"

Marc didn't work to much purpose toward the end of his long life (he was ninety when he died). He played with the idea of making a musical out of his old success *The Farmer Takes a Wife*, and he frequently talked about something called *A Stitch in Time*, but nothing came of either, and he was beginning to feel the pinch when, forty years after *The Green Pastures* opened, it brought him a happy windfall. Rummaging through a disused closet, he turned up the long-lost original script. He offered it for sale, and it was snapped up for $7,500.

Marc's skits for the annual Dutch Treat show always rattled the chandeliers. One of his funniest was "The Captain's Night Dinner on the Weehawken Ferry." I can't remember the dialogue verbatim, but it was roughly like this:

The curtain rises to show the passengers in evening dress, strolling about the deck.

FIRST LADY (leaning over the rail and pointing): *"There's one!"*

SECOND LADY: "There's another! Oooo, what a *big* one!"

FIRST LADY: "Not as big as the ones you see in the Harlem River!"

SECOND LADY: "No? Are they very big up there?"

FIRST LADY: "The biggest! E-*nor*-mous! You wouldn't believe!"

SECOND LADY: "You seem to know a lot about them."

FIRST LADY: "I ought to. My husband's in the business."

SECOND LADY: "The manufacturing end?"

FIRST LADY: "No. He's a model."

According to Art Samuels, Connelly couldn't bear to be second in anything. It came out when the two of them and their wives and several other couples took a cruise to Sweden in the summer of 1933. Backgammon was the new fad. Even before the ship had cleared the Narrows, Marc, who fancied his skill, challenged all comers. Art accepted. Game after game, the dice ran counter-Connelly; and Samuels began to ply his needle: "There must be *some* way we can even this up, Connelly! It's too easy! It's like slapping a sick baby off a chamber pot. Money doesn't mean that much to me. I'd rather have fun! Shall I play left-handed? Or why don't I give you two throws to my one? You name it!"

The fish fry proceeded, with Connelly as the fish, until finally Samuels threw a combination that would let him close his board against the man that Connelly had on the bar. Instead, he said, "Watch this, Connelly! What you're about to see is known as the Samuels Contempt Play. I use it against only the most pitifully incompetent opponents." He deployed his men so as to leave four blots, then ordered, "Throw, Connelly! Throw! And may God have mercy on your soul!"

Connelly, fuming, threw. When he realized that he hadn't hit a single one of Samuels' men, "He burst into tears," Samuels said, "and ran to his cabin, howling like a wolf."

But there is one field in which neither Samuels nor Sullivan nor Kaufman, for all their gifts, was fit to hold Connelly's coat: as a raconteur he was supreme. In Marc's magic hands, even the stock characters in the stalest story—the Hobo at the Back Door, the Old Maid in the Upper Berth, the Traveling Salesman and the Farmer's Daughter—even these would have stood up before you, alive and breathing.

I have been privileged to hear some of our greatest contemporary storytellers at their best. I have heard David Niven's story of his meeting with General Sir Bindon Blood at Boodle's, in London. I have heard Jimmy Cagney's story of the old queen in the red plush hat, pacing up and down the platform of the railroad station. And I have heard Marc Connelly's story of the two gladiators from far Hibernia, Patricius and Michaelis, waiting their

turns in the Colosseum. For all the talent of Niven and Cagney—
both of them professional actors, remember—I would have to
award the gold medal to Connelly.

I won't repeat his gladiator story here or even try to, any more
than I'd try to demonstrate Jack Nicklaus's chip shot. However,
rather than give *no* hint of Connelly's genius, I'm going to quote
from an earwitness account of an impromptu speech of his, my
excuse being that, unlike his stories, it had never been rehearsed.

The sample comes from a letter sent me by Caskie Stinnett
(who wrote the foreword to this book), a former editor in chief of
Holiday and of *Travel & Leisure*, and a former president of the
Society of American Travel Writers. He was its active president,
fresh from having chaired its 1968 convention in Portugal, when
he wrote me about Connelly, as follows:

> One of our meetings was held at Figueira da Foz, a seaside
> village just west of Lisbon, with a casino and some hotels.
> Our group was shepherded into the dining room of one of
> the hotels, where the mayor and other civic leaders were ex-
> pecting us. Since they spoke no English, and we spoke no
> Portuguese, it was suggested that each of us introduce him-
> self and state his newspaper or magazine affiliation—an in-
> terpreter would translate.
>
> Everything went well until it came around to Marc. He
> had no earthly right to be present. He wasn't one of our
> members. He wasn't even a travel writer. I had invited him
> along just for the ride, as it were. But, before I could stop
> him, he stood up, gave his name, and stated that he was
> editor in chief of *Popular Wading*, "America's leading mag-
> azine of shallow-water sports. We are also," he added, "the
> official publication of the American Splashing Society, an
> organization that we do *not* refer to by its initials."
>
> He went on, "Last year, our article on 'immersion foot'

won us an award from the American Medical Association, and I am sure that no one among you fails to recall our series when General Douglas MacArthur waded ashore in the Philippines."

Marc reviewed *Popular Wading*'s scoops and glories at some length, with special praise for its featured column of chic après-wading chitchat, "Hi 'n' Dri." Then he moved on to an account of *Popular Wading*'s circulation war with its competitor, *True Wading*. "*True*'s editorial formula is extremely limited," he said. "They cover the area only to the ankle, whereas *Popular* goes all the way to the knee. Waders seeking adventure in deeper water had to turn to us. Inevitably we drove *True* to the wall."

There was more, much more, Caskie's letter went on, but he was too weak with laughter—and too embarrassed—to retain it. He got no sympathy from me. This was the second time he had foolishly given Connelly a chance to kick over the traces, and the second time Connelly had done so. The first time was on the run from Hong Kong to Macao, in a Red Chinese hydrofoil:

The trip began as peacefully as a Rotary luncheon [Caskie wrote me]. I was on deck, Marc having disappeared below, when an agitated Englishman asked me if "the rotund gentleman" was my companion. Fearing the worst, I said yes, he was.

"Well," the Englishman said, "I was standing by the railing there a moment ago when your friend came up and whispered, 'We're going to take over the boat at three-oh-five! Pass it on!' What the hell did he mean by *that*?"

I told him to calm himself—I'd handle the matter; and went below to find Connelly. He was lecturing—in English —to a group of Chinese who plainly couldn't understand a single word he spoke. I ordered him hoarsely to follow me

up on deck *at once*! At the stairwell, he turned to the bewildered Chinese and said, "Don't go away! I was just coming to the best part, and I'll be right back."

I'd give a pretty to have heard those addresses, especially the
one on wading. My loss is not necessarily irretrievable. If ever I
have a fulfillment-guaranteed wish to spare, it will be for Marc to
record the complete text for me. I'm confident that de Lawd God
Jehovah will consider the reverent, affectionate way in which
Marc portrayed him, and will let him do so; and then will open
the Pearly Gates long enough for Marc to scale the recording
down to me and the rest of us, like a Frisbee; and then de fish fry
will proceed.

FRANK SULLIVAN

1892-1976

The Sage of Saratoga

Frank Sullivan hard at work

IT wouldn't be fair to say that Frank Sullivan was stout and bald and small, but if you suffix an *-ish* to each of those adjectives, they become valid. His eyes were gray-blue behind strong glasses; he was the last person I knew who wore a pince-nez, though he changed to plastic frames in his last years. His chubby cheeks gave him the look of an amiable chipmunk. This was one of his two stock expressions; the other was a scowl of mock severity. He was sweet-tempered, warm, quiet, gentle. Marc Connelly called him "the least bitter of men," and *The New York Times* said that he was "invariably gay and cheerful." James Thurber dedicated *The Years with Ross* to Frank, "with the love and admiration I share with everyone who knows him." I count myself among them, even though I suffered more vilification and abuse at his hands than ever Stan Laurel suffered at Oliver Hardy's. A few extracts from his letters to me will make my point:

I have been reading the *Journals* of André Gide with much interest. Around 1923, he was pretty stuck on a young boy named M. How old were you then? Were you ever referred to as "M"?

An invitation to the 1938 Dutch Treat show ended with this:

> ... You may sit at our table, but only on the understanding that you be placed below the salt. I make this stipulation not from any motives of snobbery or outmoded class-distinction, but as a simple act of kindness to you, as I realize that you would only feel uncomfortable and out of place amid the flow of wit and easy, debonair talk that will be the rule with us *above* the salt.

And an account of a party he had been to ended,

> ... But enough of my social triumphs. They can only serve to make you even more dissatisfied with your drab and inferior position in society. Was it not Oscar Wilde who once said of you, "Joe Bryan is invited to all the best houses—once"?

Sullivan was a native and part-time resident of Saratoga, New York. After relating a conversation with an employee of the local sewage disposal plant, who complained that "nowhere near the normal amount of sewage had been passing through his department," he wrote me,

> I wish you were here for a few days, so that you could resolve the poor fellow's problem. Boy, how that plant would hum if you were around!

One of his most offensive letters was this one:

> I have just come across a news item from the South Pacific [where I was at the time] which says that whales are being

tickled by submarine soundings into giving off large amounts of ambergris. I have a splendid idea which I shall contribute to my country to further the war effort: it is to detail you to the task of whale-tickling.

I have long felt that you had a natural talent for something, but I never could quite make up my mind for what. Now it comes to me: you have just the right temperament to tickle whales. You have tact and patience and discretion, all of which qualities would be necessary in dealing with whales, which are notoriously sensitive creatures. You and whales would get along capitally!

I trust you to do a thorough and workmanlike job. Do it the hard way: dive down and tickle them from beneath. Don't try to carry a lazy man's load by persuading them to come to the surface and turn over on their backs so that you can walk around on their bellies, tickling them at your leisure. Besides, I wouldn't trust even a whale on its back, with you in one of your randier moods. . . .

I wrote him that his letter had caught up with me in the Solomon Islands. It was a curious coincidence, I said, that a vigorous local movement was gathering momentum just then. These islands were so insanitary, so malodorous, so generally inhospitable and unpleasant, that we were petitioning to have their name officially changed to one more appropriate. A very slight modification would do it: "Solomons" to "Sullivans."

Primess forbids me to quote more than a few short sentences from another of his wartime letters:

I don't want to hear any more about your "hardships" in those tropical paradises! Do you think it is all peaches and cream back here on the home front? By no means! Listen, Burns: before a man can get a new tube of toothpaste, he has to turn in a used one. The same for shaving cream. The same for contraceptives.

(signed) Second Lieutenant Francis J. Sullivan, late of Company H, 303rd Infantry, 76th Division.

"Burns" or "Brine" or "O'Brien" or "III" or even "Fudgeface" were among his usual ways of addressing me; the dateline might be "Sullivan's Bluff," or "Convent of the Visitation, Lhasa, Thibet"; and he usually signed himself something like "Nym Crinkle," "Jorrocks," "Marmaduke Mizzle, the caraway seed merchant of Mincing Lane," "Horace Greeley," "Fulton J. Sheen, D.D. (PS: Feed my lambs)," "F. Shapiro," or simply "The man whose miniature your wife wears next to her heart." (It wouldn't have surprised me if she did. When he mentioned her name in his annual Christmas verses in *The New Yorker*, "Greetings, Friends!" she was so pleased that local photocopiers turned cherry red, running off copies for her.)

Art Samuels showed me a letter in which Frank invited him and his wife to Saratoga for a weekend:

> ... It is understood, of course, that in the case of all houseguests visiting me, I may exercise the *droit de seigneur* the first night. I waive that right immediately and emphatically as regards Samuels, but not, however, as regards Mrs. Samuels.

When he was temporarily short of fresh insults, he often fell back on a favorite standby, the Civil War. On his letterhead, "135 Lincoln Avenue, Saratoga, New York," he never failed to underline "Lincoln" in his letters to me. An invitation to dinner was baited with the promise that I would be seated between Mrs. Surratt and Belle Watling. One of his books, *Broccoli and Old Lace*, is inscribed to me "with the thanks of W. T. Sherman and

F. Sullivan." When I moved to Bucks County, in eastern Pennsylvania, he wrote:

> I have been constrained to report you to Secretary Stanton, as a Southern sympathizer living far too close to Gettysburg. You will shortly receive a notice of eviction, to remove for the duration to a place well outside the security lines. Your present home will be used by our General McClellan as headquarters. You will understand that we can afford to have none but those of unimpeachable loyalty living within the Union lines in these critical times. Yipp-pe-e-e-e-e! That's our Federal yell.

"The rumor that Fort Sumter has been fired on" also made him happy, "because it's terribly dull here in Saratoga, and an incident like that would give us Sumter talk about during the long winter evenings." This letter was signed

Stonewall Sullivan
Late Colonel 47th Reg't
Discalced Cistercians.

Another "rumor from authoritative sources" made him even happier: General Lee was a fag, in love with General Grant, and what Lee actually said at Appomattox was, "I surrender, dear!"

The only retort—a feeble one, I admit—that I could make to this vile allegation was to tell him that because he was "an older man," I could not in honor horsewhip him as he deserved, "on the steps of the Junior Conservative" (Sullivan was a Wodehouse fan, like myself), so I could only challenge him to meet me at Moriarty's for ten rounds and slug it out, toe-to-toe, with each man paying for alternate rounds, or slugs.

The Moriarty brothers' saloon, at 216 East 58th Street, was a favorite resort of ours in Prohibition days. The liquor was reliable and moderately priced; credit was available for friends of the house; women were not admitted under any circumstance; and the proprietors—Mort, Dan, and Jim Moriarty—never hustled the customers or bothered them. Nor did anyone else; the brothers, big men all, saw to it that you could drink in peace, undisturbed by shouts and brawls.

On the debit side, the premises were a dim, dingy basement room with a bar, a few plain tables and chairs, and nothing else, not even a waiter. There was a handyman, Joe Morgan (popularly reputed to be the son of J. P. Morgan and a French maid), but Joe didn't bring you your drinks; you fetched them from the bar yourself. The only food obtainable was stale ham sandwiches (mysteriously known as "Long Island duckling") and hard-boiled eggs.

Under the circumstances, I don't know why we kept going back to Moriarty's, but we did. Lucius Beebe, Paul Mellon, "Prince" Mike Romanoff, Noel Busch, Bob Benchley, Corey Ford, Finis Farr, and dozens of other merry gentlemen were regulars. Finis remembered being introduced to Sullivan there. Dan Moriarty said, "Finis, I want you to meet Frank Sullivan, the best friend I got, be Christ!"

Moriarty's was Sullivan's home from home, his shelter from the stormy blast. His loyalty may have been less to the saloon than to the proprietors, since his "people" and theirs came from the same bogside. I have heard this, but I can't vouch for it. I *can* vouch for Sullivan's pride in his Irish blood. His letters mention his family again and again:

> ... I never saw a one of my four grandparents and know little about them, except that my mother's father, Grandfather Shea, wore knee-breeches when he came to this country, and was thereafter for many years President of the Father Matthew Total Abstinence Society of St. Peter's Church, Saratoga. Surely it's a wonderful thing that I tuk after me father's family and never had any truck with total abstinence!

When Maggie Falter, the wife of John Falter, the painter, sent Sullivan for Christmas a pair of carpet slippers that she had embroidered with shamrocks, he could hardly be stopped from wearing them downtown in the snow (though this may have indicated his affection for Maggie as much as his pride in the shamrocks). Another of his special friends, Russell Crouse,* brought him a shillelagh from Ireland. Sullivan took it to a banquet of the Saratoga chapter of the Friendly Sons of St. Patrick (whose members, he reported happily, included a Manny Finkelstein, a Dr. Weinberg, and a Sven Dahlberg) and to his joy was forthwith appointed Keeper of the Shillelagh. Buck also brought him a rosary which Pope John XXIII had blessed. Sullivan said, "I wouldn't part with it for a king's ransom, if you could find a king worth a ransom."

He wore his religion comfortably and lightly. He wrote me:

> I had a surprise at Mass today. The celebrant preached about *you*. He didn't exactly mention you by name, but there was no mistaking whom he meant when he spoke of "the scurrilous and degenerate minds who send pornographic material through the mails to children." I am a child at heart, so I qualified. He was referring of course to the clipping you sent me. [I don't recall it.] I would have risen in my seat and denounced you, except that that is some kind of Quaker practice, to let the congregation speak out, and we don't allow it in our church. Just put your dough in the collection plate and shut your trap, is our motto.

I hadn't realized that one of his uncles was a priest until Maggie Falter showed me a letter in which he mentioned it:

* "Buck" Crouse was the author of *Lavender and Old Lace, Call Me Madam*, and many other hits. He and Sullivan had met when they were young reporters on the New York *World* and had been beloved friends ever since. One of Sullivan's books, *A Moose in the Hoose*, was written for the three Crouse children and dedicated to the whole family.

... I have read a tragic item in the NY papers about a fire and panic in a parish hall in San Francisco—seven or eight lives lost. My heart skipped a beat when I read the name of the church: All Hallows. It was founded and erected many years ago by my uncle, Father Dan O'Sullivan [*sic*], a saint, and rebuilt by him after the disaster of 1906 had knocked it down. He was pastor there until his death in 1928. Well, there was nothing I could do, but it made me feel a bit sad.

The relative closest to him, and the one who survived longest, was his sister Kate, twelve years older. I never met her, but Frank's letters painted me a clear portrait. He said she was like David Copperfield's great-aunt Betsey Trotwood, whose chief occupation was rapping on her window and keeping the Minster Green free of children. Kate would sit by the front window, and whenever she saw a boy taking a shortcut across the strip of grass, she'd rap and scowl at him, waggling a finger and mouthing dire threats— and then fetch him in for a slice of cake.

Frank said that on morning after winter morning, he'd have put on his overcoat and muffler and gloves and hat, and be looking around the front hall for his galoshes, when here came Kate, with her invariable question: "Going out?" *

Frank also reported on the repairman who arrived to fix their TV. He asked Kate, "What seems to be wrong with it?"

"Well, for one thing," she told him, "a lot of the programs are lousy."

When Harold Ross came to Saratoga and met Kate (Frank wrote me),

---

* I thought of Kate Sullivan when I read *The Uncollected Wodehouse* and came across this passage:

" 'You are going, mademoiselle?'

"As Ruth was wearing her hat and making for the door, and as she always left at this hour, a purist might have considered the question superfluous."

it was love at first sight. They understood each other immediately. I went to the kitchen to mix drinks about 10 minutes after Ross showed up. He and Kate stayed on the porch, and I heard him say, "Now, Kate, goddam it, make Frank do some *pieces!*" That's how quickly they struck an accord. It will always be one of my favorite memories.

Kate had a stroke late in 1956 and died the following spring. Her death brought me one of the few sorrowful letters I ever had from Frank:

> ... She kept track of all my friends, insofar as the news in the *Times* and *Herald-Trib* allowed it. She breakfasted about an hour earlier than I, and by the time I came down, she had read the *Trib* and was ready with something like: "I see that Corey Ford is writing a book," and I would say, "Kate, please don't tell me what's in the paper. Let me read it for myself."
>
> That brief set-to would start the day, and I miss it more than I can say. Oddly, it is in the morning at breakfast time that it is most lonely. Well, I am now the last survivor of a once lively family, and must get used to that melancholy distinction.

After Kate's death, I don't think Frank ever left Saratoga, except for necessary trips to a hospital in Albany. His house on Lincoln Avenue had been his home base ever since the *World* shut down in 1931. For some years after that, he was in and out of town, staying at the apartment on East 51st Street that he shared with Corey Ford, or visiting Art and Vivian Samuels, or putting up at the Cornell Club (he was an A.B. of Cornell, class of '14). Even then he was always homesick for Saratoga, and as soon as winter broke, he hotfooted it home.

If the word "hotfoot" was ever misused, it was right there. I should have said "coldfooted," because when it came to travel,

Sullivan's feet were icy. He was a self-confessed locomotorphobe. Any form of transportation made him uneasy and even frightened him. His annual spring return to Saratoga took him three days, by his own account. The first day, he would steel himself and get as far as Grand Central Station before his resolution collapsed, and he bolted. The second day, he'd buy a ticket and actually take a seat in the coach, where he crouched, sweating, until "All aboard!" triggered him to dash out and away. The third day, his nerves jumping, his teeth gritted, and his stomach in knots, he made it to Saratoga. Though the subject must have been painful, he managed to joke about it; he told Marc Connelly that he was working up to a voyage to Europe "by stepping over larger and larger puddles."

His last trip of any length was in October 1936, from New York to Boston, for the opening of *Red, Hot and Blue*. The authors, Howard Lindsay and Russell Crouse, managed to tease Sullivan into coming with them. They put him in a berth on the night train and stood guard against a possible attempt at panicky flight until the stop at 125th Street was safely behind them. Next morning, when the porter fetched his bags, Sullivan saw they were plastered with labels from Shepheard's Hotel, Cairo; Raffles, Singapore; the Excelsior, Rome; the Imperial, Tokyo; and a dozen others. And when they reached the Ritz Hotel, he was handed a telegram from *The New York Times*, inviting him to relieve Russell Owen as their correspondent with the Byrd Expedition at the South Pole. Lindsay and Crouse had wangled the hotel labels from American Express, and Ford had faked the telegram. Sullivan related all this to me in high spirits, on the reverse of a Ritz Hotel laundry list. It had been "great fun," but his travels were about over. He settled back to enjoy his own house (after those years of apartments and clubs), and small-town life, and the Worden Bar and Grill, and the company of Monty Woolley, Clarence Knapp, and his other local friends.

These and his locomotorphobia weren't all that kept him home.
Another powerful influence was his feeling about New York: he
disliked it and mistrusted it. Two months after the Boston trip he
wrote me:

> All the reports I hear from your New York make it more
> disgusting than ever. I *was* coming down as soon as I had got
> my chow chow and currant jelly put up, and my dandelion
> wine jarred, but after reading that Lucius Beebe * had decreed
> that pink crepe de Chine Tuxedos must be worn this winter
> by the well-dressed man, I just thought I'd stay up here in-
> definitely and hell around in my old green plaid Mackinaw.

A final *possible* factor—I emphasize "possible"— was a hor-
ripilating incident that happened to him in New York in late
1932. The proprietress of a bookshop on Madison Avenue, a
friend of his, asked if he would come in one afternoon and sign
copies of his new book for her customers. He accepted. For some
weeks previously, the newspapers had been splashing their front
pages with a lurid story from Honolulu. The wife of a Navy officer stationed there had reported being raped by five Hawaiian
beachboys, whereupon her husband and her mother—"Mrs.
Montague," let us say—had tracked them down and killed one of
them. Well, Sullivan was signing away that afternoon when a
well-dressed, gray-haired lady brought him a copy of his book and
asked him to inscribe it.

Sullivan picked up his pen. "With pleasure, madam. To
whom?"

"Mrs. Montague—Angela Montague."

Satan himself must have guided Sullivan's hand. Without hesi-
tation he wrote, "For Angela Montague, from Duke Kahana-
moku." Mrs. Montague read it and blanched and ran out. She was
that Mrs. Montague!

* A newspaper reporter, bon vivant, and *arbiter elegantiarum* of the period.

When Samuels heard about this blood-curdling gaffe, he abruptly abandoned his usual nickname for Sullivan, "Spotty," and began addressing him as "Mrs. Post" or "Emily" or "Lord Chesterfield." But Sullivan, the least malicious, least cruel of men, was so plainly distressed that the merciless Samuels took pity and gave over.

Sullivan once described New York as "a city so decadent that when I leave it, I never dare look back, lest I turn into salt and the conductor throw me over his left shoulder for good luck." His obituary in *The New York Times* quotes him as having said, "I wouldn't live in New York if you gave me Philadelphia. A small town is the place to live. I live in a small town 180 miles from New York, and while I wouldn't say it has New York beat a mile, I would put the distance at six furlongs."

—Which, conveniently for him, was about the distance from 135 Lincoln Avenue to the Saratoga race track. I say "conveniently" because Sullivan was a passionate horseplayer. He was no Pittsburgh Phil, but his attendance at the two-dollar window was devout. He had caught track fever early; his first job, at ten years old, was as pump tender and water boy in the betting ring. "I had this stool," he said, "and three tin cups—I think I invented germ warfare—and a cigar box for tips. There were days when I made as much as twelve dollars."

His most unforgettable customer was the beauteous Lillian Russell: "*There* was a woman! They don't build girls like that nowadays. You can't get the material, and even if you could, the contractors and the plumbers would gyp you and substitute shoddy." He described his meeting with Miss Russell to Red Smith, the *New York Times* sportswriter:

She had a box in the grandstand, near a flight of stairs. Sometimes I'd go and stand looking at her for two or three minutes. One day a man told me to take a drink of water to

Miss Russell, but when I started up the stairs, a Pinkerton stopped me.

"Miss Russell," I told him, "has asked for a drink from the betting-room spring."

"Go get a glass," he told me. "Miss Russell doesn't want to drink from that tin cup."

"Oh, yes, she does!" Miss Russell said. "Let the little boy through."

She gave me fifty cents.

I was in Saratoga for a few days during the 1961 season and I used to stroll over to Lincoln Avenue every morning for a chat with the Sage. (I don't know who first dubbed him "the Sage of Saratoga," but the sobriquet caught on fast, and before long we were speaking of him simply as "the Sage," just as we spoke of P. G. Wodehouse simply as "the Master." I like to remember that Master and Sage admired each other wholeheartedly. The Sage often said that the Master was "the funniest man writing today," and the Master said, "There is only one Frank Sullivan. I could do with a dozen. To my mind—and that is a mind not to be sneezed at—he is America's finest humorist.") Well, this morning I found the Sage bouncing with excitement. A horse named Banker Bob, was among the day's entries, and since both of us knew and strongly admired Bob Lovett, a partner at Brown Brothers Harriman, Sullivan took this as a wink and a nudge from On High, and warned me not to let the gravy train pull out without me. It didn't. Both of us got aboard, and Banker Bob did himself—and us—proud.

Sullivan was more superstitious (though only at the track, so far as I ever noticed) than a Neapolitan midwife. He was always on the alert for signs and portents, and was instantly responsive to hunches. A few days after Banker Bob's triumph he reported:

I had him in the daily double that day, remember?—$38. This season I had four daily doubles. If you are near a pari-mutuel window on September 22, don't fail to get down a double on 6–9! Why? Because it's the birthday, 69th, of you-know-who. It's bound to pay off. This will be the last chance I'll have to play the double on my birthday, using my birth-day digits, for two years, since there is no 7–0 double, and 70 is what I'll be on 9/22/62, the Lord willing. You may think all this is necromancy, and it is, but the day you and Mrs. B. got here, and I met you in the clubhouse, I had just collected a double of $140 by betting 6–8, which was (and still is) my age.

A week after the glorious sixty-ninth, he wrote me again: "I sent cash to my agent at Belmont to play the 6–9 double, and 9–10 came in, so I didn't quite hit it on the nose." No, not quite.

The 1967 season at Saratoga brought him an honor headier even than Lillian Russell's smile: the New York Racing Asso-ciation presented him with a silver plaque and invited him up to the stewards' box to watch the first and only running of the Frank Sullivan Purse. To cap the day, he held a ticket on the winner, Hail the Queen. He had made sure of it by buying one on each of the eight entries.

Sullivan's friends knew that he set great store by birthdays, and we tried not to let one of his slip past without recognizing it, although we well knew that we risked getting this sort of ac-knowledgment, as I once did:

Your telegram on my birthday today will suffice until you can find time to send me some more substantial gift. Thank-ing you in advance

Mr. Sullivan

One year I happened to see an ad in which a photo studio offered to take any small portrait snapshot and print it up like a sheet of postage stamps. I had a snapshot of Sullivan, so I mailed it in. Back came the sheet, with one hundred stamps, ten to a row. I sent a row each to Corey Ford, Arthur Krock, Nunnally Johnson, Finis Farr, Marc Connelly, and others of his friends (I'd have included Admiral Nimitz and Mignon G. Eberhardt, if I'd known at the time that they were Sullivan fans) and asked them to stick one or two stamps, without comment, on their birthday letters to him. I did and they did, but I don't think Frank ever noticed, alas! Certainly, he never mentioned it to any of us.

That was his sixtieth birthday, in 1952. In 1955, he wrote me:

> Thank you for congratulations on my reaching 63. I really do not mind being 63. But if I did mind, you can bet your bottom dollar that I would not *be* 63. Or if you didn't care to bet your bottom dollar, you could just bet your bottom, if you could find any takers for so raddled and scrawny a relic. I have no plans except to go along quietly until I reach 76, and at that age I will start painting American primitives and become known as Grandpa Moses or Old Black Joe. My work will be sold at three grand per canvas and you may, if you like, pay me now for the two or three paintings I know you will wish to have.
>
> I plan to come to New York to get new glasses and a new navel some time after the World Series. Shall we meet Under the Clock? *

The only painting he seems to have done was on his eightieth, which he celebrated at Siro's, in Saratoga:

> We painted it a pale pink. Gene and Lucille Markey, who usually drink my birthday with me, couldn't come this year,

---

* The clock above the Biltmore Hotel lobby was a popular rendezvous, especially for preppies, in the 1920s and 1930s.

but they sent a magnum of champagne. The fun ran riot, and the naked geisha girls who emerged from the huge pie in the center of the table were just as cute as they could be. One of them said she was about to celebrate her eightieth birthday too.

Siro's was a restaurant a few minutes' walk down Lincoln Avenue from Frank's house. The owners, Harry and Eleanor Kircher, doted on him and watched over him. One evening, he told me, another birthday party was given there, this one in honor of a boy about eight. His father asked what he would like to eat—he could have anything he wanted on this special day. Whereupon, said Frank, the boy set up a chant:

> A Coke and a steak
> And a birthday cake!
> A Coke and a steak
> And a birthday cake!
> A Coke—

Frank said it rang in his head for days, like

> Punch, brother, punch, punch with care,
> Punch in the presence of the passinjare.

(It's beginning to ring in my head right now!)

I had a little trouble impressing on him the date of *my* birthday, but once I'd managed to do so, he responded nobly. One year he sent me a childhood photograph of himself, with curls, sailor suit, and an angry glare. The inscription is, "For Joseph Bryan, III, from his illegitimate son Frank Sullivan."

Something else he gave me, something I treasure just as much, is an original drawing by his old colleague on the *World*, Milt Gross, the creator of the "Louie Dot Dope" cartoon strip. (Memorable sample: Louie's mother is notified that he has "run avay vit de countess"; she faints; it turns out to be "de puppularity countess.") My drawing shows an elderly Jew (labeled OUR YOUTH) in a yarmulke, with his long white beard (BAD HABITS) caught in the door of a safe (RUIN). The inscription reads, "To Frenkie dollink, pruppietor from de Blotz, witt luff, MILT GROSS." Everyone who sees it asks, "What on earth does it *mean?*" I tell them what Frank told me when I asked the same question: "It means that Milt Gross was a very funny guy."

A final note about birthdays: On one of mine Sullivan wrote me, "I raise my glass and drink to you, and then dash it into the fireplace. It is made of plastic. I can retrieve it later."

He enjoyed birthdays, but he wasn't sentimental about them as he was about Christmas, which he enjoyed even more. He reread "A Christmas Carol" every Christmas Eve; he wrote his annual Christmas verses for *The New Yorker*; he sent out Christmas cards by the hundreds; and the promise of a good Christmas party would rouse him from his hibernation and bring him running, even down to New York. Here is his account of one (1954) that must have been extra-special:

I went to a Christmas party at Howard and Dorothy Lindsay's and had a grand time. The champagne flowed, and everybody was taken with the urge to get up and do a stunt, and there were some capital stunters (or stuntsters) present. Buck Crouse sang, or rather illustrated, "Put Them Together, They Spell Mother," as sung by Paula Lawrence, meanwhile contorting himself into the letters M, O, T, etc. I have known Crouse over 30 years, and never knew before that he could make an R of himself. Lindsay has a remarkable accomplishment: he remembers the *second* verses of popular hits of yesteryear. He sang the second verse of "In the Shade of the Old Apple Tree," which I don't suppose had been sung since it was written. The hit of the evening was when Max Gordon's wife, Milly, sang a song from when she was a Follies girl: "Would You Like to Mail a Letter in My Box?" I was all ready to do *my* stunt, which is playing the "William Tell Overture" on my cheeks, but nobody asked me. There's the story of my life in a nutshell.

Christmas 1958 was another to be cherished. Just before it, "Jim Thurber telephoned me [to ask] about dedicating his book on Ross to me. The news took me completely by surprise, and is by far the nicest Christmas present I could imagine getting." (It's in this dedication that Thurber speaks of the "love and admiration" that Sullivan's friends had for him.)

He had begun writing his "Greetings, Friends" verses on the *World* in the late 1920s; he took them over to *The New Yorker* in 1932, and he wrote them there every Christmas for the next thirty-four years. He pretended to be bored with them at the end, but I don't think he was, really. It gave him immense pleasure to salute his friends in print—his friends and strangers, too, if their names made convenient rhymes. He treated me and, later, my wife kindly in the "Greetings," but his goodwill toward me stopped short of his Christmas card, which read: "All my Christmas affection, known as Joyeux Noël, goes to Mme. Bryan, and only a small part to her husband. (signed) Scrooge J. Sullivan."

He turned his Scrooge side toward Christmas in 1964, when he wrote to Maggie Falter:

> I am abolishing Christmas shortly, but I thought I'd send you a wish for a happy one before I put an end to the whole racket. I might reconsider if you could arrange to have these goddam radio and television stations quit playing "Partridges in a Pear-Tree" and tearing that lovely old hymn, "Silent Night," to tatters. But you can't do it. Nobody on earth can buck the Gibraltar of radio-television stupidity and cheapness. Do I sound like Scrooge? I'm not so sure Dickens was

right in reforming Scrooge and making him a damned old
fool full of sweetness and light at the end. Dickens never had
a radio that played "Hark, the Herald Angels Sing" 22,000
times in the month before Christmas.

The Scrooge mood didn't last, of course. Presently Sullivan was
admitting to Maggie, "Christmas was very fine this year. I am
really so sold on it that I'm going to write to the *Times* and suggest that we have it again next year."

His health could never have been described as "blooming,"
thanks in some measure, I suspect, to his having forged a long
chain of hangovers, though Frank himself would have denied this
emphatically. He was far from being a lush, but like Bob Benchley, Dottie Parker, and Nunnally Johnson (and myself), he enjoyed an occasional glass or so. Henry Redmond wrote me:

> I stopped in Saratoga on my way north, and Frank took me
> on an all-night tour of the local watering-spots. Next day
> around noon, I went to his house, feeling like death taken
> seasick. Frank was sitting on the porch in a dressing-gown,
> looking even worse than I felt. He said, "I'm not at all well.
> I must be coming down with a cold."
>
> I said, "Do you suppose that last covey of brandies we
> flushed had anything to do with it?"
>
> He looked at me with amazement and indignation. "What
> *utter* nonsense!" he said.

As he approached his seventies, he began suffering from a series
and variety of afflictions: bronchitis, proctitis, diverticulitis, a
colonic infection, and others. He wrote Maggie, "My bronchitis
won't go away, though I have asked it to, very nicely. It goes away
on Mondays, Wednesdays and Fridays and comes back, with a

friend, on the other days." He wrote me that the infection gave him

> a rough and painful two weeks. Don't let anybody tell you that pain or suffering ennobles one; it just makes me peevish, complaining and anti-social. Also, I am willing to give you all my rights in milk toast, free and clear, in perpetuity.

I was having a glass with Corey Ford one summer evening in New York; Sullivan's name was mentioned, of course, and Corey told me that he was laid up with I forget what. Next morning I bought a bottle of Scotch—the label boasted "Every Drop Twenty Years Old!"—and sent it to him with get-well wishes. Weeks passed. Not a word. I was invited to Saratoga that August, and my first morning there, I stopped in for an eye-opener with the Sage.

Apropos, I asked rather cautiously, "Did you ever get that Scotch I sent you?"

He bristled. "Certainly I got it! Why? You didn't expect any thanks for it, did you?"

"No," I said meekly. "Er—no."

Sullivan tapped me on the knee. "Look, Brice: I was *sick*! Do you send a sick friend twenty-year-old *flowers*? No! You send him nice, fresh flowers. Do you send him twenty-year-old *candy*? No! You send him nice, fresh candy. And yet you send *me* twenty-year-old whiskey! If you want to be thanked, damn it, send me a bottle of nice, fresh whiskey!" He added, "It's not too late yet."

But it would be too late before long. Although many of us thought that his only serious affliction was hypochondria, he had the last word. Soon after his eighty-third birthday, in 1975, he went to the hospital with a recurrence of his colonic infection. Home again, he fell out of bed and broke two ribs, and was returned to the hospital. He had often joked about retiring to "the Petroleum V. Nasby Home for Aged and Indigent Humorists," but this was not to be. He died in the hospital in February, and was buried from St. Peter's Church, Saratoga—the one where his Grandfather Shea had been President of the Father Matthew Total Abstinence Society.

APPENDIX I

When Sullivan signed a letter "The Artful Dodger" or "Mr. Murdstone," as he often did, it meant that he was on one of his annual Dickens kicks. He *loved* Dickens (so did Dorothy Parker, who wrote:

> Who call him spurious and shoddy
> Shall do it o'er my lifeless body).

A rereading of *Martin Chuzzlewit* brought this observation from Sullivan: "That first chapter, where Mr. Pecksniff gets knocked on his ass, is a darb, if I may borrow the critical phrase used by Dr. Henry Seidel Canby in referring to the incident." As for *David Copperfield*:

Nobody ever stops to ponder that although Wilkins Micawber has become a symbol of futility and mismanagement, he is the one who puts everything to rights, the only one who has the prudence and courage to do it. If his plan to expose Uriah had misfired, he really would have been destroyed. Nobody but poor old Wilkins had the guts to go after Heep, although it does seem that Copperfield might have found a way to get old man Wickfield out of Heep's clutches, and get Aunt Betsey's 8000 pounds back. And Mrs. Micawber is about the most lovable girl in Dickens' galaxy. She's a sweetheart!

Another of his favorite women in fiction was the startling Miss Lucilla Teatime, in Colin Watson's detective novels about Flaxborough, England. I introduced Frank to them, and he liked them so much, he put Watson's name in his next "Greetings, Friends" verses.

His favorite women in real life were Maggie Falter (who has allowed me to quote from some of his letters to her) and Beatrice Lillie. After seeing one of Miss Lillie's shows, he wrote me, "I went backstage afterwards and hugged her. I asked her to run for President, and she said she would. This is the greatest limey girl since Boadicea!"

*A*PPENDIX II

Sullivan told me a story about Milt Gross, who drew the "Louie Dot Dope" comic strip, when they were on the *World* together. F.P.A. was also on the *World* then. His full name was Franklin Pierce Adams—so he said, though his appearance contradicted the implied colonial American ancestry. He and Gross passed in the corridors several times a day, with Gross always greeting him, "Good morning, Mr. Adams!" or "Good afternoon, Mr. Adams!" and Adams never responding. Before long Gross's popularity reached a peak that could not be ignored. Then, for the first time,

F.P.A. spoke to him. "Morning, Mr. Gross," he said, holding out his hand, "my name is Franklin Pierce Adams."

Gross put on a low-comedy Jewish squint and accent. "Dot ain't vot *I* hoid!" he said.

This must be one of the very few times on record that F.P.A. was abashed; usually it was he who did the abashing (accent on the *bash*). If I had to prepare a scale of verbal savagery, I'd put Parker, Woollcott, and Kaufman—all of them deft with the scalpel and stiletto, and brutal with the bludgeon and blackjack, and each a combination of snapping turtle, cobra, and wolf—in a Murderers' Row at the top, with F.P.A. somewhere near them. Corey Ford would be near the bottom. Benchley, Sullivan, and Don Stewart, the Sunshine Boys, wouldn't be on the scale at all.

Corey told me about a mutual friend of ours, P———, who twice incurred an expression of F.P.A.'s displeasure. P——— was a nice enough fellow, but incurably loquacious. As Corey said, "His garrulity made a babbling brook seem like a millpond, and Niagara like a trickling faucet." In the summer of 1945, P——— had been anesthetizing the Players for week after week with his strategy for invading Japan—and then the Bomb exploded.

One member's response to the news was, "This will cut P———'s conversation down by nine-tenths."

F.P.A. said, "A drop in the bucket!"

On the other occasion—again according to Corey—the same logorrheic P——— had been discoursing for an hour or more when he unexpectedly said, "Well, to make a long story short—"

"Too late!", cried F.P.A., "too late!"

APPENDIX III

When Sullivan was in New York, he spent a lot of time at the Players, on Gramercy Park. It was—is—one of the coziest, most congenial clubs in town, a hangout for such of his friends as Ford, Falter, Connelly, F.P.A., and Rollin Kirby. Many of the stories Frank wrote me (or told me) involve the Players and its members. One of the happiest is about Mr. M.,

> a non-resident member who has been on a toot and was still on it when I left yesterday. He had become the official hair shirt of the club, insinuating himself eagerly on every little gathering, and displaying a genius for boring the crankier and most fastidious members, and breathing foully on them. I thought he was a god-damn nuisance until the following happened:
>
> Rollin Kirby, Tony Brown and I were sitting on the balcony outside the reading room, chatting and cocktailing, when Mr. M. burst out and rebuked us incoherently—something to the effect that he couldn't write a letter to his wife because we were disturbing him. For a minute it looked as though he were about to join us, but he staggered away.
>
> When we got up to go in to dinner, Kirby's eye found a sheet of letter-paper on the writing desk, blotted and stained like a 3-year-old's attempt to write a note to the teacher. We all had a look at it and are ready to testify that it read as follows:
>
>
>
> "Dear Wife, Think of you constantly.
>
> Your obdt servant,
>
> Sam'l Johnson."
>
>

Another of Sullivan's Players stories is about Dave McKinley,

a lovable old retired buccaneer of a publisher who hangs out
at the club and is the most accomplished, most artistic cusser
I have ever known. He has a four-year-old granddaughter for
whom he is crazy. Naturally, the tot has picked up some
lovely language frescoings not usually found in the vocabu-
laries of four-year-olds. Dave never had any desire to teach
them to her; they just ripple out of him in a beautiful, limpid
stream in the ordinary course of conversation, and he can't
do anything about it.

Well, he was walking with granddaughter one day, and
when she went out of her way to step on an ant, he thought it
might be the moment to give her a little lecture on being
kind, even to ants. So he told her it was a wrong thing; the
ant had no defense against her; it was one of God's creatures
too, and in some ways it was quite an admirable insect. Then
he got into the life of ants—how they keep house, and have
cities, with electricity and hot and cold running water, and
politicians and tarts, and how they teach us a lesson about
staying busy.

As he warmed up to his subject, he became pretty moved
by it himself. After about ten minutes of one of the most
touching talks on nature and insect life since a bee stung
Thoreau, he finally stopped. During all of it, the little girl
looked up at him, entranced and adoring. He waited for her
questions. There were none. She just said fondly, "Grandpa,
you old son of a bitch, I *love* you!"

✐PPENDIX IV

I once met the Master, P. G. Wodehouse. It was at his god-daughter's house in New York, and that's about all I am able to report. His mere proximity so addled and dazzled me that I have no recollection of anything he said, beyond his expressing a fond-ness for "an occasional nip of bourbon." This—*this* was the genius whose imagination had taken the quantum leap from ordi-nary humor to the point where Psmith shows Eve Halliday around the grounds of Blandings Castle:

> We are now [he tells her] in the southern pleasance or the west home-park or something. Note the refined way the deer are cropping the grass. All the ground on which we are now standing is of historic interest. Oliver Cromwell went through here in 1650. The record has since been lowered.

This was the poet who named Sir Preston Potter's mustache "Love in Idleness," as if it were a garden flower, and named Lord Bromborough's mustache "Joyeuse," as if it were a mighty sword. It was this demigod here in front of me—he, and no other—who "hung up the telephone with a nasty, wristy motion." And I just stood there in my daze, seeing, hearing, and speaking nothing, like those three sanctimonious Japanese monkeys.

It was not then, but on another evening, that his goddaughter told me this story: When "Plummy" and his wife first came to New York, he sent her to find an apartment while he was work-ing. There was one restriction: the apartment had to be on the ground floor.

She protested, "But *why*, Plummy? Ground-floor apartments are so noisy and dirty!"

"I know," he said, "but I can never think of anything to say to elevator boys."

APPENDIX V

Here, abridged, is a review I wrote of Frank Sullivan's last book, *Well, There's No Harm in Laughing*. It is reprinted by permission of *The New York Times Book Review*, where it appeared on October 22, 1972.

The line of humorous writers in America is long and proud. It begins in the period of the Civil War, with the primitive *faux naifs*: Bill Arp, Josh Billings, Petroleum V. Nasby, and Bill Nye. Mark Twain was next, standing alone and overshadowing his contemporaries. Then, as the century turned, came Kin Hubbard, Finley Peter Dunne, George Ade, Ellis Parker Butler and Irvin S. Cobb. Don Marquis was a bridge to the post–World War I group—the "New Yorker" group, to give it a convenient name—led by Ring Lardner. Was anyone ever as wildly funny as Lardner? No, no one—except his compeers: James Thurber, Corey Ford, Ogden Nash and Robert Benchley. All these dear, delightful men are dead now—but there are, finally, three more who survive: Donald Ogden Stewart, S. J. Perelman and Frank Sullivan.*

I say "finally" because I see no one on the horizon to succeed them; and I say "survive" because it is a thin, gray, pejorative word, eminently suitable for lazy scuts who show no sense of public obligation. Stewart, who published his delirious "Perfect Behavior" in 1922, has published nothing since 1929. A murrain on him! Another murrain on Perelman, who isn't publishing half enough. The man who wrote "I loved him like a brothel" ought to be chained to a wall and have high-school basketball scores droned at him until he cried for mercy and his typewriter. As for Sullivan, our topic

* These three, too, have died since this review was published.

for today, *three* murrains: one on his publisher, Doubleday; one on his editor, George Oppenheimer; and the third—the stickiest and most stinging—on himself.

I denounce Doubleday for trying to gull Sullivan's Loyal Legion by using the title "Well, There's No Harm in Laughing" for this verbatim reissue (as the title page admits) of "Frank Sullivan Through the Looking Glass" (1970); I denounce Oppenheimer for including verses and pieces already in print elsewhere, when he could have used the space for more, many more, of Sullivan's incomparable letters, ones not yet in print anywhere. And I denounce Sullivan for sitting on a silken cushion up there in Saratoga, eating strawberries and cream, and never once putting down his silver spoon to give us another "Vanderbilt Convention" or "Gloria Swanson Defends Her Title" or "Mrs. Washington Crosses Her Husband" or, one of the brightest stars in his heavenly crown, "Nocturne in Beekman Place."

Vain, deluding hopes! The man whom P. G. Wodehouse called "America's foremost humorist"—and Wodehouse knows whereof—has almost stopped writing. He is turning out only two pieces a year: one for *The New York Times* on the opening of the Saratoga season, the other his Christmas poem for *The New Yorker*. Worse, he is putting it about that he won't dole us even this meager fare, come 1973. If he had made his announcement a few years ago, we might have persuaded Admiral Nimitz, who was one of his most devout readers, to threaten the erstwhile lieutenant with a keelhauling if he didn't turn to. Now it is too late. Sullivan, once the shadow of a great rock in a weary land, has, like Topsy, "jes' folded his tents an' stole away." Silence holds in thrall the golden throat of the Spa's Sweet Singer. There is a rift in the lieut.

So, with no new pieces in the offing, the Loyal Legion will

have to content itself with these letters—which is like saying that with no more cookies in the jar, we'll have to eat angel food cake. For a sample slice, nibble at the letter asking Alexander Woollcott to sponsor him to a real-estate firm. Then read the one congratulating Marc Connelly on his election to the National Geographic Society. If a funnier letter was ever written, almost certainly it was Sullivan who wrote it. And if it isn't in this collection, it's waiting somewhere for Oppenheimer to put it in the next.

"The next"? Why not? The lode of Sullivan letters is almost inexhaustible. As a correspondent, he makes the previous champion, Horace Walpole, seem as uncommunicative as if he'd had to write with a chisel on marble. Besides, the lucky people who get letters from Sullivan never throw them away; they keep them forever, to warm their hands and hearts by. No bitterness comes in Sullivan's envelopes, no sneers or snarls, no gossip or spite; no "black humor" or "comedy of insult"; nothing but sunniness and gentle merriment. (God rest ye, gentle merriment!)

Oppenheimer, to your post! Duty calls! (Do you hear that whipcrack in my voice?) If you want to ask Sullivan's help, the time will never be riper than now. This is the season when he reaches his prime, as he himself admits: "The autumn coloring is at its height and I am simply beautiful, all red and gold. People come from miles just to see me." (I am told it is a sight never to be forgotten, without the help of tranquilizers.) Moreover, it suggests a title for the forthcoming Volume II—forthcoming, or 20,000 Sullivan fans will know the reason why: "Sullivan in All His Glory."

The last sentence brought me an indignant letter from Mignon G. Eberhardt, the author of *Call After Midnight*, *Jury of One*, and other excellent mysteries. She wrote, " '20,000 fans'? Two hundred thousand! *Two million*!" Correction accepted, gladly!

DOROTHY PARKER

1893-1967

Bittersweet

Dorothy Parker at a Hollywood Party
(UPI/BETTMANN NEWSPHOTOS)

THIS is going to be about Dorothy Parker, but I'll need a minute to get around to her. Even then, please don't expect an analysis of her personality, or speculation about her ultimate place in American literature. All I intend to do is set down, informally, a part of what I remember about her, including some of her remarks that I've never seen in print, and that I think deserve saving.

Well, then, when I was a youth in Richmond, Virginia, I had a friend named Alan Campbell. His house was near ours, and we were together often, until he went off to the Virginia Military Institute, and I went elsewhere. Ten years passed before I saw him again. I had become the second-string theater critic for *Time*, and one evening in the 1928–29 season, I was sent to review a steamy drama called *Congai*, which involved an Indo-Chinese half-caste (Helen Menken) and her handsome son, Ouven. The son looked familiar, despite a thick layer of Max Factor's "Light

Egyptian." The program explained it: "Ouven . . . Allen [*sic*] Campbell." I remember almost nothing about the play except, irrelevantly, that Ouven wore a maroon blazer; but I remember going backstage for a pleasant reunion. Thereafter Alan and I ran into each other from time to time, and it was at one of our chance encounters—I'm coming to the point at last—that he introduced me to Dorothy (whom he had just married, I discovered later, or perhaps was just about to marry).

The occasion was a dance in New York, in October 1933. I date it by the fact that, a week earlier, *The New Yorker* had published a profile I had written about Rosa Lewis of the Cavendish Hotel in London. The first person I recognized at the party was Alan. He said, "Come along at once! Dottie Parker is here and she's dying to meet you."

Dying to meet *me*? Dorothy *Parker*? I followed Alan to where she was sitting. I don't know what he said, but she waved me away. "Joe Bryan? Oh, no! Oh, *no*! Whoever you are, you're certainly not Joe Bryan! If this is a joke, buster, it's not funny!"

I babbled "Yes, I am!" or maybe "Honest, it's me!" but she went right on: "Oh, no! Not little Dorothy. Not with the Curse of the Parkers hanging over her head! Dorothy's never going to meet the man who wrote that marvelous Rosa Lewis piece! *That's* reserved for rich, attractive girls. *They* get to meet Joe Bryan, but not poor, plain little Mrs. Parker!"

I stood there like a great gowk, still mumbling that inane "Honest—" until finally she said, "You *swear* you are?" Then, to the room at large, "Go away, all you dreadful people, and leave this *special* man with me! Go away, *all* of you! —And as for *you*," she said, wheeling on me, "*you sit down*!" I sat. She stared at me, and a moment passed before she said, "You're going to think this very strange. I've just met you, and here I'm about to ask you an impertinent question. It's not 'Will you collaborate on a play with me?' but 'How soon can you start?'"

Imagine it!—the famous Dorothy Parker, the brilliant poet and short story writer, the wittiest woman in New York, asking an unknown cub to collaborate with her!—Not *asking* me; *ordering* me! In the years ahead, I often heard her describe herself, when embarrassed, as "dimpling and blushing, digging my toe in the sand, twisting my handkerchief in my two great things of hands." That's what I did then. We agreed to meet at her apartment at eleven the next morning, and I went home wrapped in a pink mist.

Her apartment was at the extreme end of East 49th Street, downtown side. She'd said "eleven," but I couldn't possibly get there before ten thirty, so I had to walk up and down, killing time. On the stroke of eleven, I told the doorman, "Mr. Bryan to see Mrs. Parker, please."

He rang her. She was a long time answering, but finally he said, "Mr. Bryan, madam . . . Mr. *Bryan* . . ." He turned to me: "Will you spell it, sir?" I spelled it, and he repeated, "B, R, Y, A, N, madam . . . Yes, madam." He turned to me again: "Mrs. Parker asks what you wish to see her about." I don't know how I made myself heard over the noise of my heart cracking, but I must have succeeded, because presently I found myself in the elevator, even though I was already achingly aware that she'd have no recollection of our glittering plans from the evening before. It proved to be worse than that: she had no recollection even of our having *met*.

I saw Dottie many, many times afterwards; indeed, she lived with my wife and me for a while; but never once was that first evening ever mentioned. For all that she retained of it, it had never happened.

A number of playwrights and novelists who knew Dottie well used her as a model for a character—usually a wisecracking woman, with either good looks or their remnants; she drinks too much; if she isn't suffering through an unhappy romance at the moment, one is just behind her; and often the threat of suicide hangs in the air. (Yes, Dottie had looks in her younger days. Mrs. Pat Campbell told her, "You're a pretty, pretty cobra!") One of her first and most lifelike incarnations was as "Lily Malone," in Philip Barry's *Hotel Universe*. Barry describes Lily as "able to impart to her small, impudent face a certain prettiness," which was bang true of Dottie; and he gave Lily lines that are purest Parker. For instance:

ALICE: What a fool I am, really!
LILY: (Sweetly.) Please, dear, let *me* say that.

That same year, 1932, "Mary Hilliard" in George Oppenheimer's *Here Today* was drawn from Dottie. Ruth Gordon created the role; she must have enjoyed it, because she later wrote *Over 21*, in which "Paula Wharton" was Dottie again. Dottie once said she wanted to write her autobiography, but was afraid that George and Miss Gordon would sue her for plagiarism. Her bitter title for it would have been *Mongrel*, presumably because she was cross-bred, her father being Jewish and her mother Scottish (Alan Campbell's father was Scottish and his mother Jewish). George Kaufman and Moss Hart, in turn, put her onstage as "Julia Glenn" in *Merrily We Roll Along* (1934). The stage directions describe Julia as "a woman close to forty [Dottie was forty that year]. She is not unpretty, but on her face are the marks of years and years of quiet and steady drinking—eight, ten hours a day. . . . She wears something from about three years ago, and which wasn't quite right then." A man offers to get her a drink and asks, "What are you having?" and Julia says, "Know what I'm having? Not much fun." Dottie as ever was!

She was also "Daisy Lester," a nightclub singer, in Charles Brackett's *Entirely Surrounded* (1934)—a *roman à clef* dedicated to her. Daisy is a speaking likeness of Dottie—Daisy, with her "great, melancholy eyes . . . a tiny, dark figure in a blue dress with peasant embroidery on the sleeves." Listen to this line of Daisy's, and you'll hear Dottie's own voice:

> You couldn't have turned a dog away in that storm. Not even Mrs. Herrick, and I may say that Mrs. Herrick looked like an old belle who'd spent the best years of her youth turning dogs away.

If you saw Audrey Hepburn in *War and Peace*, fatten up her image and age it and—however absurd it may sound—you'll have an approximation of Dottie as she looked then, in the mid-1930s: the same height (about five three), the same wistful black eyes, the same black bangs and topknot. But whereas Miss Hepburn was slim and trim and chic, Dottie was always tousled, and a little—well, *dingy*. Moreover, she was addicted to dirndls ("with peasant embroidery on the sleeves"), a costume that made her seem both dumpy and dowdy. Not that this ever bothered her. Her idea of dressing up for the evening was to add a tulle scarf to whatever she'd been wearing all day. If it is true that women dress to impress other women, this explains Dottie's indifference to fashion. She didn't care a damn what women thought of her or her appearance. What *men* thought, yes, but not women. She didn't like women. As far as I know, only two of her close friends were women: Bee Ames (who had been married to Donald Ogden Stewart) and Lillian Hellman. Dottie's friendships were liable to sudden, violent reversals. If she ever turned on Miss Hellman, I never heard about it; but she repaid Bee's long years of loyalty and generosity by making a woman very much like her the butt of a cruel short story. I myself can strip my sleeve and show the marks of Dottie's claws. Come to think of it, she had a couple of marks of her own: a small blue star tattooed on her right shoulder, and scars across her wrists. I don't know anything about the tattoo, but it was no secret that the scars came from a halfhearted attempt at suicide with a razor in the 1920s. A later attempt—no more resolute—with sleeping pills moved Benchley to warn her, "If you don't stop this sort of thing, Dottie, you'll make yourself sick!"

Pretension always invited her derision. Her "Diary of a New York Lady" crucified a woman we all knew—silly and affected, but harmless—who had somehow offended her. Later, Dottie said of her and her set, "Their pooled emotions wouldn't fill a teaspoon." The wife of a friend of mine, unfortunately given to sprinkling French phrases through her chatter, once said *"Tant pis!"* in Dottie's hearing. Ever afterwards, Dottie made solicitous inquiries about her: "How's old *tant pis* these days? Still full of it?" Yet she herself crossed her 7s, continental-style, and she gave at least three of her poems titles in French, one with a word misspelled.

Any collection of her slashes would show that though several of the most famous had men for their targets—"He's a pony's ass," for instance, and "He's a rhinestone in the rough"—most were aimed at women. There comes to mind the lady who "spent her time in London sliding down a barrister." Another lady—she had finally married the gentleman who had been sheltering her for some years—received this telegram from Dottie next day: WHAT'S NEW? A sentimental occasion like a wedding always brought something absurd from her—or like Christmas, as witnesses the telegram she sent my wife and me from Hollywood: IN ORDER TO WISH YOU A MERRY CHRISTMAS I AM INTERRUPTING WORK ON MY SCREEN EPIC, LASSIE GET DOWN.

Theater people seemed to provoke her special displeasure. I don't need to quote what she said about Katharine Hepburn's acting in *The Lake*; it's Dottie's best-known quip. When someone mentioned Meg Mundy, then starring in *The Respectful Prostitute*, Dottie affected never to have heard of her: "Meg Mundy? What's that, a Welsh holiday?" She said of a certain English actor, a notorious homosexual, "He simply buggers description" (apropos, she also said that "Verlaine was always chasing Rim-

bauds"). Clare Boothe Luce, stepping aside to let Dottie precede
through a door, rashly remarked "Age before beauty!" She said
it with a laugh, but Dottie was not appeased; she snapped, "—and
pearls before swine." She also said, "'Clare—Booth—Luce':
sounds like the motto of a girls' school."

To be sure, almost any quip would be mothered on Dottie, if it
was witty enough and savage enough—unless, of course, it had a
Washington angle, in which case it became Alice Longworth's.
The two ladies intersected at one point. Mrs. Longworth said that
Calvin Coolidge "looked as if he had been weaned on a pickle";
Mrs. Parker, on being informed that he was dead, asked "How
can they tell?"

My wife and I lived in or near New York from 1932 to 1938,
and we ran into Dottie occasionally at a friend's or at some restaurant. One evening we were having nightcaps with Frank Sullivan
at 21 when Dottie entered alone and, seeing Frank, whom she
loved, came to our table. Frank welcomed her with "Hello, you
Jew-hater!"

Dottie flung herself on his lap and clawed at his fly, demanding,
"Which side does it open on?"

Presently St. Clair McKelway brought over a man whom he
introduced as a psychiatrist. This was at a time when almost everybody was complaining about the shortage of apartments—almost
everybody but Mac, who announced that only a few hours' search
that morning had turned up a perfect one: inexpensive, comfortable, excellent location. Dottie touched the psychiatrist's arm: "A
patient for you, Doctor!"

Her apartment was at the New Weston hotel. I remember the
housewarming. Sullivan's present was a neat little package of egg-
shells, coffee grounds, orange peel, and soggy crusts. "There's
nothing like garbage," he explained, "to make a house a home."

Dottie asked Benchley what she should do with it, since she

hadn't yet bought a garbage can. Bob said, "Put it in your bed and pull the sheet up over it."

"Never!" Dottie said nobly. "That's the coward's way out!"

I went to the apartment one winter afternoon. A wispy young writer had just left, and Dottie gave an incredulous account of his visit. His blue sneakers had surprised her—it had been snowing all day—but she had been dumbfounded by his voice, which was "so high, it was audible only to a dog's ear." Her first Christmas at the New Weston, someone asked if she had hung up her stocking. "No," she said, "but I hung up the hotel."

I think it was Corey who told me that one. In those days, before World War II, such remarks of Dottie's as I heard were quoted to me by mutual friends who saw her oftener and knew her far better than I—people like Ford and Sullivan, Kaufman, Woollcott, Don and Bee Stewart, and Bob Benchley. Particularly Bob. There was a special friendship between him and Dottie. His full, formal name was Robert Charles Benchley, but for some private reason she always called him Fred. The poems in her *Sunset Gun* include "For R.C.B.," and her *Death and Taxes* is dedicated "To Mr. Benchley." She was with him when he reached one of the most important milestones in his life: his first alcoholic drink— the first, as the years passed, of a formidable series they would have together.

George Kaufman was not as close to her as were the others; but it was he who told me about a dinner at Lillian Hellman's on a summer evening when Louis Adamic, author of *The Native's Return* and other books, turned up in a white cotton suit, rather rumpled, and Dottie remarked in a loud aside, "Looks like he's come to sell us some leaf tobacco!" Another summer evening, she went for drinks at the apartment on West 47th Street that Woollcott shared with Harold Ross. Charlie MacArthur was there, in a suit like Adamic's, plus an open shirt and a wide-brimmed raffia hat; he was even smoking a thin cheroot and holding a tall frosted glass. Dottie addressed him respectfully: "As the American consul here, sir—"

My wife and I saw Dottie most frequently just after the war, when we were all living in Bucks County, she and Alan at Fox Farm, near Pipersville, and we a few miles away at Fiddler's Green, near Doylestown. Sid and Laura Perelman were close by, too, and George and Bea Kaufman, and Moss Hart and his recent bride, Kitty Carlisle. After a dinner, we often played The Game— the one in which one team draws up a list of ten words or names or phrases and gives it to the captain of the other, who has to act them out in pantomime for his teammates to identify as quickly as they can. The Kaufmans and Harts (no slouches as actors themselves) often had one or two professionals from their shows down for the weekend, so competition was hot. Alan was excellent at pantomime, and Dottie was excellent at lists. I have kept a couple of hers, in her round, finishing-school handwriting. Here is one:

> *I'd die for dear old Rutgers. Peter Pan. You don't know your ass from your elbow. Fly Away, Kentucky Babe! Have you a little fairy in your home? Pride and Prejudice. Block that kick! Parallel lines meet in infinity. Misery loves company. You too, Brutus?*

Once when Dottie was doing the pantomime, she signaled that the word contained four syllables (this was permitted), and then began to nibble, delicately and daintily, at an imaginary morsel: in-grace-she-ate.

She was on her good behavior that evening. But as the months passed and her marriage fell apart, she became bitter and cruel, especially toward Alan's mother—"the only person on earth," said Dottie, "who pronounces the word 'egg' in three syllables: 'ay-yuh-guh.'" She told me once that she had seen Mrs. Campbell wearing a hat "that would have looked young on Joan"—our daughter, then aged twelve.

One day at our house she switched her sights from poor, harmless Mrs. Campbell to Moss Hart, the gentlest and kindest of men. She pretended to believe that "Moss" was not his real name and began coaxing him to admit it. Moss said mildly that it actually *was* his name; his parents had given it to him, and he'd never had another. Dottie laughed this aside: "Oh, come *on*, Mossy! This is old Dottie—you can tell *her*! What is it *really?*—Moses? Morris? You can trust *me*! Besides, it's nothing to be ashamed of. Plenty of nice people change their names! Tell Dottie now: is it Moscowitz?" *

She kept it up until anyone more combustible than Moss— which was almost anyone else at all—would have smacked her chops, but he took it quietly until she ran down. And then, if you please, she turned on Kitty! I didn't hear their dialogue. Kitty repeated it to me long afterwards:

"When Dottie realized she wasn't going to get a rise out of Moss, she came over and sat by me, sweet as sugar cane, and begged me to tell her about my debut on the stage. I should have known she was half-loaded, but I didn't, and I—Little Miss Innocence— plunged ahead. It was in *Rio Rita*, I said, the title role, and the theater was the famous old Capitol, in New York. I was all wound up, describing the thrill of walking in the footsteps of the great stars who had played there, when she put her hand on my arm and breathed, 'They made you do *that*? Oh, you poor *child*! That *huge* place, and all those people out front *staring* at you, waiting to *devour* you! Just to *think* of it makes my heart *ache*!'

"I said it wasn't that way at all! They were a marvelous audi-

---

* Moss's autobiography, *Act One*, relates how he became the office boy at "Augustus Pitou, Theatrical Enterprises." Like Dottie, Mr. Pitou refused to accept his name, and always called him "Mouse."

ence, and I enjoyed every minute of it. Dottie said, 'You don't
have to pretend with *me*, dear. How *brave* you are! What a *brave*
girl! Oh, I *admire* you so!' I can't swear there weren't tears in her
eyes. I kept protesting that there'd been nothing for me to be brave
about—that I'd absolutely loved it—but Dottie kept oozing sympathy and calling me 'You dear, brave *baby*!'—and then, suddenly, I woke up. She was putting me on, trying to see how much
of her molasses I'd swallow. I felt like a *fool*!"

Kitty wasn't the first whom Dottie had made feel like that—it
was the same technique she had used on me the evening we met—
nor, by far, was Kitty the last. She was probably saved from worse
savaging by Dottie's dropping her cigarette lighter, which bounced
under the sofa. I had to kneel to reach it, and when I knelt, my
knee joints popped and crackled. Dottie rubbed her hands together and spread them toward me. "Ah," she beamed, "there's
nothing like an open fire—!"

The Campbells sold their farm and were divorced in 1947, to
everyone's distress, especially our children's. They liked Dottie,
but they loved Alan. He played their games with genuine enthusiasm. He had a fund of riddles and jokes and nonsense jingles.
He was "cozy" and never unkind. Dottie too would entertain
them, but her principal audience was always herself, as when she
told them "the little-known fable of Aesop and the Wolf":

"Well, Aesop was walking through this forest one day, when
he came upon a great big wolf caught in a trap. The wolf begged
him, 'Please, nice Mr. Aesop, help me out of this cruel trap!' So
Aesop did, and when the wolf was free, he bit Aesop on the ankle
and said, 'Now go write a fable about *that*!' "

Another of her stories (but *not* for the children) was about
the bumpkin who went to visit his rich cousin in the big city. The
host showed him around the huge, sumptuous apartment: the
Louis Seize salon, the library, the dining room, the master suite,
the sauna, the conservatory. "And now," he said proudly, opening

another door, "here's where I keep my collection of phallic symbols."

The bumpkin goggled and giggled and gave his host a nudge: "You know what they *look* like, don't you?"

Still another favorite was about the haughty lady at a fashionable church wedding. She felt a timid tap on her shoulder and turned to see a meek little woman in the pew behind, mouthing something incomprehensible and gesturing toward the back of her skirt. The haughty lady said sharply, "What are you trying to tell me, madam? Is it—by some preposterous chance—that I have an eggbeater caught in my fringe?"

The meek little woman whispered, "Yes."

I remember a true story of hers—at least, she said it was true. She went to a dinner at Somerset Maugham's Villa Mauresque, at Cap Ferrat, where she met Humbert Wolfe, the English poet, for whose work she had profound respect (as do I). No one else there seemed to know who he was, and as course followed course, without a word being addressed to the quiet, slightly drunken little man in the rusty dinner jacket, Dottie saw that he was getting more and more restive. Finally, she said, he rapped on his glass and announced loudly, but thickly, "I have just lost a very precious emerald! I must ask that the doors be locked, and that everyone present submit to a search!"

Dottie also loved overheard remarks, and she was hurt if anyone expressed a suspicion that she had overheard the best of them when she was talking to herself. Of course, she was always armed with "substantiating" details: "It's true, I tell you! Scout's honor! I was sitting on the right side of the bus [Dottie in a *bus*? Her story collapses right there!], about four seats from the front, and this woman in the seat ahead told the other woman—may I fry in hell through all eternity if I've changed a *syllable*!—she told her, 'Mad, I don't say. Odd, I do—sitting nude at the piano!'

"I couldn't have made that up, could I?"

Yes, she could have—Dottie, and nobody else.

Granted that she was wonderful company, life with her was life on thin ice. You never knew when she would turn on you and denounce you as a fascist, an anti-Semite, a warmonger, a geoplanarian, a neo-Malthusian, or something equally ridiculous. Almost any epithet would serve. It didn't need even a smidgen of justification. The barb of her wit made it stick where it hit, and the victim was tagged forever after. He had been given instant immortality—of the wrong sort—like the man from Porlock, and the courtier who farted in the presence of Queen Elizabeth I, and the Hollywood producer of whom Dottie said, "He hasn't got sense enough to bore assholes in wooden hobbyhorses."

She was never a girl to back away from a word just because it wasn't in Elsie Dinsmore's vocabulary. Sid Perelman told me that during one of his hitches in Hollywood, the studio assigned him an office adjoining Alan and Dottie's. Alan's desk was near the common wall, and Dottie's was at the far side; thus, Sid couldn't help hearing most of Alan's remarks, whereas Dottie's were only a mumble.

One afternoon he heard Alan say brightly, "I've finished that scene now, Dottie! I'll read it to you, and you can tell me how you like it." He read. "Well, what do you think?" Her answer was a muttered monosyllable. Then Alan's voice again, shrill and clear and anguished: "Dottie, I've asked you *ten thousand times* not to use that word!"

I'm not sure what Alan did immediately after the divorce. I remember going to see him in New York when he shared an apartment with Tom Heggen (who wrote *Mister Roberts*), but that was for only a short while; Heggen died in the spring of 1949. Dottie came to stay with us that summer—rather, with my wife; I was working in Washington and was home only on weekends. Our household consisted of us and our three children, Mamie the cook, and four dogs. Mamie had been a dresser for the Dolly Sisters. She was small and black and was a quiet drunkard. When the fit was on her, she simply kept to her room, even though it might be an evening when we were having guests to dinner or, more likely, the next morning. Dottie called her "a tower of Jell-o." On one of Mamie's "mornings," it fell to me to get breakfast. I asked Dottie what she'd like. "Just something light and easy to fix," she said. "How about a dear little whiskey sour? . . . Make it a double, while you're up." "While you're up" was one of her pet additives. She'd tear a strip off some poor wretch, then add reflectively, "And his wife's a shit too, while you're up." Another of her pets was "for my sins," as in, "I had to go to this *dreadful* party, and there, for my sins, I saw—" *All* parties were becoming "dreadful." I think she continued to go to them only because they gave her something to do, and because they offered her fresh targets. She took her dog to one of them, where it promptly vomited on the rug. Dottie explained to the hostess, "It's the company."

The Doylestown of Dottie's summer with us had a ceremony called "viewing." When someone died, friends and even acquaintances were expected to call at the bereaved house and view the corpse. The first we heard of this aboriginal custom was when our daughter Joan reported in gleeful excitement that the grandmother of a schoolmate had "passed"; viewing would begin the following afternoon, and "Please, Mummy, will you take us, *please?*" My wife was horror-struck, but she finally surrendered under a flurry of lefts ("Everybody in school will ask why we weren't there!") and rights ("Aw, gee, Mummy! You *never* let us have any fun!"). Next afternoon was scalding hot, my wife told me; she and Dottie dropped the children off at the crape-hung door, and waited in the car, both of them melting in the furious heat. When the children came back, my wife asked, "Are you glad you went? How did the old lady look?"

Joan glanced at her mother's damp, rumpled dress and sniffed, "She looked better than you do!"

Dottie rushed to the rescue: "Maybe, but don't forget she's been on ice all day!"

My friend Stockton Rush and his son John, aged six, stayed with us one weekend while Dottie was there. Saturday night was a rough one. Sunday morning, when Stockton tottered down to breakfast, he asked me shakily, "Be all right if I cut my throat?"

Dottie came in just then. She told him, "Move over on the blade and make room for me!"

All that day she watched young John Rush playing with our children. She was fascinated by the way that he—like "Pigpen," in the "Peanuts" comic strip—accumulated layer upon layer of grime "without seeming to try. I could take John into 21," Dottie said, "and leave him at the center table while I went to the ladies' room for no more than a moment, and when I came back, he'd be covered with *tar*!"

When her stay with us ended, I brought her bags downstairs for our drive to New York. One was a large, heavy Vuitton. She watched me struggling to fit it into our small car and remarked, "I know! They feel like they're full of wet sand before you've packed even a handkerchief."

I saw her again, just after Dame Edith Sitwell gave a reading in New York and, recognizing Dottie in the audience, bowed to her and paid a generous compliment to "your grett Ameddican pwettess, Miss Doddothy Wadden." (Those are not misprints; I have transcribed the line exactly as Dottie, still enraged, quoted it to me.)

"'Wadden'!" for Christ's sake!" she snarled. "Why, that goddam limey—!" and went from strength to strength.

Someone teased her, "It's no use getting sore! You've got to expect public recognition like that. After all, you're an international celebrity."

"Yeah," Dottie said. "That's me: the toast of two continents— Greenland and Australia."

She herself once gave a reading or a talk; I didn't hear it, but I remember her account, often repeated, of the woman who came up to her afterwards and gushed, "Oh, Miss Parker, I can't *tell* you how many sleepless nights your books have saved me!"

More and more she was surrendering to self-pity, self-mockery, self-diminishment, and to openly and bitterly reviewing her old loves. She couldn't keep her tongue off them, as if they were so many aching teeth. The names of only a few have stayed with me: John Garrett, Charlie MacArthur, John McClain, Alan Campbell, Ross Evans. I can't contribute even a minor footnote to her romances with Garrett and MacArthur; I never knew either of them, so I didn't pay much attention to her breast-beatings and recriminations. But although Dottie and McClain had blown up before I met her—*just* before—and she had already married Alan, McClain and I were close friends, and I could hardly help being exposed to, and absorbing, some of the lingering radiation from the fallout.

John was the male equivalent of a Rubens nude: a big, blond, handsome hunk of "roast beef and cold cream." His friend David Niven called him a Teddy bear. A single glance at him was all that Dottie had needed: she hadn't dropped her handkerchief at his feet so much as flung it into his lap, and John had picked it up. His good looks were only one of his assets: he was jolly; he chuckled; he had a nice wit and nice manners and a gentle drawl. Marion, Ohio, was his hometown. He had arrived in New York by way of Brown, where he played football, and Kenyon; and when I met him (about the time that Dottie did), he was reporting ship news for the *Sun*, in a column called "On the Sun Deck." He and I were almost exactly the same age; we had many mutual friends; both of us liked to think that we were writers; both of us were from "the sticks": and both of us enjoyed an occasional glass of the old and bold. In short, we saw a good deal of each other, and I could hardly help watching his side of the affair with Dottie develop.

It went smoothly and merrily at first. Ardor matched ardor. In addition to the physical satisfaction, John was flattered (and somewhat dizzied) at being taken up by this famous, brilliant woman and introduced to her famous, brilliant friends; and Dottie, for her part, was proud to parade him, an attractive ten-years-younger man, as proof that she was still seductive. But eventually the day came when John's ardor began to flag, whereas Dottie's did not. If anything, it increased. She became voracious and insistent. She telephoned him every few hours, even at his office, with your-place-or-mine suggestions, until John, in desperation, found himself beginning to plead imaginary assignments and fake engagements.

He didn't have to fake many or for long. He was that precious rarity, the personable Extra Man, with clean fingernails and a smooth tongue; and hostesses were quick to grab him not only for their dinner parties but—as the word got around that he was a *beau sabreur*—for other, more private, entertainments. Dottie's diagnosis was "His body has gone to his head!"

So, dining and weekending, drawling and chuckling and flirting, up John went, leaving Dottie behind to curse and wail, to call him a climber and an ingrate. At fashionable estates from Old Westbury to Bernardsville, guest books began to carry this entry, in John's clear, beautiful handwriting:

> From east to west,
> The nation's guest
> —John McClain

Dottie said of an extremely rich Long Island hostess at whose house he had become almost a weekend fixture, "He'll be back as

soon as he has licked all the gilt off her ass." But he on honey dew
had fed, and he didn't come back. It was over.

Alan Campbell caught her on the rebound, or perhaps *she*
caught *him*. Anyway, they were married in October 1933. He was
utterly different from John, less lover-husband than a housekeeper-
companion, always at hand to straighten her hat, escort her to a
party and back, and mix her Bromo the next morning. The marriage lasted until 1947. I don't know where or how she met her
next, Ross Evans. She first brought him to Fiddler's Green in 1949:
a pleasant, shambling hobbledehoy with huge, lump-toed Army
boots that instantly inspired our children to call him "Li'l Abner,"
in tribute to Al Capp's lamented naif, Abner Yokum. Dottie soon
thought better of Li'l Abner and, to our delight, remarried Alan a
year later. This time they stayed married.

Bee Stewart told me a story about Dottie that has been printed
before, but since this is the authentic version and is a credit to the
three people concerned, I'm going to repeat it:

In one of Dottie's flat-broke periods, early in the 1930s, Bee
telegraphed her friend John Gilbert, who was then at the peak of
his fame and prosperity, I WANT TWO THOUSAND DOLLARS FOR
SOMEONE WHO SHALL BE NAMELESS. Gilbert sent the money at
once, asking no questions. Well, the talkies came in, and soon it
was Gilbert's turn to be broke. He asked Bee if she thought he
could collect any of his many loans. Bee notified Dottie, who
promptly returned the two thousand in full—whereupon Gilbert
sent her an enormous basket of red roses with a card saying,
"Thank you, Miss Finland!" (Younger readers may need reminding that after the Great War, Finland was the only nation that
paid its war debt to the U.S.A.)

Alan died in Hollywood in June 1963, and his body was sent
home to Richmond, where I had returned to live. His family asked
me to be a pallbearer, with several others of his boyhood friends.

I assumed that Dottie would come to the funeral, so I telephoned Hollywood and left an invitation for her to stay with us. No answer. The next I heard, she was in New York, in a suite at the Volney Hotel. At first, I used to ring her when I came to town and ask if I might stop in for a drink, but she was always "just going out"; and if I called well in advance, it was always, "If *only* you'd phoned five minutes earlier!" I was reassured to learn before long that she was avoiding almost everybody, so I stopped bothering her.

The last time I saw Bee Stewart, a few weeks before her death in 1980, she told me about Dottie's in 1967. She came to Bee's apartment one evening and sat around drinking vodka until Bee decided it would be best to get her home and to bed. She loaded Dottie into a taxi and paid the driver to make the delivery. Half an hour later, her phone rang and she heard a mumble: "My bes' frien'! Mos' loyal frien'! *On'y* frien'! Goo' nigh'!" Next morning, June 7, a maid at the Volney found her dead. Dorothy's Yellow Brick Road had ended in potholes and mire and squalor, and no kindly Aunt Em and Uncle Henry were waiting there to hug her and comfort her.

She left no family, nor any estate except her literary rights (which went to the NAACP), nor any personal possessions except a few books and some clothing. Over the years, she had bought little and kept less. Almost everything given her, she handed on to someone else—including six original drawings by James Thurber, which she gave to me. Bee said that she was buried in a cloth-of-gold caftan given her by Gloria Vanderbilt. She had composed her own epitaphs long ago:

EXCUSE MY DUST

and

THIS IS ON ME.

FRED ALLEN
1894-1956

The Guy with Blitzwits

Fred and Portland Allen

WHEN I was a young cub on the Chicago *Journal* in the late 1920s, I was sent to a press reception for Jack Osterman, a comedian newly imported as master of ceremonies—or "m.c.," as I quickly learned to say—at some nightclub or perhaps at a revue. Which, I have forgotten, but I remember that when the Chicago *Tribune*'s theater critic, "Mae Tinée," made her entrance at the party, Osterman dropped to his knees in front of her, pulled her skirt over his head, and shouted, "Call for your proofs on Thursday!"

The guests fell in screaming windrows. "This," I was assured on all sides, "is the funniest man alive!"

In my innocence and inexperience, I was willing to agree, although I privately felt that *somewhere* there must be *someone* funnier than this—some "mute, inglorious Milton" Berle. I was right. The incomparable Fred Allen was already a veteran of vaudeville, although it wasn't until 1931 that I first saw him, in *Three's a Crowd*, and until 1941 that I met him, in order to write this piece for *The Saturday Evening Post*. It appeared there in the issue of October 4, 1941, under the title "Eighty Hours for a Laugh." I have revised it and expanded it for this book.

A late friend of mine, Herb Sanford, a former radio and television executive, so shared my admiration for Allen that he gathered a sheaf of tributes to him by men of proven taste and judgment. Here are three of them:

John Steinbeck: "Fred Allen is unquestionably our best humorist, a brilliant critic of manners and morals."

Herman Wouk: "Allen is America's greatest satiric wit in our time."

James Thurber: "You can count on the thumb of one hand the American who is at once a comedian, a humorist, a wit, and a satirist, and his name is Fred Allen."

All I can add is my fervent endorsement.

On Monday, October 24, 1932, there was a sudden minor boom in the business of repairing radios. A number of sets had gone mysteriously awry the night before. The victims had all been tuned to Station WABC, and all agreed they first noticed the distortion at a few minutes past nine. "It's hard to describe," they said, "but it was sort of a *snarling whine*."

Scientific listeners suspected a corrosive ray from outer space. Certain others professed no surprise that the quality of electricity, even, had begun to deteriorate under President Hoover's administration. The repairmen were as bewildered as the owners. They were glad to replace grids and wires and tubes, but they could find no accountable defect. Not until nine o'clock the following Sunday night did WABC's audience realize that the "snarling whine" was the normal voice of a newcomer to the air, Fred Allen.

Thomas Love Peacock, who knew Shelley, wrote that his voice

"was not only dissonant, like a jarring string, but he spoke in sharp fourths, the most unpleasant sequence of sounds that can fall on the human ear." O. O. McIntyre, who knew Fred Allen, wrote that he sounded like "a man with false teeth chewing on slate pencils." Allen's voice was harsh, but it was purgative. Ears clogged with radio's usual grease-and-treacle tones were scoured as ammonia scours a drain. People tuned in Allen for relief. They discovered that he was funny. He continued to be funny, and they continued to tune in. His weekly audience rose to an estimated 20,000,000, and his vinegar drawl soon became as familiar as FDR's organ roll.

Allen's face was the ideal backdrop for his voice. It might have been labeled "villainy's ledger." The avarice of a Scrooge, the treachery of a Quisling, the malignant cunning of a Fu Manchu—all were written there, in an alphabet of pouches, squints, and seams. Beerbohm's iniquitous Lord George Hell wore an angelic mask; Allen's mask was iniquitous. Behind it was a kindly, devout Catholic who seldom drank, never gambled, and quietly gave away far more money than he spent on himself.

Like a gangster, he had a powder burn on his hand; a property man had been careless with a blank pistol. Like a stool pigeon's, his eyes were shifty and darting; he used to be a juggler, and most jugglers have darting eyes. Like a brawler, his teeth were chipped; one of his juggling stunts was to hold a fork in his mouth and catch turnips tossed from the audience.

His first words that night in 1932—the first he ever uttered into a microphone—were: "Good evening, ladies and gentlemen! I want to welcome you to the opening of our Theater Petite. . . . You'll have to excuse me if I seem a bit nervous. I didn't sleep well. I dreamed I drove downtown in my car, and all night long I kept moving around to different parts of the bed, so I wouldn't get a ticket for parking."

An associate of Allen's once described him as a G-man—genial, gentle, and generous. "Modest" should have a synonym beginning with *g*. His response to a fan letter from Groucho Marx was genuine astonishment: "He thinks I'm good!" His clothes were subdued. His only jewelry was a wristwatch given him by the actor-playwright Jack Donahue, and a simple gold ring, a high-school graduation present from his aunt. The Allens spent their winters in a small New York apartment, their summers in a small cottage at Old Orchard Beach, Maine. Fred said, "The difference between our beach and Bailey's Beach, at Newport, is that there the tide won't come in until it's been properly introduced, whereas here the sea gulls use your bathroom." The Allens didn't own an automobile. Shortly before they went to Hollywood, Fred asked an agent to reserve them a couple of rooms at some inexpensive hotel. The agent suggested a twelve-room house. Allen wired back, DON'T BE ALARMED. YOU DON'T HAVE TO LET ON YOU KNOW US.

A minor Hearst columnist once reproached him for stinginess. Allen was panic-stricken when he saw the paragraph, but only for fear that one of his beneficiaries would rush to his defense and thereby expose his secret charities. His roll of regular pensioners once ran to more than thirty names. His wife said, "The WPA saved him." But to the end he supported six families, and it was an exceptional week when casual panhandlers didn't cost him another hundred dollars or more.

If somebody caught him in an act of kindness, he ducked behind a screen of cynicism. A friend was walking with him when a truck bore down on a daydreaming newsboy in front of them. Allen dashed out and snatched him to safety, then snarled, "What's the matter, kid? Don't you want to grow up and have troubles?"

His counterfeit misanthropy never intruded on his programs. Analyze an Allen script, and the humor is light and gay (and always *clean*). But analyzing the humor is something else.

"It can't be done," Allen once declared. "All I know about

humor is that I don't know anything. Sure, you read that 'There are only seven (or eleven) basic jokes,' but I've never found anybody who could tell me what they are. At a guess, two of them probably deal with comparison and exaggeration, because these are at the bottom of a lot of our humor. For example, 'He tripped the heavy fantastic; his dancing sounded like a log jam in a dry river,' and 'He was busier than an octopus going through a revolving door,' or 'She was prettier'n a peacock backing into a sunset.' Another one is probably incongruity. A great illustration of that was in *Once in a Lifetime*, when the character in clerical robes sends a boy out to buy him a *Racing Form*.

"But what are the others? Well, some things are funny in themselves. Take stuff you eat: an apple isn't funny; neither is a potato or a loaf of bread. On the other hand, eggs *are* funny—remember the gag about the impatient Democrat who couldn't wait for the egg, and threw a hen at Wendell Willkie?—eggs and tomatoes and grapefruit. But what makes them funny? Is it because they're limp? W. C. Fields said it's funny when something bends, but not when it breaks. That's why a beret is funnier than a silk hat, so you call a silk hat 'an undertaker's beret,' and it becomes funny.

"Or is it because eggs and tomatoes and grapefruit are squashy, which means a mess, which means somebody will have to clean it up, which means trouble? If that's so, another fundamental form of humor is somebody's trouble—somebody else's, of course. But I don't know. There's a lot of guesswork in this business."

It was prophesied in the late 1920s that radio comedy would perish of self-cannibalism. A vaudeville comedian playing Brooklyn would tell how a horse fell dead on Paerdegat Fourth Street, and how the unschooled cop who had to write the report asked him to help drag the carcass around the corner to 80th Street. The next week, playing Philadelphia, he would substitute "Wingohocking" for "Paerdegat Fourth," and "Broad" for "80th." These were the only changes in his act, week in and out, sometimes year in and out. But when he went into radio, he found he had to have a completely new act every week. Many vaudeville favorites couldn't stand the pace. Others managed to keep up only by hiring teams, even mobs, of gagmen and scriptwriters. The vaudevillians themselves became mere mouthpieces.

Allen's staff of four writers admitted that their jobs were sinecures. Each told how, at his first few conferences, he wore himself out trying to jot down the spate of gags in Allen's casual conversation—they seemed too good to be lost. And then each realized that the supply was unlimited, that Allen turned out gags as unremittingly as the magic salt mill. One of his writers paid him this tribute: "That guy's got blitzwits!"

Allen said, "The best form of comedy for radio is a knowing, satirical approach to the events and foibles of the day." In preparation, he read nine daily newspapers and four weekly magazines, and clipped any items that lent themselves to comedy treatment. Further, he sifted the chatter of friends and passing strangers for odd incidents and bits of humor. His pockets bulged with these memoranda, scribbled on scraps of paper and the backs of envelopes. When he sat down to write his weekly script, he had a hundred or more notes and clippings. About six slips survived the winnowing. These he dramatized, decorated with gags, discarded, and redecorated. Every line that his microphone carried was the third or seventh or tenth version of the original, and the callboy's warning always found him in a frenzy of final editing.

He never missed Sunday morning mass, and when, presently, the show was moved from Sunday night to Wednesday, mass was the only reason he left his New York apartment between late Friday night and the first rehearsal on Monday afternoon. That night and Tuesday he made a thorough revision. When the company met for its second rehearsal, at ten o'clock Wednesday morning, he was showing the strain. He chewed a cigar, changed to gum, changed to cut plug—"but only because I own two shares of spittoon stock." Sometimes he had a bowl of soup at lunch, but he was too busy and too nervous to eat a solid meal until after the broadcast. The editing was done by seven, and Allen went home for a shave and a change of clothes. At eight, he was back in the studio basement for a last-minute rehearsal and some last-second polishing. At 8:50 he went on stage to introduce his associates and warm up the audience. At nine he was on the air.

Now his nervousness fell away. So did his fatigue. He was the host at an informal party, and he wanted everyone present to enjoy it as much as he did. One night when he was unwrapping a stick of gum, he noticed a small boy in the front row eyeing it.

Allen stopped the program cold. "Have some!" he said, tossing it across the footlights. Then, to the theater at large, "Anybody else?"

These impromptus were the delight of the audience, but the despair of the men in the control room, to whom any delay was disastrous. One of the inconsistencies in Allen's character was the fact that whereas his offstage life followed a timetable as inflexible as a planet's, onstage the passing minutes meant no more to him than to a beachcomber. He was the most incorrigible ad-libber in radio, and the best. At every broadcast, three or four people—not celebrities—were invited to be interviewed. Allen seldom knew their occupations or even their names until the moment he met them in front of the microphone, but he never failed to greet them with a pertinent quip. For the operator of a beauty shop, it was, "I trust you make a pretty penny!" For the owner of a pool parlor, "You're going to rack and ruin!"

He was always careful to put his guests at ease and keep his quips innocuous. He dropped the slapstick and drew a verbal dagger only during his "feud" with Jack Benny. Many of his fans insist that here he reached the peak of his genius, and they will quote—between gasps and eye wipings—passages like this: "Benny's arm looks like a buggy whip with fingers. I've got veins in my nose bigger than that arm. As for his legs, I've seen better-looking legs on a bridge table. At a cannibal dinner, Benny wouldn't be on the menu!" Other fans dismiss the Bennyisms as run-of-the-mill stuff. For the true, vintage Allen, they say—slapping their knees and strangling—you must turn to his account of playing a theater "so deep in the woods, the manager was a bear—he paid us off in honey. The audience threw owl eggs at us. Woodpeckers ate up the straight man's cane, and the only review we got was in *Field & Stream*."

Allen's ad-libs were particularly frequent and fluent at the second broadcast—midnight, for the Pacific Coast—because many of the studio audience had heard the first one at home, and it took new material to make them laugh. When he drawled, "This is Fred Allen saying 'Good night,'" at a few seconds before one o'clock Thursday morning, his working week was over. His new week began in another few seconds; two of his writers were waiting for him as he came offstage, to discuss ideas for the next script. It was usually half an hour before the conference could begin, because the audience and autograph hunters refused to let him go. And after the conference, when he was at last allowed to start for his apartment, it took him another hour to get there through the swarm of voracious panhandlers blocking the theater exit.

His inability to turn down even the most arrant bum corrupted the whole brotherhood. They came to regard his weekly dole as their legal right. One of them sent a boy to collect for him, with a note saying that he was too busy to come himself. Another expected hospital expenses because he had slipped and broken his leg on his way to the pay line.

When Allen was asked why he tolerated this extortion, his

answers were evasive. Only once did he give the real reason: "I've been poor myself." Then he grinned. "Why, I can remember, when I was a baby, my teething ring was vulcanized in three places, and if I wanted something to eat, I had to creep out and fight a bird for it."

He was born near Boston, on May 31, 1894. The parish priest first knew him as John Florence Sullivan. Other people were to know him by four other names. It will be less confusing to call him "Fred Allen" throughout. His mother died when he was four, leaving him and a younger brother, Robert. Their father, a bookbinder at the Boston Public Library, died eleven years later, leaving the same and nothing more.

The boys moved to Dorchester, to live with an aunt. Bob was too young to work, but Fred was already a veteran employee in the children's department of the library. The job was a present from his father for his fourteenth birthday. At twenty cents an hour, working Sundays and three nights a week (he was still going to school), he was able to contribute $4.80 a week to his aunt's household expenses. She always insisted that he take back enough for a ticket to the local vaudeville theater, his only amusement.

It became his absorption. He found the juggling acts fascinating. Soon he had borrowed some plates, begged a couple of cigar boxes, and scraped up three dollars to buy a silk hat. The seller explained that a hat had to be specially balanced for juggling— therefore the high price. Allen learned years later that the local Salvation Army had a cellar full of such "specially balanced" silk hats, and would have sold him any number at fifty cents apiece.

After hours of practice over his bed (so that a dropped plate wouldn't break), he was ready to volunteer for an entertainment the library employees were putting on. The other acts were novices, but Allen considered himself an experienced trouper on the strength of a previous performance, when he was seven, as one of the Wise Men in a parochial-school play. These were his lines:

> Myrrh is mine. Its bitter perfume
> Breathes a life of gathering gloom—
> Sorrowing, sighing, bleeding, dying—
> Sealed in a cold stone tomb.

The sophisticated library audience would demand a different mood, so Allen, now sixteen, worked up a patter. It opened with "Well, summer is going, and winter drawers on." He pinned particular hopes to "I could tell you a secret about a can of condensed milk, but I'm afraid it would leak out." He was also rather pleased with "A doughnut will float, but it looks like a sinker," and with "He's a good boy. Everything he steals he brings home to his mother." He was prepared even for the improbability that applause would be meager: "Who spilled embalming fluid in here?" As it turned out, he didn't have to use the line.

When he graduated from high school, he was the only member of the class in short pants. The principal asked him to get long ones, so the other boys wouldn't seem mentally deficient. Now he was free for daytime employment, in addition to his job at the library. He found it in a piano store, sweeping up, collecting bills, and running errands, for eight dollars a week. Three nights of his week were still open, so he looked for a third job, preferably one connected with the stage. The job didn't come through for another year, but when it did, in the spring of 1912, it was better than he had dared hope: the great Sam Cohen, Boston's Belasco of the Amateur Night, agreed to give him bookings.

Amateur night, an institution now as dead as the minstrel show, was having its heyday in 1912. Once a week, every neighborhood

theater closed its regular program with a series of amateur recita-
tions, mandolin duets, clog dances, and the like. After the last act,
all the performers lined up onstage, and the manager stepped behind each one in turn, holding over his head an envelope marked
"$25" and cocking an ear toward the audience. The performer who
got the loudest applause got the envelope; the runner-up got one
marked "$10"; the third man got one marked "$5." All three envelopes were empty; each contestant, winner or loser, got fifty
cents, plus another fifty for dinner, plus a dime for carfare.

Allen kept the notebook in which he listed some of his early
bookings. The first page reads:

Hub	April 9	Good (speak up louder)
Copley Hall	April 18	"
Hub	May 29	2nd
Eagle	June 5	Good

It was a rough, tough game. Allen said, "The toughest were
the 'sympathy acts'—performers who had no ability, but were
given the envelopes out of sympathy, while talented kids went
home with nothing. There wasn't a trick they wouldn't pull to get
a hand. One boy, a buck-and-wing dancer, used to wear socks that
he'd cut the heels out of, and when he did a twist, he'd hike up his
pants so that his audience would see what a poor, hard-up kid he
was and would beat their palms raw. Another kid was a tough
little hunchback. He'd sing 'Mother Machree' in a thin tenor, and
when he came to the end, he'd give the hump an extra twitch. He
always won first prize! There was also a middle-aged woman on
crutches. She carried them to the theater like so much lumber, and
tucked them under her arms when she came out to sing 'Only a
Bird in a Gilded Cage.' It was dog eat dog, I tell you!"

Neither the manager nor the audience showed mercy. A contestant might be reaching the climax of a dramatic monologue

when he would be dismayed by a burst of laughter. Behind him, a stuffed fish five feet long would have zipped across the stage on an invisible wire, missing his head by inches; or the curtains would have parted silently to reveal a sign: "Maybe he's good to his mother"; or two hundred boxing gloves would fall from the flies and litter the stage. Most humiliating of all, the manager would thrust a hook from the wings and drag the poor devil away. Allen remembered a night when he was juggling with something less than his usual dexterity, and the manager stalked out and demanded sourly, "Where did *you* learn to juggle?"

Allen said, "I took a correspondence course in baggage smashing."

The audience loved it. Right then Allen conceived the idea that someday he might add a few gags to his juggling act.

He had played amateur nights for a year when Sam Cohen invited him to become his representative at a chain of outlying houses. As befitted his new importance, Allen bought a pair of needle-toe shoes, tilted his hat, and began frequenting the Hotel Rexford, Boston's unofficial theatrical headquarters, "where all the little guys went to hang around the big and medium-size guys." Among the medium-size guys was Harry La Toy, another juggler. La Toy was "temporarily at liberty," and while he waited for a booking, he taught Allen a few new tricks in return for free meals. (Allen said, "La Toy had short arms and he carried his money low in his pockets.") One day La Toy sent him a hurry call. He had agreed to fill out a bill that night, at cut rates and under an assumed name, but a more profitable engagement had just been offered him. If Allen would like to take the old one in his place, he could keep two dollars of the five-dollar fee.

Allen jumped at it and, as "Paul Huckle, European Entertainer," he made his first professional appearance. It passed, he said, like a heavenly nightmare. Next day La Toy called him again. "Kid, you're in! A lot of agents have been asking who this Huckle is. I told 'em you were from out west, just here to see your folks. Come on down and sign up!"

Allen signed for four weeks' work at twenty-five dollars a week, twice what he had been making before. La Toy sent him to have lobby photographs taken, and had a fresh name for him when he returned. Allen never knew where "Paul Huckle" came from, but "Fred St. James" was inspired by the St. James Hotel, on Boston's Bowdoin Square.

He resigned his jobs with Cohen, the library, and the piano store, and opened at the Scenic Temple, in East Boston. He had made all his amateur appearances in ordinary clothes, without greasepaint, but an actor on the same bill warned him that a comedy juggler had to wear a funny makeup, with funny clothes and a red wig; otherwise, people wouldn't know he was a comedian. It so happened, the actor went on, that he had an extra wig in his trunk, and Allen could have it cheap. Allen bought it and built his "character" around it: the wig down low on his forehead, eyelids whitened, clown mouth, front teeth blacked out, seedy tailcoat.

His first week went off smoothly. So did the second and third. Then fell disaster. He was dressing after the Monday matinee at the Superb Theater, in Roxbury, when the manager brought him his photos and sheet music. He had recognized Allen as a former amateur, and his customers, he said, would resent an amateur being presented as a pro.

Allen was too ashamed to report to the booking office. He got a job with a plumbing-supply house, but he didn't let his juggling go stale. He practiced in a storage room during the lunch hour and gave occasional exhibitions at small clubs and smokers, but it was seven months before he was confident enough to make the rounds of the agents again.

Booking was slow, and he was determined to wait until he

could get three consecutive weeks. The day he got them, he signed the contract, quit the plumbing house, and hopped the train.

"That was my last traffic with mercantile enterprises," Allen says. "Right there I took a shortcut to an ulcer."

The next afternoon he was laying 'em in the aisles in Bangor, Maine, with his tennis balls and cigar boxes, and "I don't have to look up my family tree. I know that I'm the sap." He was barely nineteen.

An English juggler named Griff was responsible for Allen's radio career, though Griff never knew it. They never met. Their closest contact was when Allen saw Griff's performance at a theater in Boston in the summer of 1913. Jugglers are rated by the number of balls they can keep in the air. Allen could juggle four; Griff could juggle six; Cinquevalli could juggle eight; Frank Dent, the greatest of them all, could juggle eleven. Watching Griff, a middle-aged man, display his six-ball "shower," Allen suddenly wondered whether it was worth it—whether he, still in his teens, should devote his next twenty years to mastering two extra balls. From that moment, he began to play down his juggling and play up the comic patter that accompanied it.

The first step in his new campaign was to change his name again. John Florence Sullivan—later Paul Huckle, and now Fred St. James—rather than discard the current name entirely, along with whatever publicity value might have accrued, informalized it to "Freddy James." The second step was to order letterheads with the legend, "Freddy James, the World's Worst Juggler." The last step was to open a correspondence with all the theatrical agents in New York, sending them gags and bits of comic verse. Allen didn't care if few of the agents troubled to answer. His object was to introduce his name and din it at them until they remembered it, against the day when he would be ready to crash the big time.

It took him a year on the New England circuit to save up the necessary stake of one hundred dollars. Forty of this he banked; the rest he took with him, after getting a Boston friend to guarantee a return ticket in case of emergency. He arrived in New York on a Saturday; on Monday he was working. The letterheads had opened the door.

It wasn't an important door. It led only to theaters in Hackensack, Rome, Ithaca—towns of that size—but he was making sixty dollars a week where he had made twenty-five in New England and, far more exciting, he was now a New Yorker.

The sixty-dollar pay scale was steady, but work wasn't. Allen's ledger for 1914 shows that for every week he worked, he laid off two. His windowless room in a shabby hotel on West 40th Street cost him only four dollars a week, and he ate in a restaurant that managed to serve liver and bacon, coffee and doughnuts, for only a dime. Even so, starvation was baying at his heels when he unexpectedly became able to save a critical two dollars a week by taking in a roommate. The roommate was used to doubling up; he was half of an act in which two men danced in the same suit of clothes. There were days when even two dollars a week for a room and a dime for a meal were out of reach. Allen remembered one long stretch when six more actors slept on their floor, and all eight of them lived on a cache of salami and raspberry jam in the bureau drawer.

At least three times he was on the point of wiring for his return ticket, but something always turned up to postpone it. In his last and worst crisis, he was actually writing the telegram when an agent snatched him away from the desk and rushed him to replace a cancellation in Paterson, New Jersey. Allen made the curtain and finished out the week. In gratitude, the agent gave him the break he had been praying for: four weeks on the Poli time.

"Time" in vaudeville was the equivalent of "league" in baseball. As there are two big leagues, so were there two big times: the Keith time in the East, the Orpheum in the West. And as there are many minor leagues, so were there many small, or family, times. The Poli time was Springfield, Worcester, Hartford, Bridgeport, New Haven, Waterbury, Wilkes-Barre, and Scranton. The four weeks, at a new high of $125 a week, gave Allen such prestige that a Loew's agent booked him into the big houses in Cleveland, Toledo, Detroit, and Chicago. From there he went on the Western Vaudeville circuit, down through Kansas City, Hutchinson, Topeka, and Wichita, to Shreveport; and in Shreveport he received a telegram that he had to read twice.

Sir Benjamin Fuller, owner of the Fuller circuit in Australia, had caught his act in Chicago and wanted to sign him for a six months' tour, with a guarantee of sixteen weeks' work at twenty-five pounds a week (about $115 US) and round-trip fare thrown in. Allen pondered. Summer was coming on—this was in 1916—and bookings would be hard to get. He wired his acceptance.

The record for the theatrical broad jump is held by W. C. Fields, who spent twenty-nine days getting from Fremantle, Australia, to Rochester, New York, where he joined the cast of *Watch Your Step* and was fired after opening night. Allen is the runner-up; it took him twenty-eight days from Shreveport to Brisbane. He said, "My stateroom was a form-fitting gullhole (on a ship, a pigeonhole is a gullhole)." He once finished an engagement at Perth, Western Australia, and found that he was booked to Auckland, New Zealand. The ship from Perth to Adelaide took five days; the train from Adelaide to Sydney took three days; the ship from Sydney to Wellington, New Zealand, took five days; and from Wellington to Auckland was overnight by train.

When he got back to Sydney, his headquarters, he wore a sailor hat into his agent's office. "Did I sign for vaudeville," he wanted to know, "or before the mast?"

He had expected to stay "down under" only six months; he stayed eleven. The shortage of actors because of wartime enlistments, plus the fact that as a "single" he cost managers only one fare, increased his value to the extent of a renewed contract. But it was a lonely period. To help pass the time, he began reading in the local public libraries—drama, poetry, novels, everything he could lay hands on. He also began a collection of joke books that eventually totaled four thousand. He sifted them as he read, entering the best jokes on file cards, until he had enough to string together in a continuous patter. He had left the United States as a juggler who occasionally made funny remarks; he came back as a comedian and ventriloquist who occasionally juggled.

One of his best new props was "Jake," a dummy. A ventriloquist's usual finale is drinking a glass of water while his dummy continues to talk. Jake talked, then sang a solo in a voice astonishingly like Caruso's, then seemed to become a one-man chorus, and ended with a brilliant imitation of Sousa's band playing "The Stars and Stripes Forever." The strain of this prodigious feat was always too much for Jake; he came apart in Allen's hands. The chair came apart too, exposing the gramophone under it. The act was called "Just a Young Fellow Trying to Get Along."

Allen began his American tour on the West Coast, intending to break in his act there and polish it before taking it to New York, but the West Coast theaters liked his nonsense and held him over, week after week. Meanwhile, he aimed another publicity campaign at the big eastern agents. First he sent them business cards:

FREDDY JAMES

Acting Done Reasonable

12 Minutes in One—Benefits a Specialty

These he followed with a twelve-page pamphlet entitled *What I Know About Show Business, by Freddy James*; all the pages were blank. Then from St. Louis he mailed out a hundred two-ounce bottles of brine, with the label "Perspiration taken from the body of Freddy James after playing four shows a day at the Grand Theater." When he finally reached New York, in 1919, he had decided on a step that he had taken three times already: changing his name. He was afraid that if he looked for a booking as "Freddy James," he would be offered the same salary as before he went to Australia.

An agent named Edgar Allen agreed: "Why don't you take my name?"

Sullivan-Huckle-St. James-James took it; he was "Fred Allen" thereafter.

His publicity campaign paid off; the break came within a year. He hit the big time on the Keith circuit with such headline acts as Rooney & Bent, Frank Van Hoven, Joe Cook, Sophie Tucker, Donahue & Stewart, and Nora Bayes. His salary went up to $175 a week. A year later it rose to $250, when the Shuberts hired him for the rival circuit they had just organized.

By then he had abandoned juggling entirely and converted his act to a monologue with banjo accompaniment. A monologist's greatest problem is a smooth exit; the banjo was Allen's solution. He had bought his first banjo at an auction in New Zealand and practiced it a year before someone told him that it was true for only the first five frets.

The new act opened on a dark stage, with a spotlight on this placard:

Mr. Allen Is Quite Deaf
If You Care To
LAUGH OR APPLAUD
Please Do So
LOUDLY

The light then shifted to reveal Mr. Allen huddled in an Inverness cape that hung barely below his armpits, a grotesque high-crowned derby, and a voluminous suit. He was always careful to explain that his suit has been tailored in New Rochelle, "and of course I'm a much bigger man there than I am here." His morose face was chalked white. He held a limp umbrella in one hand. The other was cupped behind his ear. If applause was sparse, he would whine, "Thank you, Mother!"

What is probably his best extemporaneous crack was made in these days. He was sitting in the footlights of the Palace Theater in New York when a mouse ran across the stage and stopped beside him, in full view of the audience. Allen picked it up gently and put it in his pocket.

"I didn't know my act was that cheesy," he said. "I thought I was doing a monologue. It should have been a catalogue."

A good many people sided against the mouse. Among them was J. J. Shubert, who liked the act enough to put it in *The Passing Show of 1922*. After that, engagements for revues came fast. Between revues he played vaudeville again, but after his first broadcast, in 1932, he appeared on the stage only twice, both times in benefits. He never discussed the movies he made, Hollywood not being an enthusiasm of his. He once dated a letter from there: "Hollywood, August %."

His lifelong ambition was to write. He contributed a preface to a friend's book and a series of columns to *Variety*, but he wanted something more enduring. As far back as 1925, he had enrolled in Boston University's summer school for a course called "English Vocabulary and Rhetoric," expecting to do parallel reading that winter and return to the classroom a year later, to complete his preparation for a writing career. He never did; his popularity defeated him. Season after season his bookings kept him solidly in the theater. It was a choice between giving up study or the stage, and the stage was essential to the support of his dependents. "Their seven stomachs outnumbered my head," he said.

Six of the seven were longtime pensioners. The seventh was added in 1927, when he married her. She was Portland Hoffa,*

* Portland was named for Portland, Oregon, where her family was living when she was born. Her sister Lebanon commemorates their move to Pennsylvania.

whom he had met in the chorus of *The Passing Show*. He wrote a part for her into his vaudeville skit, and she was in his act thereafter. From their wedding day until Fred's death, the Allens were never apart for more than a few hours. Their pleasure in each other's company classified them as eccentrics in the profession. Portland shared Fred's life so completely that they even had their one superstition in common: on New Year's Eve they solemnly ate a herring and wished each other luck.

She also shared his wonder at commercial radio's growth after the blight and diseases that afflicted it in childhood. The preliminaries to Allen's first broadcast never ceased to hag-ride his dreams. When the two-year run of *Three's a Crowd* closed in the spring of 1932, he poured weeks of work into writing a trial program for himself, Henry Morgan, Roy Atwell, and Don Voorhees's orchestra. They rehearsed until they were note-and-letter perfect, then invited an interested sponsor to attend their audition. He sent word that he was too busy, but for them to have a recording made, and he'd try to find time to listen.

They sent him the recording. He listened to the first few minutes, then stopped the machine. "Don't like any of it," he snapped. "But wait. Get me that man with the flat voice."

Those were the days when someone who had spent his life marketing noodles would engage Jascha Heifetz, say, for a radio program, and thereby feel privileged to change the tuning of Heifetz's violin. Allen's sponsor was no exception. He wanted Allen to dress as a Keystone Comedy cop and belabor people with a stuffed club as they entered the studio, so that they would expect a comedy act. It took Allen four days to talk his way out of it.

A later sponsor was obdurate. His wife liked organ music, so the comedy mood that Allen struggled to create was periodically destroyed by lugubrious embroideries on the *vox humana*. Allen said, "Playing an organ solo midway through a comedy show is like planting a pickle in the center of a charlotte russe."

Although he never wrote or uttered a line that could be contorted into an indecency, he was constantly subjected to a niggling, nice-Nelly censorship. For example, in a bit of harmless dialogue between himself and "a bearded lady," the sponsor insisted he make it abundantly clear that the two of them were not behind locked doors. Allen's name for such busybodies was "memo merchants"; one who was particularly bothersome he dubbed "Vice-President in Charge of Waving Fingers at Comedians." Lesser nuisances, mere "maestros of confusion, disciples of consternation, and nabobs of *non sequitur*," he called "ulcers." Bottommost were "yucks." "A yuck," he said, "is someone too little to hit, and too wet to step on."

Censors could mangle his scripts, but they couldn't anticipate his ad-libbing. Although some of his best gags were spontaneous, some of his spontaneous gags backfired. When he mentioned a would-be pharmacist who "flunked in chow mein," the drugstore trade took up arms. When he spoke of a Philadelphia hotel—not by name—where "the rooms are so small, the mice are humpbacked," the local hotelkeepers' association demanded a retraction. More serious yet was the time when he interviewed a man who had been a doorman at the Astor Hotel for thirty years.

"I once got hundred-dollar bills as tips," he recalled.

"Yes," sighed Allen, "back in '28, those Wall Street men used to think nothing of buying a restaurant and throwing it to the waiter as a tip. I guess some of them still chuckle about their financial pranks as they sit around up there in Sing Sing today." Brokers were thick-skinned only to someone else's troubles, it appeared. Allen wrote an apology to President Martin of the New York Stock Exchange. It ended:

> . . . i have considered committing hara-kiri on the two points recently gained by bethlehem steel. [Allen never used the capitals on his typewriter.] i have also thought about calling a conference, since a conference is a gathering of im-

portant people who, singly, can do nothing, but together can decide that nothing can be done. both ideas were abandoned in favor of this letter to you.

Mr. Martin posted it on the Exchange bulletin board.

On Christmas Eve 1940, Allen had a debilitating conference with some "ulcers." That night the studio audience was stickier than usual. Suddenly he interrupted his program to announce that he had a priceless Christmas present for his listeners. And gave them one minute of dead silence.

APPENDIX

A few days after the *Post* published this piece, I received a letter from Fred. It was written on the startling stationery that Al Hirschfeld had designed for him and, as always, was single-spaced, lower-case throughout:

> you will be happy to learn that the reaction to your piece has been excellent up in boston. fortunately for my selfish purposes, the same issue contains a story on cardinal o'connell [of Boston], and when the local folks buy a post to digest the cardinal's views, they are bound to turn another page or two, rather than waste a wet finger, and they came across your story . . .

During World War II, Fred wrote me from time to time; his letters were always amusing, as when he complained that his desk "looks like the floor of a hillbilly privy," and when he reported having seen a notoriously conceited actor "walking down lover's lane holding his own hand." On Christmas 1942, he sent me a small leather jewel box from Cartier, containing one coffee bean "to help relieve posible suffering from the shortage." It reached me in Brisbane, Australia, and I remembered with lively sympathy Fred's account of his stay in that dull city during the Great War. He closed one of his letters with "formal good wishes and a continued normal metabolism and organic peace to you, sir!"

One of my lasting regrets is that I was out of the country during the debut and early years of "Allen's Alley." The fact that I caught some of the later programs makes my regret all the more poignant, for "Ajax Cassidy," "Mrs. Nussbaum ("Mine husband Pierre"), "Titus Moody," "Senator Beauregard Claghorn," and "Falstaff Openshaw, the Bowery Bard," were certainly the greatest troupe of drolls ever collected on one stage, and too many of their glorious lines are lost to me forever.

Still, the Alley left me with a few precious memories. One is of the Bowery Bard's poem, "Come with me to the belfry, Nellie. We'll kick the gong around." Two others involve Mr. Moody. The first is his complaint that he was so anemic, his finger didn't bleed when he cut it—"it just puckered and hissed." The second is his account of the time when a hurricane blew his cow, Bessie, up onto the roof of the barn. The eye of the hurricane arrives, and Mr. Moody climbs up to rescue Bessie. He is still on the roof, struggling with her, when the hurricane returns—

ALLEN: Pray continue, Mr. Moody! The suspense racks our
nerves!
MOODY: Well, I grabbed aholt of the first things I could
reach.
ALLEN: And?
MOODY: Got both sleeves full of milk.

Fred's blood pressure had been too high for some years, and his twelve- and even fourteen-hour workdays did nothing to lower it. In June 1949 he broadcast his final show, then went into semiretirement. He continued to make guest appearances, frequently on "What's My Line?" but he saved enough of his new leisure to write two books of memoirs, *Treadmill to Oblivion* (1954) and *Much Ado About Me* (1956).

A quarter hour before midnight on March 17, 1956, he started out on his regular evening stroll along West 58th Street. He had gone only a block when he was stricken with a heart attack. Passersby carried him into the lobby of a nearby apartment building, and someone rang for an ambulance. Before it arrived, the elevator came down; one of its passengers was the New York *Post* columnist Leonard Lyons. He cried, "My God, it's Fred Allen!" Fred died a few minutes later.

For a devout Irish Catholic born Sullivan, what better day to die on than St. Patrick's? The funeral was held at St. Malachy's, on West 49th Street, "the Actors' Church," where Fred and Portland had been married. A thousand mourners found seats; another two hundred crowded the aisles, another eight hundred stood outside. Modest in death as in life, Fred had requested no eulogy and no flowers, and had left instructions that he be buried in a plain coffin. His wishes were respected.

DONALD OGDEN STEWART

1894-1980

The Commie Comic

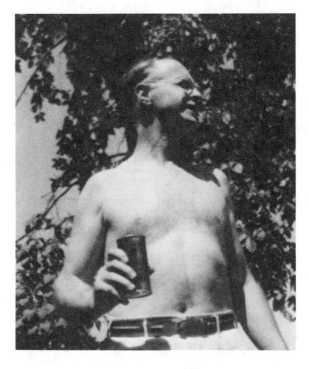

Donald Ogden Stewart attired for summer, 1941

THE Don Stewarts, the Bryans, and another couple took a cruise to Haiti and Santo Domingo in January 1936. I knew the Stewarts slightly and liked them, and during our cruise they captivated me completely. If there was ever a more attractive, amusing, delightful pair—! Beatrice was smart and pretty, Don was smart and witty, and both of them had cloudless dispositions. Never in all the years ahead did I see either of them angry or sour.

Don was a big man, around six feet and 190 pounds, with blue eyes behind wire spectacles. His nickname at Exeter was "Duck-Lip," and one glance told you why: his upper lip was unusually wide and deep—and was always stretched in a grin. He liked to speak of himself in the third person: "Don't look now, but Donald is going to pour himself the dearest, sweetest little drink." Many of his remarks began "Don't look now—," and everything and everybody he liked was "dearest" and "sweetest," whether it was

London or chop suey or Bob Benchley. He had two all-purpose names, "Toots" and "Sweetie," which he used for everyone impartially, man or woman, friend or stranger. And one all-purpose gesture: his hands held chest-high, palm facing palm about six inches apart, and always moving parallel, as if he were demonstrating the length of a fish, or holding a skein of yarn, or doing Fred Allen's juggling trick with three cigar boxes. It was his only gesture, and he used it constantly, regardless of its irrelevance to what he was saying.

If Bee had any faults, I never noticed them. Don had two. The milder one became obvious early: a sometimes embarrassing tendency to turn bawdy in the wrong company or at the wrong time. Still, he was so funny, and so apologetic when he saw that he had given offense, that only a professional prude could get stuffy about it. I remember an evening when someone mentioned a certain writer whom Don happened to dislike. "Don't look now—" he said. "Don't look now, but he's a horse's ass!" A primmish lady overheard him and was plainly shocked. Don was instantly contrite. "I'm terribly sorry, Toots," he said. "I didn't know you mind the word 'horse.'"

I'm sure the lady didn't want to laugh, but she did. She did *not* laugh when he left the room a few minutes later, explaining that "Donald has to go do tiss-tiss."

Don's other fault, or flaw, was slower to appear, but was more grave and less defensible. This was his infection with Communism. It may have been dormant when we went to the Caribbean, but I had no hint of it until some years later. Again we were on a cruise, though this one was for only a few hours. We and the Stewarts and perhaps six other couples had been invited to dine on a yacht that would steam up Long Island Sound and then steam back. This was a *yacht?* To my innocent and popping eyes, she looked like a quarter-scale *Leviathan.* Picture it: this huge, comfortable ship gliding up the Sound under a full moon, with everyone in evening dress, eating caviar and drinking champagne. It was as if our host and hostess were obeying stage directions that read, "The key to this set and scene is *luxury*. Everything must be the richest and most sumptuous procurable."

Don was already quite tight when we came aboard, which meant that he was at his funniest and bawdiest. A song hit of that year was "Love in Bloom," as featured by (I think) Jack Benny. Someone began humming it, but Don took it away from him and improvised his own lyric:

> "Can it bē Louise
> Who spreads disease
>   To every man in the room?
> Oh, no, it isn't Louise;
>   It's Rosenblum."

He should have known better. It was too early in the evening for that, and the laughter was strained. I think this hurt Don's pride. I don't know how else to explain what he did next: he picked up a glass of champagne and waved it at the whole group of us, slopping a good half of it. "Listen, Sweeties!" he called. "Listen! This is important!" Everyone turned toward him. He waved the glass again, as if to include the guests, the magnums, the bowls of caviar, the yacht, everything. "Enjoy this while you can," he said, "because 'comes de Rewolution,' we're going to take it all away from you!" He slapped one of the men on the shoulder and roared with laughter. Everybody laughed with him. "Comes de Rewolution" was a famous comedy line of Fanny Brice's, so it never occurred to us that Don wasn't kidding. But he meant it. I realized this long afterwards, when his Communism was open and acknowledged, and something brought to mind our evening on the yacht.

That cruise was as far in time from the other as Long Island Sound is far in leagues from the Caribbean. Our only worry at the first was whether Don would get loaded and start telling blue jokes in the ship's bar. He announced often and loudly that he was "on the wagon," although he was drinking two bottles of Dubonnet a day—"Don Stewed"—and made no bones about it; "every sane man" would agree that Dubonnet was "practically nonalcoholic and therefore didn't count." It never made him drunk; it merely loosened his tongue. Not that it needed loosening. With or without booze, he talked a rainbow-colored streak from breakfast to bedtime, pouring out a stream of nonsense and quips and funny stories. He wasn't "onstage"; he didn't "grab the mike"; it was just his nature to entertain people, and he did it supremely well. He and Bee made a perfect team; she led the laughter, not as a claque, but because he was so funny she couldn't help it. More than that, this paragon of wives never "helped" him tell his stories, interrupting to correct an unimportant name or date.

I can't select any single sample coin from the treasure that Don showered on us every day. Yes, I can: we were driving through a cane field in Santo Domingo one morning, and suddenly there at the roadside we saw a boy of about fourteen. He was chewing a piece of cane and he was wearing a short shirt, nothing else—short enough to show his impressive erection. Don broke our astonished silence. He waved his hand and said cordially, "Morning, little girl!"

That simple remark immediately took its place beside what he'd said to me when we first met: "You're from Richmond, they tell me. My grandfather spent some time there. [Pause.] In Libby Prison. [Pause.] For forgery."

I was to learn later that Don and his bosom friend Bob Benchley liked to use their grandfathers as straight men, the way George Jessel and Milton Berle used their mothers. Benchley wrote of "my grandfather Private Benchley, formerly Corporal Benchley—" and Don, on this same trip to Santo Domingo, insisted on addressing a rather stiff banquet for local cane planters: "You fellows are lucky that Donald's grandfather isn't still alive!

He had diabetes so bad that if he even lifted his leg, the sugar market would crash, and you'd all be wiped out."

At that time Don was the highest paid screenwriter in Hollywood, at five thousand dollars a week, so it isn't surprising that Hollywood was a fairly steady topic with him. He spoke of "Clark" (Gable) and "Irving" (Thalberg) and "Bart" (Herbert Marshall) and "Sam and Frances" (the Goldwyns) and "Grace" (Moore) and "Dick and Jessie" (the Barthelmesses) as casually as I spoke of my cousins and classmates. It was intoxicating stuff to a Richmond boy; but despite myself, I couldn't help wondering if he *really* knew all these dazzling people that well. The quick answer is, yes, he did.

Don never referred to his youth. All I knew was that he had been born in 1894 in Columbus (like Jim Thurber), Ohio, and had gone to Yale (class of '16), where he had been a Big Man— big enough, at least, to be tapped for Skull and Bones. He wrote for the *Lit* and he had the reputation of being an aggressive puritan. If someone told a dirty story, Don would leave the room. (Bob Benchley was like that too when he first went to Harvard; both men recovered soon and permanently.) What greased Don's slide into comedy and bawdiness I have no idea. I have heard that at the end of his Exeter days, or soon afterwards, his father, a judge, made a financial misstep and died of the disgrace. Don laughed it off by saying, "Fortunately for me, it happened just when I was well on my way to becoming vice-president of the Second National Bank." But why or how did this inspire him (if indeed it did at all) to buzz off to Paris and write his hilarious *Parody Outline of History*? His career was as full of these U-turns as his character was full of inconsistencies and contradictions.

He explained *what* happened, but not *how* it happened. He said, " 'Crazy humor' was becoming popular just then, thanks to Ring Lardner and George S. Chappell, and I seemed to have a talent for writing it."

An understatement. *A Parody Outline*, published in 1921, was such a success that he went to Vienna, grew a red beard, and wrote *Perfect Behavior*, another parody, this one of Mrs. Emily Price Post's *Book of Etiquette*. Other "crazy humor" books followed: *Mr. and Mrs. Haddock in Paris, France*; *Father William*; and *The Crazy Fool*. Don's favorite among them was *Aunt Polly's Story of Mankind*. The flyleaf of the copy he gave me is inscribed, "This is the best book I ever wrote." He rated it so highly, in fact, that he urged his English publisher to plug it for a Nobel prize.

My own favorite is *The Crazy Fool*, which is about a young man named Charlie Hatch, who inherits a lunatic asylum. A reporter comes to interview him:

"What do you think about something?"
Charlie: "I think something is just wonderful and—"
Reporter: "What does the American farmer want? Does the modern girl smoke too much? What is that on your necktie?"

During Don's short business career, he had met Scott Fitzgerald in St. Paul. He saw him again in Paris, with Ernest Hemingway, and their friendships took fire. The character of "Abe North" in Fitzgerald's *Tender Is the Night* is said to be based chiefly on Ring Lardner, but it has unmistakable elements of Don; and in Hemingway's *The Sun Also Rises*, "Bill Gorton" is drawn from Don intact. Read the dialogue in the trout-fishing scene in Spain, and you hear Don speaking with Gorton's voice.

The Stewart-Fitzgerald friendship lasted until Fitzgerald's death. The Stewart-Hemingway friendship had a shorter life. It came to an abrupt end one evening in October 1926, in Paris. The Archie MacLeishes were giving a party for the Hemingways, the Stewarts, and a few other guests; and Hemingway, unurged, chose to read aloud some verses he had written, "To a Tragic Poetess"— a cruel attack on Dorothy Parker for what he considered her false emotions after having an abortion. No one present saw any excuse for Hemingway's gratuitous, brutal mockery, but it was Don who stood up and denounced him. Hemingway's retort was to declare their friendship finished. So it was. But Don's loyalty to Dottie endured.

Another of his friends, Philip Barry, also realized the uniqueness of Don's "crazy humor," and not only wrote him into a new play, *Holiday*, as "Nick Potter," but invited him to play the role. It was perfect casting. The stage direction says that Nick is "about 34, with an attractive, amusing face." Don was exactly thirty-four when *Holiday* was produced, and if you happened to be looking for an attractive, amusing face and saw Don's, you'd know your search was over. Further, Barry's witty dialogue could have been recorded by an eavesdropper on Don's natural conversation. For instance, Nick warns a friend against an elderly curmudgeon. "Be careful," he says, "or he'll come down on you like Grant took Bourbon!" Pure Stewart.

Opening night was in November 1928. Don said, "I'd never been on the stage in my life, Sweetie! I made my entrance early in the second act, opening a door and bringing in some champagne. The audience were supposed to laugh. Well, they did." They laughed at him throughout, especially when he ended a long, "crazy-humorous" speech with what would become one of our national catch lines: "—and that, children, is how I met your grandmother."

The step after *Holiday* was toward writing his own play. It was called *Rebound*; it starred Hope Williams; and it, too, was a hit. The movies were becoming the talkies now. They needed dialogue that people could listen to, not just read from subtitles, so a crash-gong rang for dialogue writers, and Don was one who answered, in 1930. The producers heard him loud and clear. He started off with an adaptation of *Holiday*, starring Katharine Hepburn (it won Don an Oscar in 1940); then another of Phil Barry's plays, *The Philadelphia Story*, also for her; and then *Marie Antoinette*, for Norma Shearer; and more successes, including *The Prisoner of Zenda* (written in collaboration with John Balderston), and still more.

Somewhere around then Don brought me out to Hollywood. Never mind what I did for my paltry salary at M-G-M; it was worth it to me, because it showed me beyond any doubt that I had no gift for screenwriting, and I'd be wise to aim my ambition elsewhere.

My life was lived outside the studio, at the Stewarts' luxurious house on Beverly Drive. Don and Bee were Hollywood's darlings; they were inexhaustibly merry and bright, they loved to give parties, and the biggest stars flocked to them: the Ronald Colmans, Virginia Bruce, Kay Francis, Herbert Marshall. Don's first entrance on the stage, "bringing in some champagne," was a warm-up for his social life in Hollywood. The Stewarts were constantly invited out—they were sure to make a party "go"—and in their kindness they always arranged an invitation for me. We went to a birthday party at Sam and Frances Goldwyn's; and to a dance at Ruth Chatterton's; Grace Moore and her Spanish husband came to our house; we went to dinner at Dick and Jessie Barthelmess's; Clark Gable and his wife, Ria, came to our house. That night, Don, with a huge grin, denounced Gable:

"These goddam limey juveniles, coming over here with their phony accents! 'Clark' Gable, forsooth, like a solicitor's 'clark.' The kid's name is 'Clerk,' I tell you, C, L, E, R, K. I'm not going to string along with this phoniness anymore. From now on, he's 'Clerk' to me—Clerk Gable, Clerk, Clerk, Clerk, just as God wanted him to be! And that goes for Bart Marshall, too! 'Bart': I ask you! Hey, Bert Marshall, come here a minute!"

They loved it. So did everyone else.

Don could never resist an opportunity to clown. At the Goldwyns', he "read" a roll of toilet paper as if it were ticker-tape: "My God, the bottom is out of Amalgamated Tub! Ruin! *Ruin!*" At

one of the Stewarts' own parties, a drunken young actress, fresh
from starring on Broadway, scrambled onto a table and shouted,
"I'm the only natural blonde in the goddam room, and I can prove
it!", and forthwith hoisted her skirt above her naked thighs.

Don picked up a spoon and went to the table. "Say 'Ah!' Toots,"
he told her.

At another party, a girl said to him, "I feel foolish dancing with
you when you're wearing that long overcoat. Take it off, won't
you?"

"If you want." He took it off. He was wearing nothing under it.

I had the good fortune to be with Don at the historic moment
when he made a quip that has been credited to half the wits of our
time. The Stewarts and I had been invited to a big bash at Ruth
Chatterton's. It was broad daylight when we got home. A flock of
white pigeons, pets of their young son Ames, were strutting on the
driveway, waiting to be fed. Don took off his hat as he approached
them. "Any messages for me?" he asked.

The pigeon incident always reminds me of when the Stewarts
were in Paris, shopping on the Left Bank. Bee saw a beautiful
ivory crucifix, and Don bought it for her. The shopkeeper assured them that it would be delivered to their hotel that afternoon—Monsieur was not to give himself concern: it would be
there *without fail*!

Don said airily, "Oh, *nous ne sommes pas pressés*, Toots!—
We're not in *that* much of a hurry!"

Of the many contradictions in Don's character, one of the
strangest was his combination of prodigality and parsimony. If
there can be such a thing as a spendthrift miser, Don was it. He
and I went to dinner one evening at the Vendôme, an extremely
expensive Hollywood restaurant. The way to our table led past
one where half a dozen of his friends were ordering their after-
dinner coffees. They hailed him, and he asked if we might have

our cocktails with them. We did, and when their waiter brought their check, Don snatched it away and signed his own name to it—for their six dinners!

By my frugal standards, this was above and beyond the call of courtesy or friendship. And yet he was embarrassingly tightfisted about expenditures that anyone else would consider petty. He never bought even a newspaper or a postage stamp without entering it at once in his pocket ledger. He and I played tennis every afternoon until the original box of a dozen balls had come down to two, both of them abraded to baldness by the concrete court; so I bought a box for us. "Gee, that's swell!" Don said. "We'll start on them when the others wear out." One of the gossip columnists printed this slander: "The Donald Ogden Stewarts opened their safe last night and gave a party." He had it wrong: Don never closed his safe—certainly it opened wide enough and stayed open long enough for him to give me and my wife a pair of magnificent Great Danes—but he was painfully loath to open his change purse.

As Hitler's rantings grew louder, Don joined the Hollywood branch of the Anti-Nazi League and became its president. (He was also head of the Screenwriters Guild.) He wasn't joking now. On one of his trips to New York, around 1935 or '36, a friend mentioned that he was about to sail for Europe.

Don asked, "What ship?"

"The *Bremen*."

Don was outraged. "The *Bremen*! If you take that German liner, Toots, I swear to God I'll send you a radiogram: NEVER MIND GOERING. GET H!"

I don't know when Don's Communism came to the surface, but I know that he began going to party meetings and rallies, because the story flashed around New York that before taking Bee to a rally in Union Square, he told her to turn her mink coat inside out.

For Don—funny, clever Don—to say something as absurd as that, and say it seriously, meant to me that *he* was inside out. It must have meant so to Bee, too. Don said, "My dear wife, who was marvelous, couldn't take it anymore." They were divorced, and in 1937 Don married someone whose political philosophy was more congenial: she was Lincoln Steffens's widow, Ella Winter, an Australian and a passionate Communist sympathizer. (Steffens and Ida Tarbell were the first and probably the best of what are now called "investigative reporters," but what Theodore Roosevelt then called "muckrakers." It was Steffens who went to Russia and reported, "I have been over into the future, and it works.")

Ella was such a vigorous and relentless proselytizer that an evening with the Stewarts came to mean an evening when you had to listen to the Glories of Communism and the Evils of Capitalism. Such wit and gaiety as Don now showed would not have been out of place in Lenin's tomb. He became the vociferous spokesman for every liberal and labor cause in Hollywood. It was said that F.D.R. began each day "by ordering orange juice, coffee and the first ten telegrams of protest from Donald Ogden Stewart." His friends began to drift away. Then the McCarthy hearings began (the "witch-hunts," as the Stewarts' circle called them) and Don and Ella skipped the country in 1950 and turned up in London. There, in Hampstead, they took the "dearest, sweetest little house," except that it was a big house, with a garden, big and rambling and comfortable. They stuffed it with Ella's collection of modern art, including a Picasso and some Paul Klees, and they lived there happily ever afterward.

Don never lacked for work. The English movie studios were greedy for his talents; the producers didn't care whether his politics were rose-red or snow-white, so long as he wrote good pictures for them, and he did. —Or so I was told; I don't know the name of any of them, or whether I saw them, or the name he signed to them; I know only that he didn't sign his own.* Although I saw him once or twice a year for his last twenty-five years, he never volunteered any information about his films, and I never questioned him. Nor did he bring up Communism; he gave me an impression that the subject was as dead as Stalin. Instead, we talked about the old, sunny days in New York and Hollywood and the Caribbean and on Long Island, and his quips and my laughs came as thickly as ever.

Don and Ella each found time to write an autobiography; hers was called *And Not To Yield*, and his *By a Stroke of Luck!* In it he insisted that whatever success he had achieved—and professionally it was brilliant and abundant—was due wholly to luck and nothing else. One of the last interviews he ever gave (to a reporter from the London *Sunday Times*) has this quote:

> My whole life has been lucky—wait a minute, Sweetie;
> any sentence beginning "my whole life" is to be distrusted,
> so we'll scrub that. Just say I was shot in the ass with luck. . . .
> The main thing is, Toots, I didn't have anything to do with it,
> it just happened.

If there is life after death, Don's luck holds. He and Ella were inseparable in life, and "in their death they were not divided." He died in the Hampstead house late on Saturday night, August 2, 1980, and Ella died just after midnight that Monday. Their bodies were cremated, and the ashes were scattered over the garden.

Ella's son, Peter Steffens, wrote me, "Don remained good-humored to the very end, displaying his magic capacity to make everyone feel happy—the doctors, nurses and all about him." All except his bereft friends.

---

* I have just learned that one was *Escapade*, written under his father's given names, "Gilbert Holland."

APPENDIX I

In the 1920s and '30s, there was a fashionable lying-in hospital in New York, Miss Lippincott's (shouldn't it have been *Mrs.* Lippincott's?), where all the chic young mothers-to-be went for their confinements. One Christmas Don's presents to Bee included a reservation at Miss Lippincott's, prepaid, for September 25 of the following year.

When I lived with the Stewarts in Hollywood, their two children, boys, were also there: Ames (Bee's maiden name), then about eight, and Don, Jr. (also known as "Duck" and "Dee-Dee"), about three.

Dee-Dee was too young then to make much of an impression on me. I remember him only as being almost a platinum blond, and as wandering across the tennis court heedless of any match in progress. Much later, I heard about a letter that Don is said to have written him when he reached fourteen:

> Dear Dee-Dee: The time has come for you to learn about the flowers and the bees. There is a gentleman bee and a lady bee, though I don't know which is which. As for the flowers, we get ours from Plaza Florists. So much for *that*.
>
> Affectionately,
> *Daddy.*

Ames was a heller. Once when Bee was in Europe, and Don was working at home, he telephoned her: "Ames is here on my knee, darling, and wants to tell you something. Go ahead, Ames. Say, 'Hello, Mummy!'" Silence. "Ames, say, 'Hello, Mummy!'... *Ames!*" Silence, while the transatlantic phone ticked away at a dollar a tick. Don shook the stubborn wretch and ordered him, "Goddammit, *say 'Hello, Mummy!"*

Ames said, "Hello, Daddy."

He broke a neighbor's window one afternoon in Hollywood when I was there. Next day, a Sunday, Don had to go to the studio for a special job, and hoping to capitalize on the occasion, he explained to Ames that instead of playing tennis with him as planned, Daddy had to work overtime and make enough money to replace the window that a certain naughty boy had broken. (The money that Don made could have replaced the Rose Window at Rheims.) He ended, "Aren't you sorry that poor, dear Daddy has to work on his day off, just because of you?"

He had chosen the wrong audience for his eloquent appeal. Ames said, "If you have any money left over, buy me an air rifle."

I remember another passage between Don and Ames. One day at lunch, Ames was refusing to eat his carrots, and Don was trying the new technique of persuasion by droning repetition, thus: "Eat your carrots, Ames. Ames, eat your carrots. Your carrots, Ames: eat them. Ames, eat your carrots—" After some minutes of this, I didn't know who was going to crack first, Ames or me. It proved to be Ames. He said to Don, "Shut up!"

I was wondering what thunderbolt this would bring down on Ames's head when Don said sharply, "Don't ever say that again, Ames! Say, 'Shut up, Daddy dear!' " I'm afraid that "rigid disciplinarian" is not the right term for Don.

Ames and I were good friends, and when my short hitch at M-G-M was over, his farewells were tearful and ululant. The only way I could quiet him was to make three promises: Next time he was in New York, I'd (1) take him to lunch, (2) at the Passy (he had remarkably sophisticated and expensive tastes for an eight-year-old), and (3) let him order whatever he wished.

The Stewart family came to town a few months later, and I

kept my promise to the little blackmailer. I took him to the Passy, where he ordered and ate three dozen oysters—nothing else. He behaved beautifully, and there was not the slightest trouble from start to finish, unless you count a trifling incident that happened as the maître d'hôtel was bowing his thanks: Ames whipped out a toy pistol and shot a stream of muddy water all over his beautiful boiled shirt.

APPENDIX II

Don told me that he too had had a chilling experience with the lady novelist whom I have called Mrs. Martha Mary Baker. He and Bee were spending a week with the Gerald Murphys at Antibes. One afternoon Don chartered a sloop with a paid hand and took Bee for a sail in Golfe-Juan. What happened, Don said, was frightening and almost a tragedy; and at a dinner that evening, seated next to Mrs. Baker, it was still so vivid in his memory that he felt compelled to tell her about it:

"We were bowling along very nicely, the sailor at the wheel, and none of us paying much attention, when a fluke gust hit us from the lee side. The boom slammed over, knocking the sailor and me overboard. Bee knew absolutely nothing about boats, and here were the sailor and I struggling in the water, and the boat drawing further away every second. All this was just opposite the Clews' house and—"

Mrs. Baker asked, "How *are* the Clews?"

APPENDIX III

Don told me that in the late 1920s and early 1930s, a standard feature at a big organizational banquet—for instance, the Bar Association's—was a speech by a professional funnyman like himself or Bob Benchley or George S. Chappell or Will Rogers. The speaker's fee was a thousand dollars or more, so the boys always welcomed an invitation.

Chappell was best-known for his book *The Cruise of the Kawa*, by "Dr. Walter S. Traprock," but he was almost as well-known for turning up soused and hardly able to mumble. The chairman who had engaged him to speak at one banquet knew about this little failing and appointed a bodyguard to keep temptation at bay, from rising bell to dinner bell. The man did a thorough job; he brought Chappell to the dinner cold sober. And yet (Don told me), when Chappell arose an hour later to make his speech, he teetered in silence for a moment, then burst into tears, wailed "My little sister—!" and slid under the table. It turned out that he had given his waiter a handsome tip to bring him a water pitcher full of gin, and had been sipping away at it all through the meal. Thereafter, whenever Don and I had a drink together, one of us was sure to wail, "My little sister—!"

NUNNALLY JOHNSON
1897-1977

Script-Doctor Johnson

Nunnally Johnson escorts Lauren Bacall and Marilyn Monroe to the premiere of How to Marry a Millionaire

NUNNALLY Johnson was fascinated by bizarre names—*people's* names. So was Frank Sullivan. So am I. Whenever one of us turned up a name of special absurdity, he reported it to the other two. The cornerstone of our collection was an obit of one Reverend Mr. Casebeer, sent in by Nunnally, who had penciled a thick black line around it, with "We mourn our loss." Another of his finds was the London *Times*'s obit of a Colonel Reginald Bastard, dead at the age of seventy-nine. Nunnally sighed, "Think of seventy-nine years (minus a few very young ones) of facing up to quips, smirks, and 5,788,613 bum jokes!"

Many of our most precious treasures came from the obit columns. I had an advantage over Nunnally and Frank because I live in the South, where the baptismal font is often a wellspring of inspiration, and parents soar to realms of fanciful nomenclature where earthbound outlanders cannot follow. Thus I was able to nominate for our Golden Book Messrs. Quo Vadis Randolph, Nightlatch Tucker, Do-Funny Johnson (no relation, Nunnally hastened to assure us), Ocean Hunter, and Sweet-Legs Brooks—all late ornaments of my native Richmond.

My favorite name was Mrs. Birdie Bottom Tingle, of a hamlet in Virginia. My next favorite leaped at me from the society pages of *The New York Times*: Miss Alice Foxhall (that's close enough) had married a Mr. Knight, apparently heedless of the name that divorce would legally inflict on her. I sent the story to Nunnally, who replied, "What right to laugh have *I* got, living in the same town with somebody named Bubbles Schinazi?"

When Lady Bird and Linda Bird Johnson moved into the White House, Nunnally quickly read the wind and notified Frank and me that he wished to be known thenceforth as "Nunnally Bird Johnson."

Frank wrote me in April 1950:

I had a drink with Nunnally in New York on the eve of his departure for England, and I had a fine bon voyage gift for him. That very morning, the *Herald-Tribune* had printed the announcement that a Dutch gardener had been hired to supervise the tulip-planting at Rockefeller Center. His name is Homo Gytenbeek. It is not a typo either, as it has appeared since.

Frank wrote again:

I have nothing to communicate except the name of a recent bride here in New York: Miss Cherry Shapiro. She really should have married the fellow who figured in the conversation between two girls Dottie Parker overheard:

"Guess who I seen yesterday?"

"Who?"

"Laddie Ginsburg."

Nunnally brought our little game to an abrupt end with a clipping that Frank and I instantly recognized as the Nonpareil Nugget, a name we could never hope to surpass, equal, or even approach: Mr. Nota Pecker. Nunnally's letter said, "In case the board acts favorably on Brother Pecker, I suggest that he be appointed honorary chairman of the ladies' membership drive." It was so carried, unanimously, and the game was over. There was a flurry of renewed interest a few years later, when Nunnally queried us about the rumor that Lucius Beebe had a sister named Phoebe B. Beebe, but it took only one telephone call to track down this canard and quash it.

Nunnally's own name can't fairly be classed with Tom, Dick, and Harry, though it's familiar enough in my part of the country. I have known several Nunnallys here in Virginia. One of them kept an antique store in Bowling Green and gave me a letterhead of his, so that I could write Johnson, "Just happened to be thinking of you—"

Nunnally was a southerner himself, of course, as he could prove by speaking only one sentence or even only a couple of words. His Georgia accent (he was born in Columbus, in 1897) was as thick as Georgia grits; and his years of living in foreign lands— New York, Hollywood, Rome, London—did nothing to dilute it. When his daughter Roxie* was married in 1975, and the minister asked, "Who giveth this woman?" the whole church heard Nunnally's response: "Ah do, an' her mothah do." His friends used to tease him about Columbus. One of them asked, "That's *Tobacco Road* country, isn't it?"

Nunnally said, "Shucks, weh Ah come f'um, we look on the *Tobacco Road* folks as the country club set."

He got to Hollywood, as did so many other screenwriters, by

---

* Roxie owes her name (actually Roxana) to having been born at a time when her father was producing *Roxie Hart* (which he had adapted), with Ginger Rogers, whom he much admired, in the title role.

way of journalism. He started as a reporter on a Columbus paper, moved along to Savannah, from there to the Brooklyn *Daily Eagle*, and on to the New York *Herald-Tribune*. Meanwhile, he had begun writing short stories. *The Saturday Evening Post* bought many of them, and that's how I met him. Around 1939, a manuscript about Hollywood's stupidest and most vicious gossip columnist, the late, ineffable Louella Parsons, came to us from a new contributor, plainly an amateur. His writing was pedestrian, but his research had been thorough, and since a professional would have no trouble refining the crude ore, we bought the material and offered it to Nunnally for rewriting. He didn't do a hatchet job on Miss Parsons; it was more like surgery—he cut her into small pieces. Consider these two sentences: "In a field where bad writing is as natural and common as breathing, Louella stands out like an asthmatic's gasps. . . . She is probably the most consistently inaccurate reporter who ever lived to draw $600 a week." The waning of her malign influence dates from the week that "The Gay Illiterate," as Nunnally called her, was published.

I don't think he did anything else for the *Post* while he was in Hollywood; he was far too busy writing screen originals and adapting others. He was a skillful healer of ailing scripts; whenever one began to totter and turn pale, the cry went around, "Get thee to a Nunnally!" and Doctor Johnson would bring the roses back to its cheeks. He was a true craftsman, one who took pride in his craft. He despised screenwriters who despised screenwriting, as if it were for *Cap'n Billy's Whiz-Bang.* Nunnally told an interviewer, "Writing is a profession, wherever you do it; and anyone who doesn't take his profession seriously is a fool."

Of all his pictures, his adaptation of John Steinbeck's grim novel *The Grapes of Wrath* (released in 1940) is probably Nunnally's best-known and certainly among his very best. *The New York Times*'s critic called it "a masterpiece of the cinema, one of those pictures which by dignity of theme and excellence of treatment seem to be of enduring artistry." Nunnally himself had a special reason for cherishing *The Grapes of Wrath*: the role of Rosasharon was played by a young Memphis starlet named Dorris Bowdon. They were married in 1940 and they stayed married. They had met the year before, when she had a small part in *Young Mr. Lincoln*, starring Henry Fonda. Nunnally followed the career of the picture, and when it opened in Memphis, he learned that the theater where it played had proudly given the local girl top billing on its marquee, this:

DORRIS BOWDON

in

YOUNG MR. LINCOLN

with

HENRY FONDA

So what did the unspeakable Johnson do? He arranged to have a photo taken of the theater and marquee late on a rainy night, when the only creature to be seen on the street was a cat. And *then* what did he do? He had a headline printed:

GOVERNOR CALLS OUT NATIONAL GUARD
TO CONTROL CROWDS RIOTING TO SEE
DORRIS BOWDON'S LATEST SCREEN HIT

And finally, after he and Dorris were married, he posted photo and headline on the family bulletin board, where no one entering the Johnson house could fail to notice it.

To return to John Steinbeck: John told me that soon after signing the contract for *Grapes*, he went to Hollywood to discuss the treatment with Nunnally, whom he had never met. Their dinner at Chasen's began with cocktails at the bar. Nunnally enjoyed drinking, as John saw at once, but he had a very light head, as John did not see. They were chatting over their third cocktail when in came a man whose face struck John as unusually interesting. He nudged Nunnally: "Who's that?"

Nunnally said, "His name is Robert Benchley. I don't think you'd care for him. He drinks"—and toppled off the bar stool onto the floor.

Nunnally maintained that the writer and the director make the picture; actors are indispensable, of course, but regrettably so. He was once heard to describe his plans for a new production—costumes, location, background music—in minute detail, ending up, "And then we'll get us some actors."

When one of his pictures was "in the can," the leading man, a vain, swaggering ham, told Nunnally what a privilege it had been to work with him, "and be sure to call on me if I can ever help you again."

The world "help" was a mistake. "Yeah," Nunnally said. "I'll keep you in mind. Can you type?"

An actress whom he both liked and respected was Marilyn Monroe. He saw in her much more than a sexpot; talent was there,* and he was convinced that if he could only give her enough confidence in her ability, she could become a great star. She, in turn, liked and respected Nunnally and trusted him; she even wanted to put her career in his hands. It was too late. This was in 1959, and he was already committed to taking Dorris and the children to Europe for a tax-saving stay. His last night in Hollywood, Monroe telephoned him at the Beverly Hills Hotel to ask if she could consult him just once more. Nunnally told her he was sorry, but he had engagements that evening and was flying to New York early next morning.

"Well, then, can I have breakfast with you?"

He hesitated before saying, "Okay, but I'll be finishing my packing."

"I'll be there at seven o'clock sharp," she said.

Monroe had never been known to be on time, or even near it,

---

* He proved his belief by starring her in *How to Marry a Millionaire*, with Betty Grable and Lauren Bacall.

but next morning punctually at seven the desk clerk rang Nunnally and said there was a young lady to see him.

"Send her up."

"I can't do that, sir. The Beverly Hills doesn't allow young ladies in gentlemen's rooms."

"Hell," Nunnally said, "this isn't a young lady! This is a call girl. Send her up!"

While Nunnally packed and they drank coffee, he tried to pump confidence into her: "You can do it!" he kept saying. "I *know* you can! I believe in you—*you* must believe in *yourself!*"

He strapped up his bags and told her good-bye. They never met again.

Before one of his trips east, he wrote Sullivan (I have condensed the letter):

> I am coming to New York at the end of this week and will be at the Plaza Hotel. I'm wondering if you will be coming down to the metropolis, as it would be good to meet you in person. [By then, Nunnally and Frank had been bosom friends for at least twenty-five years.]
>
> But how should I describe myself, so you'll know me? After all our correspondence, you can imagine how often I've wondered what you look like, just as I have no doubt you've wondered about me. As I think I told you once, my eyes are blue, with just a glint of hazel in certain lights. "Cute" is the word that most of my friends apply to me, but that sounds as if I were tiny, and I am not at all tiny, though you could hardly describe me as large. My own feeling is that I am kind of large cute.
>
> Ordinarily I could help you by describing the way I do my hair, but just now I am in a spell where I change the arrangement almost every day, to suit my mood.... This is futile. I simply cannot bring myself to observe myself objectively. Besides, who knows which of the myriad me's will

be present the day we meet? To save trouble, I might wear something distinctive, like my green, and to make doubly certain, a red, red rose in my lapel. And I'll carry a sunflower in my left hand and a Remington Rand adding machine in my right. I don't see how you can possibly miss me.

Yours till then—

The Johnsons first took a villa in Rome, then an apartment in London—two apartments: one for him to work in, the other for them to live in. (Nunnally complained, "I don't know why Dorris has to have so many places, when all I need is a card table and a typewriter.") He wasn't under such pressure now, and his correspondence with Sullivan and me picked up. Here is a letter from London, dated April 1964:

The vital statistics are hardly worth mentioning. Dorris (remember?) and I are still married. Our oldest daughter, Christie, married a Swedish steeplechase jockey (there are only three steeplechase races a year in Sweden, and he hasn't placed in one yet, so you can imagine what an affluent marriage *that* is) and is now living in a bog outside Göteborg. This is a girl who was educated for gracious living at Sarah Lawrence! [Nunnally spoke of his jockey son-in-law as "the Swedish martingale," and told me that he'd had a message from him early in the honeymoon: "I managed to get your old Jaguar up to ninety."] Roxie, 18, is at a small co-ed college in Illinois, Shimer, which distinguished itself last winter by establishing a new national intercollegiate record of 61 straight losses at basketball. Not that this disturbs her; she has a single, simple aim in life—to marry a millionaire. God go with her! Our son Scott, 15, who tried Andover for a year and a half, is now back at the American School here and was just voted the best-dressed man on campus and the worst math student. He's majoring in staying out late.

(I have never met Nunnally's son and daughter by his two previous marriages, but I've known Dorris's three children for upwards of twenty-five years, and I take my oath that their father's implications are the foulest kind of slander.)

I saw Dorris and Nunnally several times when they were living in London. Once I brought them a clipping from *Country Life*: "the song of the willow warbler," as reported by a correspondent:

> Sip, sip, sip, see!
> Tee, Tew, wee, tew!
> Witty, witty, wee-wee, weetew!

We thought it had possibilities as an icebreaker at stiff dinner parties, but we realized we'd never get to the last line without breaking up.

The studios that Nunnally worked for when he and his family returned to America in 1968 I'm not clear about; it doesn't make much difference now. Somewhere along the line he went to Twentieth Century–Fox, and Finis Farr quoted him as saying, "This job makes a nice umbrella—and it's been rainin'.'" Then he went to Universal with Bill Goetz and Leo Spitz. Peter Lind Hayes told me that a newspaperman called at Nunnally's office to interview him about the new job, and remarked, "Bob Goldstein just passed your window, Mr. Johnson. What does he do here?"

Nunnally said, "Bob? He spits for Goetz and gets for Spitz."

My wife and I went to Beverly Hills for a few days in the summer of 1975, and the Johnsons had us to dinner. Johnny Mercer was there—such a nice guy that I forgive him for not singing my favorite of his songs, "The Death of J. B. Markham"; and my old chum from the Chicago *Journal*, Arthur Sheekman, with his wife, Gloria Stuart; and Groucho Marx. My wife had never seen Groucho offstage. When he stormed in, late, and flung his overcoat at Nunnally, shouting, "Have this cleaned and pressed and back in half an hour!" she thought she had waked up in the middle of a Marx Brothers act.

Nunnally had retired by then. For the previous forty years, he had needed a full-time secretary to cope with his daily mail. Now it had dwindled away until—he said to Peter Lind Hayes and Mary Healy—"My big problem in the mornin' is decidin' which letter to open first, the one addressed to 'Resident' or the one addressed to 'Occupant.'"

By now emphysema had begun to rack him. Dorris moved them to a one-story house, to spare him the agony of struggling up a flight of steps. Early in March 1977, Peter telephoned him and asked, "Nunnally, what do you want?"

Nunnally managed to gasp, "Anything Ah can get!"

Two weeks later he died—not long before the publication of Alistair Cooke's *Six Men*, which was dedicated to him. Nunnally would have liked to know that.

A passage from Boswell applies to Nunnally as well as to Samuel: "Johnson is dead.—Let us go to the next best:—there is nobody; no man can be said to put you in mind of Johnson."

APPENDIX I

I met Arthur Sheekman the morning I started work on the Chicago *Journal*, in 1928. When I reported in, the publisher told me, "Your main job will be second-string editorial writer, but you'll also be a handyman. We'll give you other assignments if we need to. I'll expect you to turn out about eighteen inches of editorial copy a day."

"Yes, sir. Any special subjects?"

"No, choose your own. I don't think many people read editorials anyway."

I shared a dark office on an airshaft with the chief editorial writer, Rex Strom, and our columnist, Sheekman. Strom was big and burly and could write about anything and write well. An edit of his about Teapot Dome said that the oil rigs "danced a lumbering minuet," which I thought was good. Sheekman had the beautiful, sensitive face of a young Polish violinist, with deep, soft eyes, but his soul did not accord with his appearance, as he quickly proved.

I finished a couple of edits that counted out to eighteen inches and asked what I should do with them: clear them through the publisher or whom?

Strom said, "They go to the managing editor, Dick Finnegan. Call Mick Harris—he's the city editor—and tell him to send you up a boy."

I rang. Back came a harsh, impatient "Yeah?"

I said, "Mr. Harris, this is Bryan in the editorial room. Will you send me up a boy, please?"

"Bryan? Who the hell are you? Never heard of you! And I'll tell you something else, Brown, or whatever you said your name is: I'm responsible to these kids' mothers, and I'm not going to send any nice, clean little kid to someone who might be a rotten pervert for all I know!"

I stammered, "I—I—"

"All right! All right! I'll take a chance. What do you want? Fat boy or thin boy? Blue eyes or brown eyes?"

Harris had a voice that overflowed the telephone receiver, and Sheekman heard him. "Gimme that phone!" he said. He grabbed it from me and yelled into it, "Goddammit, Harris, you can't talk to a pal of mine like that! Do it once more, and I'll come down there and bite your ass!"

"You can't!" Harris said. "It's Friday! Har-har-*HAR*!"

I had been at work in Chicago for just under two hours.

Mick Harris and I later became good friends, after he decided that he had given me enough of the dirty assignments (including Cook County's first electrocution—a double one) that the cub always gets; and one night he called me over to his desk and invited me to join him in a drink of cherry brandy. It was so smooth and delicious, I asked where he had found it. "Bowles Harbor, Michigan," he said. "Straight from the mayor himself. I'm the only newspaperman in Chicago who knows he has an illegitimate son."

Sheekman's column, "Little About Everything," ran on the editorial page. It had been originated by F.P.A., and when he moved on to New York, Sheekman inherited it. He didn't change the formula; it continued to be a hodgepodge of jingles, puns, epigrams, couplets, riddles, "paragraphs" (now called "one-liners"), free verse, and what-all. It was indeed a little about everything. A few perks went with the job, and Arthur was willing to share them with me, in return for helping him fill out the column on a sterile day. A specially valuable perk was the couple of freebies to the parties that the Hollywood studios' local publicity men gave when their stars came through town. (All coast-to-coast passengers had to change in Chicago then.)

One party was the lunch given to introduce Miss Gertie Green, a coming star—they thought. Miss Green would be called an "exotic dancer" today; in 1928, she was a "shimmy queen." And *tough?* She may have been a Salome on the stage and screen, but she was a fishwife at the lunch table. She talked from the side of her mouth, and her every other word was blasphemous or obscene. She had a husband somewhere; one of the critics had heard that he was making pictures in Paris. "True, Miss Green?"

Miss Green snarled, "I dunno an' I don't give a shit! But if that sumbitch is makin' pitchers, you can bet you sweet ass they're the kind that sell for ten francs a package on the bully-vards!"

There was silence, a long silence. My boy Sheekman broke it. He looked around the table and remarked brightly, "Well, here it is Tuesday already!"

One other vivid recollection of Sheekman: the day he danced into our office, whooping, "Congratulate me, fellows! *Congratulate* me!"

"For what?"

"I've just had my salary doubled, that's what!" Then came the Sheekman of it: "And boy, can I use that extra five bucks a week!"

I left the *Journal* after a year. The next I heard about Sheekman, he had gone to Hollywood and married the beautiful Gloria, and was writing gags for the Marx Brothers. Our dinner at the Johnsons was the last time I saw him—or Nunnally either, alas! Both of them died soon afterwards.

APPENDIX II

Nunnally's wife, Dorris, sent me the photo that accompanies this chapter, and with it the following explanation

. . . Made the nite of the opening of *How to Marry a Millionaire.* We had the girls at our house for dinner before [the] premeire. Marilyn came alone, a bit late and mighty breathless. Nunnally suggested she could use a drink. Bourbon straight was her choice. She downed it fast. Had another and yet another. Dinner she merely dallied with. Then we rushed to waiting limos and full speed ahead to the theater.

When we stepped out at the theatre she, Marilyn, was mobbed and I was knocked down. Police quickly ringed us with locked arms. Cameramen were allowed a few moments of flashing . . . and we pranced on into our seats. Lights were hardly out before Marilyn whispered to me that she needed the ladies room urgently. I went with her and she asked me into the booth! She then told me she had been sewed into her slinky white lace dress at the studio before coming to our house and asked me to help her free the essential parts. I pulled, twisted, strained every thread while she wriggled. A sight we were! Once relieved we reversed the minuet and returned to our seats exhausted.

Next morning [Nunnally] called to tell her how great she was in the film. She answered weakly and he asked if she was o.k. Not quite she told him because her head ached and stomach churned. Why? "Because," said she, "I never drank liquor before in my life."

JOHN STEINBECK

1902-1968

Mumbles and Bellows, Scowls and Laughs

John and Elaine Steinbeck, in costume?

A new Chinese restaurant opened on West 52d Street in the early 1950s. My literary agent, Mark Hanna, invited me to dinner there, and I accepted at once. I liked Chinese food and I liked Mark. He was an old China hand; he knew the different regional cuisines; and I was sure the dinner would be delicious. It was—especially the steaming soup, which was served in a hollowed watermelon with its rind incised like a scratchboard drawing. I also, and pre-eminently, remember that Mark's other guests were John Steinbeck and his wife, Gwyn.

As often happens when I first meet somebody I have long admired, my mind went blank. I haven't the least recollection of anything that John said, though this may have been partly because he was a mumbler and I didn't hear him clearly. But I distinctly remember how he looked and sounded: strong gray eyes, bristly hair, a trick of pushing out his lower lip, deep, growly, unresonant voice.

Here (credit Ring Lardner) "the curtain is lowered for several years to denote the passage of several years."

In February 1954, then, I rented a one-room apartment in Torremolinos, near Málaga, in Spain. I am told that today Torremolinos looks like a road show of Miami Beach, with condominiums, towering hotels, boutiques, discos, and a seasonal population that thinks of itself as "the Beautiful People." But it was a quiet little fishing village in '54, with a *posada* (a state-owned inn), some modest villas and, bang on the beach, a one-story building, El Remo ("The Oar"), that housed my apartment and two others. There was a swimming pool, a bar-restaurant with a headwaiter named Cristoforo Colombo, and three waitress-chambermaids, all named Barbara.

Life there was pleasant and comfortable and inexpensive. Two of my friends, James and Marcia Burnham, had taken a villa; and of El Remo's other apartments, MacKinlay Kantor and his wife, Irene, had one, and Stephen *(Gamesmanship)* Potter the other. We had a happy month together, until the day came when the Burnhams, the Kantors, and Potter left for home, and there I was, alone, except for the Black Dog on my back.

I needn't have worried. No more than two days passed before the housekeeper told me, "An American couple arrives this afternoon. Perhaps you know them? Señor y Señora Juan Steinbeck?"

I happened to be outside when they drove up: John and a sparkling young lady. He wore a beard now, but I had no trouble recognizing him. I introduced myself, and John lied in his teeth— "Of *course* I remember you!"—and introduced me to his new wife, Elaine. We agreed to meet for cocktails. And for dinner, as things turned out. And afterwards, God save us, for some of that creamy Spanish brandy called Carlos Primero. When I finally managed to wrench myself off the pillow next noon, and started on my diocesan rounds of the afflicted and distressed, I saw a sheet of paper tacked to the Steinbecks' door: SICK ARAB—which is

what the Duke of Bilgewater wrote on the shingle he put outside
of Nigger Jim's wigwam, after painting Jim's face and hands
blue, "like a man that's been drownded nine days." John's *Sweet
Thursday* was published later that year. The copy he gave me is
inscribed:

> Vice is a monster so fearful of mien,
> I'm sure we should all be as happy as kings.
>   John (Sick Arab) Steinbeck.

That night in Torremolinos was the first of many such in the
fourteen happy years that followed, in Rome, Paris, New York,
Capri, Washington, Somerset, Richmond. I never expect to find
merrier companions anywhere than Señor y Señora Steinbeck,
nor will I ever again, I'm afraid, laugh as much as I did in our
Spanish weeks together.

There were so many stories to tell, mutual friends to catch up
on, favorite books to discuss, jokes to swap, restaurants and inns
and hideaways to recommend! Everything came tumbling out at
once, all three of us talking, voices rising, and all trying to listen
too, and interrupting, and backing up with a polite (if obviously
impatient) "No, *you* go ahead"—well, finally, we agreed that
when one of us had to break in or burst under the pressure, a
hand would be raised, and as soon as the other two of us noticed it,
the signaler would be permitted to announce, "I wish to make a
reservation to say something, please," and in due course the other
would yield the floor.

John's car was a Jaguar XK 120 coupe, low and black, and
looking like a pirate felucca on wheels. (He used to refer to himself and Elaine as "the Joads in a Jag.") The horn was a chrome
steel bull's-head that *bellowed* when he sounded it. If he stopped
in a street for even thirty seconds, every urchin in Andalusia
materialized from nowhere and swarmed over the Jaguar and tried
to detach the horn. John was fearsome in his wrath. Enraged, he'd

stick out his lower lip, contort his face into a murderous scowl, and bellow (like his horn), "*Buttered TOAST!*" The children scattered like a flushed covey.

I asked, "Why 'buttered toast'?"

"Because it lends itself to being bellowed."

I had a car of my own in Torremolinos, a Citroën, small, tough, and cheap to run. It could carry four as against the Jaguar's two, so when we toured the neighborhood—to the Caballo Blanco for roast baby pig, or to Ronda to see Spain's oldest bullring—the Steinbecks rode with me. I'm cautious behind the wheel; moreover, although my car was light, its front-wheel drive made this model famous for the way it held the road. So it mildly irritated me to notice that whenever we entered even the gentlest curve, Steinbeck, in the other front seat, would draw in a sharp breath and stiffen his knees and lock them, until his feet nearly broke through the floorboards. What the devil was this? Then I caught Elaine's eye in the mirror, and she winked. Oho!

Pinky Thompson had once suckered me with a ploy I have never forgotten, and the road that we were now on—the coast road west to Gibraltar—was ideal for reviving it. That part of the Andalusian coast is deeply scalloped and indented, and the road hugged the shoreline tightly, twisting through one hairpin turn after another. But tourism and the trucking business were already making their influence felt; the highway department had begun to pinch off the sharper V-turns, and was building bridges across them, leaving the original road to melt back into the earth. Whenever we came to such a place, my ploy was to call attention to the abandoned stretch and deliver a solemn address about it, like this:

"See there to the right? That's the old road. That's the one we'd be on now, if they hadn't built this new road. It's much straighter, notice—the new one, I mean—which makes it shorter, so naturally you save time, you save oil and gas, you save wear and tear on your car and your tires. In fact, no matter how you look at it, the new road is better. An improvement, in other words. There's forty-five or fifty stretches like this between Torremolinos and Gib, and when you add the yardage all together, you can see right away that building the new road is a mighty—good—thing!

"Look, we're coming to another stretch! This one is longer than the one we just left, so we—and all the other cars—will save even more time and gas and oil and wear and tear. And something I forgot to mention: it's smoother, too, so the driving is easier, more pleasant. What it adds up to—"

Three or four stretches of "new road," with its superiority over the old road being explained in numbing detail, is guaranteed to break down even the most patient passenger, which John Steinbeck was *not*.

He had long ago stopped stiffening his knees. Now he said, grinning, "I'll knock it off, if you will."

I said, "Done!"

Elaine cried, "Praise God!"

"Has your game got a name?" John asked. "Just 'the Old Road'? I call mine 'Pseudopedalepsy,' which I hope means 'a compulsion to press down on imaginary brake pedals.'"

(Elaine had a game of her own, which she'd learned from George Kaufman: assigning the names of dishes on a menu to fictional characters. The only ones I can remember now are Chicken Cacciatore, a cowardly *mafista*; and his girl friends, Fluffy Potatoes and Cherries Jubilee.)

John was a various man. He took interest in, and was well informed about, a surprising variety of subjects: marine biology, for instance, the Aztec civilization, flags, pigs, the Arthurian cycle, etymology. It was John who taught me that the Spanish word *hidalgo*, "a nobleman," is a contraction of *hijo de algo*, "son of somebody"; and that *chum* is short for "chamber-fellow," i.e., roommate. He said, "But I've never really trusted the big Oxford dictionary since I looked up the derivation of *padlock*. What I got was, '*pad*, of uncertain meaning, plus *lock*.' From the *Oxford*! I *ask* you!"

He had a flagpole in front of his house at Sag Harbor, Long Island—"I am a vexillophile," he said proudly—and an eclectic assortment of flags to fly from it (*not* including one from Dora's Bear Flag Restaurant in Cannery Row). When I and my wife, who is French, went to Sag Harbor for a weekend, she was flattered to see the tricolor waving on high in her honor. Next day John replaced it with

WELCOME AMERICAN

DENTAL ASSOCIATION

(He gave this one to Nat Benchley, who ran it up his own flagpole in Nantucket. In a matter of mere minutes, Nat told me, a dentist had puffed in, demanding to know, "Where's the party?")

Pigs were another of John's enthusiasms. He often spoke of them with admiration. He said that his muse was "Pigasus," and he signed some of his letters with a tiny drawing of a winged pig, not unlike Whistler's butterfly. I once sent him a clipping from a journal of animal husbandry about a maze designed to test the comparative intelligence of pigs and rats. No rat needed fewer than two hundred tries to solve it, and no pig needed more than forty. John was overjoyed.

We all left El Remo in April and met again in Seville, for the *feria*, the annual week-long fair. It happened to coincide with my birthday, so John and Elaine gave me a party—and a present. I had foolishly let slip my promise to drive two young ladies up to Madrid when the *feria* was over. Worse, I had complained that it would be difficult to crowd their tumulus of luggage into my narrow little car. So what was the Steinbecks' present to me? A complete suit of armor! True, it was child-size and was made of tin, but even so the helmet and corselet alone would have filled a laundry hamper, and the lance was well over six feet long. (For sheer uselessness combined with unwieldiness, my armor matched the bon voyage present that Hugh Troy, the mural painter and practical joker, gave to a friend sailing from New York to Cherbourg: a heroic plaster bust of Nero.)

The Steinbecks were great ones for presents. I pass over the pair of candlesticks they gave me, as merely silver and extremely handsome, and come to the shotgun cane. That's not clear? Well, it's a walking stick that doubles as a shotgun (or vice versa). You twist the curved handle (like an umbrella's) through a quarter-circle and pull it toward you, thereby exposing the breech. Slip in a cartridge (they're about the size of a cigarette), shove the handle forward, twisting it again, and you are ready to fire—the trigger is a tiny lever just under your forefinger. Where this deadly toy came from, I haven't any idea, and I never remembered to ask John; it carries no gunsmith's name and no identifying number. To answer the natural question: No, I never dared fire it, for fear it might blow my hand off.

The chronology becomes confused after Seville. I *think* our next meeting was in Rome. I can't recall the year, but the date was October 15. What fixes it is that we took a picnic basket and a thermos to the Forum that evening—there was a full moon—and after the Steinbecks' ritual toast to Ava Gardner, the three of us drank to Edward Gibbon, who recorded that "It was on the fifteenth of October, 1764, as I sat amidst the ruins of the Capitol [that] the idea of writing the decline and fall of the city first started to my mind."

John and I swapped Gibbon's orotund Latinities (or Latin orotundities) until our memories ran out of them. We agreed that our favorite was where he says, "Among the first fifteen emperors, Claudius was the only one whose taste in love was entirely"—you can almost hear Gibbon's schoolmarmish little cough as the perfect word comes to his mind—"entirely *correct.*"

There's a nice story behind "the ritual toast to Ava Gardner," a story that John always recited as a curtain raiser to the first drink of an occasion. I heard it scores of times, and this is it, as nearly *verbatim* as my flabby memory permits, though John's delivery in a headlong, mumbling monotone must be imagined:

Steinbeck speaking: "May I propose a toast?

"Here's to Ava Gardner!

"One time I was in Hollywood working on a script. Zanuck had given me an office about the size of the Taj Mahal. I couldn't work there, so I went to the Beverly Hills Hotel and got down to the script. Dorris Johnson, Nunnally's wife, phoned and said they were giving a party and would I bring Ava Gardner? I said sure. About half an hour later Dorris phoned again and said Ava Gardner couldn't make it and would I bring Ann Sothern? I said sure. I took Ann to the party and we had a good time, so when I got back to Pacific Grove [his house on the Monterey Peninsula], I phoned her and said, 'I'm lonesome. Why don't you come up and have some fun?' She did, and being a cautious girl, she brought along a chaperone, Elaine Scott. On the *first* night, we went out to dinner and had a good time. On the *second* night, we went out to dinner and had a good time. On the *third* night, Ann said to me, 'I have to go out with some other friends tonight. Will you take care of Elaine?'

"I did. I have. And I always will.

"So here's to Ava Gardner!"

From Rome, the "Joads" headed their Jaguar for Naples, where they were taking the ferry to Capri. What happened on the drive down needs John to relate, with his gestures and grimaces. Anyway, about halfway, before you get to Terracina on the coast, the highway runs dead straight and dead level. To your right is a wide canal, with bridges at intervals of about a kilometer. To your left, behind a thick windbreak of eucalyptus trees, are orchards and truck gardens which you can see only through the gap where a farm road approaches to cross one of the bridges. Well, the Jaguar is tearing along when, far ahead, a donkey ambles out from a farm road and starts across the highway. He'd be onto the bridge and safely out of the way well before they reached him, so John didn't slow down. But then he sees that the donkey is hitched tandem to a horse, and the horse to a farm wagon, with a driver who beams at the onrushing car, but otherwise ignores it. John brakes hard and figures he can just pass behind the wagon, which is now well onto the highway. But behind the wagon is tethered a cow, and the whole procession forms an impassable roadblock. John had no choice: he stamped on the brake and spun the car, praying that it would neither turn turtle nor plunge into the canal nor crash into the windbreak. It didn't. But when it had screeched to a smoking stop, its front wheels were touching the wagon's rear wheels. For a moment, John and Elaine trembled so violently that neither could speak. Not the wagon driver; beaming, he kissed his bunched fingertips toward John and uttered one word: *"Mag-NIF-ico!"*

When Charley died (he was the cocoa-colored poodle of *Travels with Charley* and the only dog, you remember, who could pronounce the letter *F*), John and Elaine came down to Washington and stayed with me while they picked an American bull terrier from a local kennel. The one they took didn't have a single black tick on his white coat, so they named him "Angel"—"not knowing at the time," John wrote me later, "that his original name was 'Gino,' which is short for 'Angelino,' which is long for 'Angel.' Last night I added a little to his name; he is now 'Angel Biddle Duke.' "

I had told the Steinbecks about my friend Hugh Troy. His genius for practical joking seemed to amuse them, so while they were in town, I invited Hugh and his wife, Pat, to dinner with us. Hugh didn't let me down. (He never did.) There used to be a novelty postcard that showed a photograph of a kitten, with a concealed device that made a silly noise when you pressed it. Hugh brought one of them to our dinner; he had pasted a photograph of John over the kitten, and had lettered it:

Squeaky American Writers
#71: John Steinbeck

John pressed it, it squeaked, and he laughed until I thought he'd be ill.

I moved from Washington to Richmond in 1958, to an old house where the trenches and breastworks that marked Richmond's outer defenses in 1861–65 still run through the grounds. The Steinbecks soon drove down for a weekend; John's bread-and-butter letter ended:

> It has come to my att'n that the battery on your north boundary, if fired from its present position, will shoot the front porch off Aunt Clary Tremont's cottage. Please traverse carriages 28° and elevate not less than 17°.
>
> R.E.L.

John's handwriting was almost indecipherable—a mumble in pencil—so when a fit of nonsense was on him, I was grateful to get a telegram instead of a letter. I have a cable which reads, DISREGARD LETTER POSTCARD FOLLOWS; there had been no letter, and no postcard followed. Tamara Geva, the Russian dancer, has her birthday on St. Patrick's Day, so John used to wire her BYELORUSSIA GO BRAGH! He made a special trip to Usk, in Monmouthshire, just to cable a friend, HAPPY BIRTHDAY TO YOUSK FROM USK. He sent a note to "Erskine Caldwell, Ersk." When William Faulkner won a Nobel Prize in 1949, John wired him JOYEUX NOBEL! When his own turn came in 1962, the avalanche of congratulatory messages included a letter from Princess Grace of Monaco. John asked Elaine to look up the proper way to address an envelope to her. Elaine did so, then asked if he knew how to begin the letter.

"Sure!" John said. "I've already written it: 'Princess Grace, honey—' "

On the Steinbecks' way back from the Nobel ceremony in Stockholm, they stopped off in London. The account that John wrote me of a mutual friend he met there was, I felt, something less than exhaustive: "Saw Nunnally [Johnson]. He was in pajamas and an opera hat." Explanation?

Elaine did rather better: "John's English publisher [Alexander Frere, of Heinemann] gave a cocktail party for him. The door suddenly burst open, and in strode Noel Coward, shouting, 'The meeting of the John Steinbeck Fan Club will now come to order! The president has just arrived!' John loved it."

He loved nonsense of any sort and would go to endless trouble to foster it. One night at his house in New York, I found this notice attached to the door of the cabinet in my bathroom:

$$C_{15}H_{19}NO_2$$
Mandragora Iscariot (fecit in noctis)
$$C_{21}H_{33}NO_5$$
Diacetyl Morphine (heroin)
(mainline with pin)
Aconite & Day (for pure fun)
Eye of Newt (powdered)
(bring to boil, strain and drink)
$$CH_3CH_2CHOH-OH-(CHO)$$
$$N(CH_3)_3OH$$
Amanita Phalloides
2 tsps at bedtime
Elixir of Hemlock, 1 cup as decreed
Chill & serve.

On one of the shelves was a smutted spoon, a candle, and a safety pin; on another, a small packet labeled "Graveyard dust, Hydrochloride (sprinkle on doorstep)," and a sign in heavy black letters:

KEEP THIS PLACE CLEAN

STERILIZE YOUR OWN NEEDLE

BAIL BONDS   OPEN NITE & DAY

I think that was the last time we sat up all night, talking and drinking. The more John drank, the worse he mumbled, but things evened up: the more I drank, the better I could understand him—though, alas, the worse I remembered what he said.

I don't recall the bread-and-butter letter I wrote after this visit, but the comment it brought from John (which I have kept) leaves its tenor in little doubt. He says:

> I am saving your hangover letter for future use. It has more, sharper, fresher figures of speech to describe a condition which is commoner than the common cold than I have ever seen in one place at one time. I treasure them as beads on a rosary of pain. But we did have a good time, didn't we?
>
> Up Anjou for Merrie Engelande!

On one of our merry evenings, something reminded Elaine of a black handyman who had worked for her family in Austin, Texas. Every Monday, without fail, he was hours late reporting in; and every time, without fail, he gave the identical excuse, never varying a single word:

"Ah was drivin' down the street las' Saddy night, and thishere big, mean-lookin' Messican, he jump on mah runnin'-bode and shove this pint bottle in mah face wit' he lef' han', an' he shove this pistol in mah face wit' he rat han', an' he say, 'Boy, ef you don't want no trouble, *you drink thishere whiskey!* Well, natcherly, Ah din' want no trouble, so—"

We agreed that the "runnin'-bode" was a touch of genius. Ever afterwards, when John or I felt "poly," it was assumed that a Messican had jumped on our runnin'-bode the night before.

John's "Code of Steinbeckery," as he called it, had several provisions about drinking. I have forgotten most of the code, but here is part of it:

1.   *Cogito, ergo cogito sum.* [Considering John's pig-fixation, I think it's reasonable to call this pig-Latin.]
2.   Always keep yourself off balance.
3-a. When the martini calls, balls!
  b. When brandy beckons, no seconds.
4.   Never let a drunk catch your eye.
5.   If you wonder whether you are U, you aren't. ["U" refers to Nancy Mitford's tests for Upperclass and non-Upperclass people.]
6.   Steinbeckery always increases.

I recommend Number 4 to everybody; it has saved me grief time and again.

I don't know which was John's favorite of his books. I think it was the one about the Arthurian cycle. I know that he enjoyed writing it more than any other. Early in March 1959, he went to England and rented a cottage at Bruton, Somerset (King Arthur's home country), to steep himself in the land; and instantly he fell under its spell. He wrote me in April:

> Our main news is that we are very happy here. Elaine loves it more than any place she has ever been. I feel more at home here than I have ever felt. And I have rediscovered my mother language, and also that I can use it and use it well.

He returned to this a few days later:

> I have refound our beloved language, its strength and dignity, its subtlety and incredible communications, its great

simple words that can go out alone without the crutches of adjectives. I wonder whether the words I have written can convey to you my joy and peace and almost shrieking sense of fulfillment? If this should be my last book—this is what I would want it to be.

If you don't come to see us here, I'll never speak to you again. If you *do* come—we'll have to see.

I went. We *did* speak again, at such length and so vociferously that our arms became tired from "making a reservation."

But for all the enchantment that Somerset and its people laid upon John, and for all his infatuation with Sir Thomas Malory's lovely, sinewy prose, and for all his hope of getting the story of Arthur down "in hot words that hiss on paper," the book refused "to march. It doesn't march," he wrote me in September, "because it doesn't jell . . . My subject gets huger and more difficult all the time. . . . [It] is so much bigger than I am. It frightens me. . . . I hope I can bring something off. If I can't—I'll break my brushes and call it a day. . . . When my brushes break, my heart will go with them."

He called it a day at the end of that month and came home. But if he left a part of his heart in Somerset, he brought a part of Somerset and much of Malory and Tennyson home with him. His motorboat at Sag Harbor was christened *Lily Maid*, and her home port was given as Astolat. The little gazebo where John worked, well away from the house, was "Joyous Garde"; a sign on its door said gruffly, AROINT!

Our weekend at Sag Harbor, John and Elaine showed us around (beginning with the French flag). It was an easy place to admire, and we did so. John pretended to be insulted: "Did you think we lived like *pigs* out here?" There were his pigs again!

We saw the sapling that he had planted over Charley's grave, with the collar and leash hanging from a branch. Right then I remembered a line John had written about Charley: "Because of his long turning before lying down, we sometimes call him a whirl poodle—much to our shame." So I told him about our peacock, Prince Aly Khan, who roosts on the edge of the roof above our bedroom, with his tail hanging down like a strip of tapestry. We call *him*, I said, "the gutter-percher."

Most astonishingly, we saw—while having cocktails on the Steinbecks' terrace—a mallard hen waddle past our feet, quite as if we weren't there at all, leading a file of eight ducklings down for their afternoon swim. Elaine said simply, "She always does that."

I thought of the Joe Cook show, where an old man comes into Joe's office, opens a desk drawer, takes out his lunch, and eats it.

Joe asks, "Who are you?"

"I'm the old man who always comes in here to eat his lunch."

This was the last cocktail that John and I had together, my last toast to Ava Gardner. On December 21, 1968, the impatient, businesslike voice of a Western Union operator said, "I have a telegram for you. It comes from New York City and is signed 'E. Lane—' "

Ed Lane? Ernest Lane? Ellis Lane?

"—The message is, 'John died peacefully yesterday afternoon.' Shall I mail you a copy?"

"Please."

The cause of death was valvular heart disease. He was only sixty-six and was still bursting with "hot words that hiss on paper."

APPENDIX I

Here are some of the inscriptions that John put in the books he gave me:

The Wayward Bus:

> God damn it, Gridley,
> Didn't I tell you to open fire?
> Well, get to it!

Travels with Charley:

> With a long howl from
> John & Charley Steinbeck

The Pearl:

> For little Joe, from Black Beauty

The Pearl (Turkish edition):

> For Bey J. B. III
> Kemel Pasha is the pash for me.
> John Effendi Steinbeck

East of Eden:

> When I shall die think only this of me
> That in some corner of a foreign land
> There shall forever be
> A little corner of a foreign land.

Once There Was a War:

> From a seasoned coward.

Bombs Away:

> Cry havoc and unleash the XXth!
> John Steinbeck, habitual civilian

(assimilated and simulated rank,
vestryman, 2nd class).

Cannery Row:
Blue skies smiling at me
Nothing but blue skies from now-ee
Blue skies singing a song—
Nothing but blue skies from now ong.

John also gave me (at my request) a photograph of himself.
The letter that accompanied it says,

This is a rather noble picture. It does not show a number
of tendencies I'm glad it doesn't show—no hint of deformity,
histomy or digitosis. May its sweet malignity bless you all the
days of your life and particularly on this your 71st birthday.
Many happy returns! John Steinbeck, April 30, 1964.

—which was my birthday, all right, but my sixtieth, as the
scoundrel well knew.

APPENDIX II

Fun bubbled from Elaine Steinbeck as naturally as water from
a spring. She had been one of the Theatre Guild's stage managers,
so a good many of her stories concerned actors. My favorite was
about the Guild's tryouts for casting a new drama. One actor gave
such a brilliant reading that the director told him, "I don't need to
hear anyone else read for the part of Captain Dalton. The role is
yours. What is your name, please?"

"Thank you," the actor said. "My name is Ernest Armpit."

"I *beg* your pardon?"

"Ernest Armpit."

The director rubbed his eyes; he seemed to be battling some strong emotion. At last he managed to say, "Mr. Armpit, this is the *Theatre Guild*. We are an organization of distinction and propriety. You cannot ask us to print a program announcing that Captain Dalton is played by Ernest Armpit! This is simply out of the question. I'm sorry, but you'll have to take a stage name."

The actor drew himself up, lifted his chin, and glared down his nose. "Sir," he said, "that *is* my stage name!"

COREY FORD

1902-1969

Once a Punner—

Corey Ford, self-appointed three-star general

FALSTAFF: "I'll tell you strange things of this knave Ford."
—*Merry Wives of Windsor*

FRANK Sullivan invited me to Lüchow's restaurant one evening in the spring of 1936,* and it was then that I met Corey Ford, the other guest. John Aubrey's description of Andrew Marvell—"middling at stature, pretty strong sett [i.e., stocky], roundish faced, cherry-cheek't, hazell eie, browne haire"—fits Ford perfectly as far as it goes, but it doesn't go far enough. To do Ford justice, you would have to add that he not only was a handsome dog, but looked much younger than his age. He was thirty-four that year. I was surprised to learn it; he could have passed for twenty-four or even twenty. Once, when he opened his door to a reporter come for an interview, the first question put to him was,

---

* A postscript to Sullivan's invitation said, "If I am late, order me some *Kartoffelmitsauerbratenglockenspiel* with a side order of prepositions taking the accusative."

"Is your father at home?" And the first time he went to the Players as a member, the doorman stopped him. "You the new busboy? Use the service entrance!"

People underestimated Ford's age all his life. He said it was because he had "one of those innocuous baby faces," but "innocuous" implies something bland, like yogurt, whereas Ford's face flickered with mischief. His features were restless. Sullivan described his eyebrows as "constantly a-twitter." They were a pair of acrobats; when he was about to spring one of his outrageous puns, his right eyebrow shot up to the hairline and bent into a circumflex accent, while the outer end of the left drew down to form an *accent grave*. Laughing, he didn't chuckle, like Sullivan, or bellow, like Benchley; he *tittered*, "Hee-hee-hee!" His shoulders shook, his features squeezed together, and out came his absurd "Hee-hee-hee!"

That evening at Lüchow's we drank beer and laughed and patted time to the orchestra, and presently Sullivan and I found ourselves arguing whether the man who played the piano was properly a *pee*-an-ist or a pee-*an*-ist. Ford's eyebrows went into their act. "I don't know about *that*," he said, getting to his feet, "but I know I've got to pee-an-no two ways about it!" His shoulders shook. He hee-hee-hee'd all the way to the men's room.

New York had punsters aplenty in those days, master paronomasiasts like George Kaufman—"One man's Mede is another man's Persian"; F.P.A.—"Take care of the peonies, and the dahlias will take care of themselves"; Clifton Fadiman, Oliver Herford, Dorothy Parker, Marc Connelly. . . . Ford may not have ranked with these superstars, but on anybody's punning team, he would have been a good utility outfielder. I rest my case on his sobriquet for Sullivan, when they were sharing an apartment: "Ford's ugly roomer."

I have kept many of his letters and postcards. Thank heaven the letters were typed! His tiny, pinched handwriting was so illegible, the *Reader's Digest* once used a specimen to illustrate an article called "The Decay of Penmanship." Here is a fair sample of a Ford letter; it came from Hollywood, where he was working on a script for M-G-M; the date is late in 1939:

> . . . I have joined a company of Boy Scouts (or, as they are known out here, "Film Scouts") and I am studying for my First Class test, which consists of tying a scenario in knots, recognizing the common varieties of poison ivy, like Joan Crawford, and starting a fire by rubbing Hedy Lamarr and Joan Bennett together [Miss Bennett and Miss Lamarr were look-alikes, successive ex-wives of Producer Gene Markey, and openly jealous of each other].
>
> Most of all I enjoy our camping trips. There's nothing like sleeping under the stars, if you can pick your stars. Our first night in camp, the supervisors hazed the tenderfeet by turning them upside down, lowering their artistic principles, stripping them of their literary integrity, and showing great wads of thousand-dollar bills as far as they could reach.
>
> All night long there is scarcely a sound but the chirping of the critics, the occasional "Oomph!" of an Ann Sheridan prowling in the underbrush, and the soft flutter of bank notes drifting down. Otherwise it's so quiet, you can almost hear an option drop.
>
> P.S. You'll be glad to learn that Forest Lawn Mortuary out here is still advertising on its billboards, "Protect Your Loved Ones from Seepage!"

I repeat, this is a sample Ford letter, but it's not a typical Ford communication. That would be a postcard, mailed from Hong Kong, Salzburg, Dublin, Madrid, or Kodiak (he was such a globetrotter, I used to call him "Ford o' Kabul River"); and the message would be a one-liner, usually a pun, such as: From Honolulu,

"I'm staying at the best hotel, of course: the Hawaiian Handsome." From Tokyo, on a photo of two geisha girls, "Lillian and Dorothy." From Santiago, Chile: "I'm coming along pretty well with my Spanish. AQUI SE HABLA ESPAÑOL means 'I have a water spaniel,' and NO FUMAR stands for 'Things Are *Not* Fouled Up Beyond All Recognition.'" From Boston, on Halloween: "Boo!" From Yucatán, "Wonderful duck shooting! I took down a case of shells and I'm taking home a case of diarrhoea." From Bangkok, "Just ran into a fraternity Buddha of mine. I recognized him because he was wearing our old school Thai." And from New York City, "Why haven't you answered this? Love from Mom and Aunt Tina and the twins and Cousin Lemuel and Doc Twitchell and all the boys. Uncle Corey."

I sent him a clipping about a service station operator with the form-fitting name Wheeler Ballance, and surmised that he might have a partner named Philip Tanks. Ford wrote back, "—or Gus Gage, or Earl Pressure, or Manny Fold (he married Sonja Horne, remember?)."

Some of our gags-by-correspondence lasted us for years. Everybody knows those giveaway postcards that show a hotel dining room or the interior of a restaurant. They're all basically the same: every table is set, every glass is sparkling, every napkin is crisp— and there's not a soul in sight. Well, whenever one of these came to hand, we felt honor-bound to write on it, "Regular monthly meeting of the Corey Ford [or Joe Bryan] Fan Club. Attendance as usual."

Another running gag started when Finis Farr sent me a postcard from Mexico City, with the message, "There must be some mistake. I asked for a ticket to *Mackinaw* City." Round-the-World Ford took it up, and presently there came postcards from Frankfurt, Germany—"ticket to Frankfort, Kentucky"; Eire—"ticket to Erie, Pa."; Toledo, Spain—"Toledo, Ohio." One of my lasting disappointments is that when my ship touched at a port in New

Zealand during World War II, it was Wellington, not Auckland. I'd have enjoyed complaining to Ford that I'd thought I was taking the ferry to Oakland.*

Still another gag that gave us long service grew from a report that one of the movie studios had considered buying Rachel Carson's best-seller *The Sea Around Us*, but couldn't decide how to make it into a picture. Easy! we said. Begin by hiring James Whale to direct and Rex Beach to write the script. Additional dialogue by George Sand and Bennett Cerf. Financed by grants from Gulf and Shell. The cast should include Ethel Waters, Buster Crabbe, Norah Bayes, Dinah Shore, and Ethel Merman. "Of course," Corey wrote, "we must sign up Mae Marsh and George Raft, and isn't there a small part for Vivienne Segal?" Finis Farr suggested a chorus of WAVES, courtesy of the U. S. Navy, but when one of us added Laura Hope Crewes, the others took it as evidence of strain, so we dropped the gag for good—and not a moment too soon.

From Ford's college days to about 1937, he wrote chiefly for the New York newspapers and magazines: the old *Life*, *The New Yorker* (he created and named its symbol, "Eustace Tilley"), and *Vanity Fair* (to which, as "John Riddell" —"a clever rearrangement of the letters of my own name"—he contributed parodies of current books). During this period he also wrote sketches for three musical comedies, *Three's a Crowd*, *Flying Colors*, and *Hold Your Horses*. In the late 1930s, he turned his hand to short stories, many of them for *The Saturday Evening Post*. He was hitting his stride with stories when the outbreak of war knocked him off it. Almost his only subject for the next ten years was the war, especially the Army Air Force. During his final phase, from 1950 on, his writing was mostly biographical and historical, except for his regular monthly feature, "A Meeting of the Lower Forty," for

---

* Newspapers for April 3, 1985, carried an AP despatch about a dreamy young man in Los Angeles who thought he was taking a plane to Oakland. Instead, what was his surprise—

Field & Stream. I haven't mentioned his three hitches in Hollywood for RKO, because Corey himself seldom mentioned them.

The pun virus infected him early, and when, barely in his twenties, he began writing parodies, the combination soon became his trademark. His first parody, published in the Columbia University *Jester* while he was still an undergraduate (class of '23), was a burlesque of the popular juvenile series *The Rover Boys.* Dick Rover, the eldest brother; Tom, "the fun-loving Rover"; and Sam, the youngest, were embodiments of the Boy Scout oath. Despite the foul machinations of Professor Josiah Crabtree, abetted by the bully Dan Baxter and his toady Mumps, the stainless, peerless Rovers always triumphed in the last chapter, and therefore were an inspiration to every pure-minded, right-thinking American boy—a legion which—alas!—did *not* include Master C. Ford.

This became shockingly clear with the appearance of his parody, *The Rollo Boys.* Again, three brothers, Tom, Dick, and Harry Rollo, fall afoul of a villainous professor and his two confederates, Ben Barsted and the toady Measles. But here the parallel splits. The Rollo brothers could have been the Marx Brothers, for all the respect they paid to hallowed traditions—or to anything else. Tom was thrown into "an old abandoned quandary"; they ate their lunch "with Gusto, who barked and wagged his tail happily"; and "Three rousing cheers were given with a will. For the contents of that will, see the next volume in this series."

Although the book was hilarious, the clownish Rollos somehow failed to ingratiate themselves with the creator of the noble Rovers, Edward Stratemeyer. Indeed, Mr. Stratemeyer talked of bringing suit. It's a pity he didn't, if only because being sued would have been an interesting switch for Ford, who was himself one of the most indefatigable litigants in the annals of the Law. The trouble was, readers found his writings so amusing, so irresistibly quotable, that they treated them like an open box of candy, and helped themselves—not only to his puns, but to his short, humorous essays, especially to one called "How to Guess Your Age." They stole it and reprinted it left and right, often under their own names, rarely with credit, and never with payment. Ford sued for plagiarism, promptly and profitably. At one time, he said, he "had more suits than Adolph Menjou," the Hollywood dandy. The hapless (and bitterly indignant) defendants included his own hotel, Arthur Godfrey, the *Journal of the American Medical Association*, seven insurance companies, and *Life* magazine. A large chain store ran "How to Guess Your Age" with "a modest admission of authorship by the president, together with his photograph." Ford won every suit, with damages; he said, "I find this a much easier way to make a living than by writing."

Another consistently productive hook on his trotline was his essay about "skid-talk," as he called it—a kind of rhetoric that didn't *quite* make sense. Its innocent inventor was "Bunny" McLeod, the wife of his friend Norman McLeod, the movie director. Bunny would say, "That's the best cookie I ever put in my whole mouth!", and "It was so dark you couldn't see your face in front of you," and "It's a wonderful picture. Don't miss it if you can!" Ford explained, "Bunny talked in blurred double exposures, in which one thought was printed on top of another." He hung on her words, and when he had collected enough specimens of skid-talk, he wrote an essay around them. The plagiarists helped themselves to skid-talk too. Rudy Vallee liked to use it on his TV shows, but hurriedly bought permissions, just as Ford's lawyers were about to pounce. Ford wrote me, "—but Bunny's best was not up to this one of Lyndon Johnson's: 'For the first time in history, profits are higher than ever before.' I've been trying to untangle that one ever since I read it."

The McLeods were two of the three—and *only* three—people in Hollywood I ever heard Corey speak of. The third was W. C. Fields. If I dared set down some of Ford's stories about Fields, a bolt of lightning would fuse the keys of my typewriter. But there are a couple—the second quite harmless—that I'd like to preserve.

Ford said he went to Fields's house at Toluca Lake, near Hollywood, and found the great man charging around the lawn in a rage, brandishing a golf club at the ducks and geese that had come ashore to graze. "Shit *green!*" he was yelling. "Shit green, or get off me grass!"

The other story has no real point. I repeat it only because it shows Fields's rhetoric at its Elizabethan best. The scene was Chasen's restaurant. Sabu the Elephant Boy was dining at a nearby table, Ford saw. Fields saw him too, and his tindery suspicions were instantly kindled. "Methinks—" he croaked, "methinks the little mahout has a mind to bestride me pro-bos-kis! Should he dare accost me—" Providentially for the little mahout, he forbore.

All his life Fields hated Christmas, and all his life he feared death, which he referred to as "the Fellow in the Bright Nightgown." It is a pathetic irony that when the Fellow came for him, it was on a Christmas Day.

A special friend of Corey's was John Falter, the illustrator and artist, who was best-known probably for his many *Saturday Evening Post* covers. What ignited their friendship is a drawing that John had presented to their club, the Players. It showed a city street on a winter's day; the gutters are piled with snow; icicles hang from the eaves; and a man carrying a statuette of a monkey is entering a shop with the sign WELDING.

John's farm, Crow Hill, was only a few miles from ours, Fiddler's Green. Corey came down there often, so we had some merry weekends. John was a virtuoso on the tape recorder; the tricks he could make one do would be the envy of a Hollywood sound-effects man. For instance, there was "The Flying Lesson," made from a script that he and Ford had written:

The instructor (Falter) buckles (sound of metal clashing on metal) the novice (Ford) into the plane and tells him, "I'm going to crank her up now. When she catches, pull this handle back, and I'll jump in beside you. Got it?" Sound of engine starting and racketing to full power. Falter's voice: "No, you idiot, you've pulled the *stick* back!" The engine roars louder and louder. Ford's voice: "How do I stop this damn thing? Like this——?" Sound of plane bumping along. Ford's voice, becoming fainter and further away: "Help! Help!" Falter's voice, frantic: "My God, he's in the air!" Sound of plane receding, then approaching at high speed and passing close by. Ford's voice: "Get me out of here!" Voice swells and fades, swells and fades, as the plane circles. Falter, moaning: "He'll kill himself! He'll never learn to fly!"; mumbles, "I wish I'd never laid eyes on that Charlie Lindbergh kid. . . ."

It was wonderfully convincing. John did the whole business by twirling an eggbeater against a sheet of cardboard, while Corey brought the mike close or drew it back.

Another Ford-Falter production was *The History of the World.* When I came in, the boys were recording the War Between the States, as follows:

Falter's voice: "Zzzzeee-*eeeee*-EEEEE! BOOM!"

Ford's voice (deep-South accent): "They have fah'd on Fote Sumteh! * Hit means—WAH!"

Brief intermission.

Ford's voice (throbbing with excitement): "And now— And now—*Pickett's charge!*"

Falter's voice (deferential): "Will that be all, General Pickett?"

Ford's voice: "Yeah, thanks, waiter. Just put it on my tab, will you?"

Brief intermission.

Falter's voice: "On to World War One!"

---

* Ford and his friend and coauthor Alastair MacBain once owned a farm in Ivanhoe, N.C. Their manager's name was—I take my oath!—Fort Sumter Falls.

Not long after "they" fah'd on Fote Sumteh, the Japanese fah'd on Pearl Harbor. Falter and I were commissioned in the Naval Reserve, and Corey volunteered for the Army Air Force Reserve. For some reason, his commission was slow to come through. He was still in New York, tugging at the leash, at the time of the Doolittle Raid (April 1942), but that didn't stop him from writing me, "I'd always heard that Tokyo is beautiful from the air, but the flak was so thick I couldn't see much." He kept pushing official doorbells and pulling official wires, but nothing happened. Perhaps it was his age; he was forty that year. The passing months disheartened him. As late as August he was grumbling, "My affiliation with the AAF is still so vague that I don't know whether to salute myself or not. I might ask Brooks Brothers to run me up some kind of reversible uniform, lined with civilian clothes." I suggested that, as a last, desperate resort, he go to England and apply to the C. Ford Highlanders, but his AAF commission came through at last, and Major Ford was off and running. Well, if not running, at least trotting—globe-trotting—complete with a beat-up "fifty-mission" cap and a ready-made vocabulary of fly-boy slang: *raunchy*, *yay big*, *roger wilco*, and the rest.

Thus began Major Ford's romance with the Air Force, a romance that lasted the rest of his life. In Ford's opinion, any member of the Air Force, even a grease monkey, was automatically a great fellow; any pilot was one of the greatest fellows who ever lived; and as for the Chief of Staff, General H. H. Arnold, he sat at the right hand of God. When Ford spoke of "Hap" Arnold, it was always with hushed, solemn reverence, as "the Boss." He wrote a book about the Boss; and another of his books, *The Last Time I Saw Them*, written in collaboration with MacBain, is dedicated to the Boss's widow. *The Last Time* is a collection of short, true stories—vivid and dramatic, authentic and deeply moving— about men on Air Force bases around the world: Greenland, India, England, Alaska, China, the Marianas, Burma, the Philippines. I don't know how many copies Corey and Mac sold, but I know that they gave all their royalties to the Air Force's Aid Society.

On one of their flights, from Gander to Prestwick, an engine caught fire when they were at "Jones's Corner," exactly halfway across. The situation was dicey for a while; even so, Ford should have known better than to describe it to Sullivan in a letter. The only sympathy he drew was, "What better place for an engine to catch fire? You have the whole damn Atlantic to put it out with!" I too once made the mistake of inviting Sullivan's sympathy. I wrote him that *The Saturday Evening Post* had commissioned me to do an article about the Battle of Midway, and it had run to an unexpected and incompressible 8,000 words. Sullivan retorted, "*Why* should it take you 8,000 words? That's the trouble with you modern writers: you over-write. Did you ever hear of Julius Caesar, who described a battle in three words, each beginning with V? Give up?"

Ford stayed in the Air Force for some years after the war, and I stayed in the Naval Reserve. We still enjoyed the interservice kidding when we met—"Hi, there, Ace!"; "Howdy, Bull!"—so when Admiral Durgin organized a symposium for former Air Combat Intelligence Officers (I'd been one) and promised us an overnight cruise on the super-carrier *Franklin D. Roosevelt*, it was natural for me to invite Ford along. I told him, "You owe it to yourself to see why you're not pulling a ricksha right now." Ford accepted and asked if he could bring along a chum of his, a kid colonel named Walker Mahurin, a fighter pilot. "Bud" Mahurin had the uncommon distinction of having been shot down in three different countries—and would make it four in the Korean War. I should add that between crashes, he himself managed to shoot down some dozen enemy planes and win a rainbow of ribbons.

Well, orders were cut, and the three of us flew to Norfolk and reported aboard the *FDR*. The date was January 25, 1950. I give it because exactly a week before, something had happened that was painfully fresh in every Navy mind: one of our proudest ships, the USS *Missouri*, had blundered aground. Worse, it was only a few cable lengths from where the *FDR* was now moored. Ford had said nothing about it, but I knew that the black-hearted devil was only waiting for the right moment. It came when I took him and Mahurin out on the flight deck and began explaining how the planes were launched and landed.

"All very interesting," Ford interrupted, "this talk about poop decks and t'gallant-bos'ns, but the fact is, I'm too worried to pay close attention. I *have* to be back in Washington day after to-morrow!"

"Me too," Mahurin said. "It's an absolute *must* for me."

I asked what all this alarm was about. Ford explained, "I simply don't dare take a chance. That's why Bud and I thought we'd better play it safe, and—no offense, you understand—"

Mahurin pulled a small paper bag from his pocket and took out a weighted string, tagged every three feet with "½ fathom . . . 1 fathom . . . 1½ fathoms . . ." and so on, up to five fathoms. It was called a "Depthometer," or something like that. I'd seen them on sale for fifty cents at fishing-tackle stores.

Ford gestured toward the *FDR*'s tremendous bridge, high above us: "If you could send this upstairs to the motorman or driver or whatever the salty term is, I'd feel a lot easier in my mind."

"So would I," Mahurin said. "Like me to explain to him how it operates? Shouldn't take more than a minute—two or three, if he's not used to working with arithmetic."

Ford's shoulders were shaking, and he was tittering "Hee-hee-hee," insufferably pleased with himself. I was hurt the more deeply because I had in *my* pocket two packets of Mothersill's Seasick Remedy, all ready for a public presentation the moment the *FDR* was under way. Now it seemed best to forget the whole thing.

A clean score like this should have contented Ford and Mahurin; but no, they had to crowd their luck. Not long after we got back I received a letter on the stationery of the Chief of Naval Operations. The key paragraph read:

I was particularly delighted with those two young Air Force colonels whom you brought along. Never in my long Navy career have I met two such brilliant people, and it is my earnest desire that they be included in our next symposium. You are to be congratulated on your choice of friends.

(signed) J. E. Durgan
Admiral, U.S. Navy

The text was palpably fraudulent, of course, and the clincher was the signature, which was suspect on three counts: rank, initials, spelling. So *I* got a sheet of CNO's stationery and composed the following:

Colonel Mahurin:

My friend Commander Bryan has shown me a letter purportedly signed by me, but which he identifies as actually having originated with you. Bryan thought I would be amused, but I find nothing amusing in the forgery of a flag officer's signature by a junior officer in a sister service. Because this juvenile prank, however ill-advised, was not maliciously intended (Bryan assures me), I will request no disciplinary action, beyond insisting that a letter of reprimand be issued to you and made a part of your official file.

(signed) Calvin T. Durgin,
Vice Admiral, USN.

cc: Chief of Staff, USAF
    Provost Marshal, USAF

As soon as my letter was on its way, I told our switchboard girl that if Colonel Ford or Colonel Mahurin rang, I was out. Ford had gone off on another trip, but Mahurin rang all right—and rang, and rang, and rang some more. He had once jeered that my Navy blouse looked as if I were "carrying a sackful of hammers," so I hardened my heart and let him sweat for a full week before "the Chief of Staff of the Air Force" phoned him and demoted him to Specialist Two and invited him to lunch. Mahurin came, but he just picked at his food.

Offsetting Ford's worship of the Air Force, something else that he brought back from the war was an abiding contempt for most of the press correspondents he had met, especially those of the "Last Man Out Of—" and "First Man Into—" school. I don't know why he despised them so; I expect it was because many of them wrote about themselves instead of about the men who were doing the work. The only *personal* dislike I ever heard him express was for a certain columnist who used to steal his best lines with never a word of thanks or credit. Ford rarely used obscenity or blasphemy or even profanity, but this thief, habitual and unabashed, moved him to all three; I'm afraid I'll have to say that Ford excoreyated him. He also had a number of impersonal dislikes, though none quite so violent. He couldn't abide perfume; any girl who dabbed him with it, even as a joke, instantly lost a friend. (He reminded me of O. O. McIntyre, who used to go white with rage if anyone tried to pick a scrap of lint from his lapel.) He also hated snow, despite his years of residence in New Hampshire; "God's dandruff," he called it, and "albino catshit." He said that New Hampshire was "a winter wonderland, the wonder being why I stay here."

His love-hate affair with New Hampshire had started back in the 1920s, when something took him to a pretty little village named Freedom, just on the New Hampshire side of the Maine border. Corey was smitten at once, partly because Freedom was where he met the delightful Parker Merrow. It was Parker, soon to be his intimate friend, who introduced him to the peculiar local ritual—local, I'm told, to east-central New Hampshire and west-central Maine, adjoining—whereby someone asks you, "D'you think they'll hev it?" and you must respond, "Waal, they've sold all the tickets!" or "The ice cream's come!" or "The rope's up!" or something equally enigmatic. It was also Parker who designed Corey's stationery:

COREY FORD
Freedom, N.H.

A Ford writ story   *Get your writings*
is a good writ story   *off of Ford*
All Kinds of Writing Done Quick and Neat
Rabbit Hounds—Bird Dogs—Guns—Cameras—Fishing Tackle
ECT, BOT, SOLD & SWAPPED

So Corey bot a few acres at Freedom and built a house of native granite. Because its luxuries included floors of rock-maple planks, some of them two feet wide, it ended up costing Squire Ford considerably more than he had allowed for—hence the name he gave it: "Stonybroke." I told him he ought to have carved about the main fireplace "Acts 22:28," which reads, "With a great sum obtained I this Freedom."

The front porch overlooked a quiet little lake that "came right up to the shore," as a lady visitor noticed. Another visitor—at least, he threatened to become one—was the intimidating Alexander Woollcott, whose private island in Lake Bomoseen, Vermont, was within disquietingly easy driving distance. Corey told me, "When he announced that he was descending on Freedom, I swallowed and stammered, 'Gee, that'll be swell, Aleck!' Woollcott gave me a fierce glare: 'That's for *me* to decide!' he said."

Corey enjoyed showing his friends around Stonybroke. He took care that they didn't miss the birdbath with its towel rack and the two tiny towels embroidered HIS and HERS, and he pointed out the patch of lawn reserved for a flower garden: "Nothing fancy, you understand, merely standard stuff: some contusias—those big purple and green ones. Laceratias. Giant double hernias. Abrasias —you know abrasias? Pink stripes on white."

This was my chance to suggest that he also plant some coreyopsis, but I didn't think of it until too late.

His English setter, Cider, was following us around. Corey stopped to tell a story, and Cider sat down and yawned. "He's heard it before," the master explained.

My own dog in those days was a Scottie, John Keats, so named because, being impossible to housebreak, he was an all-too-frequent reminder of Keats's epitaph: "—one whose name was writ in water." The first time Corey saw Johnny, he asked, "What kind of terrier is that, a Skye?"

I said, "No, a Scottie. Skyes are gray."

"Sign of rain," Corey said, with his eyebrows doing their usual gymnastics. "Hee-hee-hee!"

I have forgotten the story he stopped to tell me that afternoon, but I'm confident it was nothing more than a quick gag. He was never a professional raconteur, like Marc Connelly, who would go from one amusing "act" into another as long as he had an audience. Ford never cared for stage center. In fact, I can't remember but one of his jokes—the one about the Boston swinger who took his girl to a remote New Hampshire inn for the weekend. They registered as "Mr. & Mrs.," but as they started up to their room, something aroused the proprietor's suspicions, and he called after them, "Hey, mister! You got a license?"

The man called back, "Sure thing!" He took out his hunting license and tossed it on the counter and went upstairs again. A few minutes later, there was a frantic knocking at their door. It was the proprietor, warning, "Ef ye hain't done it, don't do it! 'Tain't fer it!"

In 1952, after some twenty years at Freedom, Ford sold Stonybroke (his ad in *The New Yorker* emphasized that it was bomb-proof) and moved across the state to Hanover, to a house not far off the Dartmouth campus, "where I'll be the only person in town who does *not* ski." (He never learned; nor could he drive a car.) His street address there was 1 North Balch. Parker Merrow designed the new stationery too:

Carey Ferd
1 N. Bilch
Handover, N.H.

After Corey had been working for weeks on a biography of the great Norwegian pilot Bernt Balchen, he wrote me that he had become so saturated with his subject, he was thinking of changing his name and address to

Corey Fjord,
1 N. Balchen,
Hanoversholm, New Norway.

A friend of mine who had an apartment in Rome offered it to me for the winter of 1954–55. When I told Frank Sullivan that I had accepted, he warned me, "Be careful when strolling in the Campagna! They tell me that Italian men are great pinchers." I found a tenant for my small house in Washington and reached Rome in time to meet Ford and take him sightseeing. Certain cities have characteristic smells; Lisbon's is coffee; Brussels's is hot cooking oil; Raleigh's is tobacco; and Helsinki's, they say, is wood sap. All are pleasant, or at least unobjectionable. But the Romaroma, reeking, pungent, and pervasive, is stale urine. When I told Ford I was going to show him the former royal palace, the Quirinal, he asked almost automatically, "Where the queers hang out?" but when we got there, he sniffed and remarked, "The Quirinal? Misprint!"

The Colosseum inspired him to the first of the series of postcards he now began sending to Sullivan, MacBain, Falter, and other friends. His bulletin read:

Half-time score:

LIONS 7
CHRISTIANS 0

St. Peter's fascinated him, particularly when he learned that its attractions include a modest bar where you can buy a Scotch and soda. His special joy was the balustrade, with its heroic statues of Christ and the Twelve Apostles. Ford could hardly wait to get a postcard view. "This shows the College of Cardinals varsity," he wrote Sullivan, "all set for their big game, the Rosary Bowl. Left, the Holy Water-boy. Right, the Holy Coach, whose motto is, 'When in doubt, pont!'" (Corey's own motto might have been "When in doubt, pun!") He followed this up with a card showing the Pope, his arms outstretched in blessing. "One team cheer for the Red Hats!" Ford's message ran. "Hip—! Hip—!" The cards were retorts-in-kind to the note that Sullivan had slipped under his bedroom door in their apartment, early one Easter morning:

Get up, lazy bones!
I've been up for hours.
J.C.

After Corey left Rome, I didn't see him again for perhaps another year; he was either traveling or confined to a hospital because of an accident or an operation. In fact, he was in and out of hospitals so often that I had a rubber stamp made:

Dear Corey:
Sorry to hear you're back in again. I hope the operation/ doctor's bill/night nurse hasn't left you weak. Get well soon!

Hospitals usually failed to depress him; when he had an appendectomy in 1940, he sent out printed announcements with a small card—"*Appendix Vermiformis Ford,* weighing 1½ ounces"—attached by a blue ribbon. He was still jocular in 1946, when he seems to have had another operation (I don't remember what it was for), because he wrote me that

> my scar will cause a ripple of sympathy whenever I stroll on the beach. I am planning to tell everyone that it was received during a banzai raid on Iwo Jima: these seven Nips came rushing at me, waving samurai swords, and I bought the first Nip's because his price was a little lower.

But in February 1956, the car in which he was riding through Hollywood with Dave Chasen had a crash, and both of them were taken to the hospital. The first I knew about it was when Ford wrote me, "The doctor put my kneecap on backwards, and now I've got to learn to walk in the opposite direction." The flippancy suggested that his injuries were not too serious, so I wired him

> TERRIBLY DISTRESSED TO HEAR ABOUT DEAR DAVE STOP PLEASE SEE IF THERE IS ANYTHING HE WANTS—FLOWERS, WINE, SPECIAL FOOD, EXTRA NURSES—AND NOTIFY ME AT ONCE STOP MONEY NO OBJECT STOP I WON'T REST EASY UNTIL I KNOW THAT DAVE IS COMFORTABLE.

Ford's injuries *were* serious, it turned out, and his response was a huffy "I am not amused." God knows there was little for him to be amused about! A week later he was "still pretty shell-shocked and feeble," and even by mid-April, "still weak and rung out like a wild bell . . . I'm afraid that you and Troy will have to arrange to be born a little later this year. [signed] Curry Fork."

He was referring to our happy discovery, some years earlier, that Hugh Troy's birthday was April 28, Corey's was April 29, and mine April 30. Ever since, we had celebrated together when it was possible, until our threefold cake eventually began to look like a bonfire. My mother came to one of these parties, and I had the pleasure of introducing Corey to her as "one of my oldest friends." Corey beamed until I added, "Most of my friends are a good deal younger." The 1955 party, when I was still in Rome, was notable for Hugh's present to Corey: a handpainted fish, thirty-four feet long. Since Corey's house in Hanover had an attached gymnasium eighty feet long, "I am probably the only man Troy knows," he wrote, "who has a place to hang such a trophy."

By the late summer of 1956, he had completely recovered from the accident and was back at work. He was slow getting started:

> I'm staying right here [at Hanover] this summer, writing a novel. Inasmuch as I've been working for 3 weeks and haven't yet written the first line, it looks like a long summer. I may give it a do-it-yourself title, like *101 Things A Boy Can Do With Human Skin.*

He gradually gathered his old momentum, and soon he was again turning out material as if he had a brilliant djinn in his cellar, working to ransom himself from captivity. A letter dated April 12, 1861 (*sic,* because it was the centennial of Fort Sumter) shows his pace:

> I've just finished a book and nine articles in two months, and am slightly bushed, so just to rest up I'm starting another book.

Even so, I was surprised and impressed when I read in his obituary that his output for his forty years of quill-driving amounted to the huge total of twenty books and more than five hundred short stories and magazine articles, not to mention his work for Hollywood and Broadway. *The New York Times* did not exaggerate when it called him "a prodigious writer."

In September 1961, he was back in the Hanover hospital, to have a tumor removed. His report began:

Dear Joe; (I don't have a full : anymore, after the operation)—

There were no ill effects, he said,

except for weakness and an abdomen which looks like the lacing on a rugby ball, and a slight rearrangement of my lower intestinal system which has eliminated several miles of old winding roads (very scenic, but dangerous in wet weather) and the substitution of a fine new six-lane superhighway which makes it possible to go from one end of me to the other without hitting a single traffic light.

In early May 1964, he hoped that I had survived our birthday better than he had: "MacBain, who is always thoughtful, gave me a wonderful present: a hangover which he made with his own two hands out of a bottle of Scotch, and which fitted me just fine." He ended with a Bunnyism: "We missed you almost as much as if you'd been there." Again on our birthday two years later, he complained that his work was being slowed by a series of headaches— "probably a sign of pregnancy." And two years after that, on his sixty-sixth birthday, "I'm now sixteen, give or take half a century." This was the last letter I had from him. On July 27, 1969, three months after his next birthday, he died from a stroke in the Dartmouth College Hospital.

Some people seem to have been born full grown just before you met them. Apparently they have no past and no family; at least, neither is ever referred to. Corey was one of these. Where he was born and where he went to school, I have no idea. I never heard him mention a boyhood chum or a college classmate, or even his father or mother; and the fact that he left his estate to

Dartmouth suggests that he had no near relatives. Although he and I were friends for more than thirty years, I never learned anything about him that needed be stamped even RESTRICTED. He did not offer confidences (nor did he invite them). He was not at all secretive, but large areas of his life were marked NO TRESPASSING. I wouldn't take a bet today against his having been a gypsy's changeling, an elbow fetishist, the compiler of a Basque dictionary, a demonolator, an unfrocked child evangelist, or even the Lost Dauphin. His letters occasionally said something about the work in progress—"I am sitting here contemplating my novel, with 50 goddam 000 words to do in three months"—but that's as intimate and confessional as he ever got. At the end of his life, I knew very little more about him than I had known at the end of that first night at Lüchow's, in the spring of 1936. After Corey's death, Frank Sullivan, who had been his closest friend, wrote me, "As well as I knew him over a long period. I'm not sure I knew him completely." Finis Farr felt the same way: "What lay behind Corey's cut-steel exterior, I simply don't know." He added, "I think of him as the best organized person I ever met. Absolutely competent. Alert and very fast on the pick up. Whatever anyone said, he got the point instantly."

I don't think Corey had any vanities—well, perhaps one: before he'd hold still for a snapshot, he'd always contrive to stick a pipe in his mouth, presumably to make himself look out-of-doorsy. He may have borne a physical resemblance to Andrew Marvell, but he was also like Charles Lamb, in that both remained bachelors and both were addicted to pipes and puns. Lamb once remarked that he wished to draw his last breath through a pipe and exhale it in a pun. Corey could have endorsed that.

It is a custom of the Players to notify the death of a member by writing his name on a black-bordered card and posting it on the bulletin board. When Oliver Herford saw one of these cards, he would read it and murmur sadly, "Always the wrong man . . ." I

like to think that when the card with Corey's name went up, someone remembered the pleasure he had given so many, and penciled
on it Herford's complaint.

$\mathcal{A}PPENDIX\ I$

Ford and I went to *Guys and Dolls* together. When the final
curtain fell and we started up the aisle, he moved ahead of me,
and I heard him muttering as he squirmed through the crowd,
"Let me out of here! I've just shot Lincoln. Let me out!"

I thought of that evening soon after Lincoln Center opened;
and I wired him, "Stay away from Lincoln Center, Ford! Rough
justice may be in the cards."

$\mathcal{A}PPENDIX\ II$

Among the long-running gags that Corey and I enjoyed, one
was based on a magazine cover that showed a country boy selling
a string of fish to a portly banker type. The theme is venerable, of
course, it has been used again and again in illustrations, and in
advertisements, but let me run through the details:

The two characters, their costumes, and their props are immutable, hallowed by tradition. The boy is about ten years old, freckled, with a tuft of red hair sticking through a hole in his tattered straw hat. He wears bib overalls, one-gallus; a slingshot hangs from his hip pocket; and he is barefoot, with a rag bandage around a big toe. One hand holds a string of "speckled beauties"; the other, a fishing pole—not a "rod"—fresh cut and peeled. On the ground is a tomato can, with a worm crawling over the side.

The banker type wears a derby, a frock coat (white piping on the vest), striped trousers, spats. A black ribbon moors his pince-nez. His fishing tackle is obviously new and expensive; quite as obvious, it has availed him nothing, as he is taking a bank note from a fat wallet, and at the same time is signaling the smirking lad to silence. If there is any title, it is something like "A Secret Deal in High Finance."

Ford and I appointed ourselves Keepers of the Flame, and whenever we saw a version of "our" picture (usually on a calendar), we checked it for authenticity: the bandage is on a *big toe?* the bait-can label shows a *tomato?* the banker's glasses are a *pince-nez?*—and if any detail varied or was lacking or otherwise failed to meet our rigid standards, off went a sharp letter to the artist, pointing out his errors and warning him to mend his ways.

APPENDIX III

Our painter friend John Falter, the sound-effects virtuoso on the eggbeater, told me a story that ought to be preserved despite its unsatisfactory open end. One of his tours of duty with the Navy was in its recruiting office at White Plains, New York, where he

was put to painting "Join Up NOW!" portraits of ruddy-cheeked
bluejackets. The account from here on comes direct from a letter
of John's:

> When the A-bomb fell, I knew I'd be discharged before
> long, so when I found a photograph of Admiral King sitting
> in some sort of ship's chair, I painted his portrait, full length,
> to amuse the art dept.

(John was an extremely fast worker; he told me that he could
turn out one of his *Saturday Evening Post* covers, which were always packed with detail, in two days or less.)

> From his cap to his knees, it was a good, strong likeness,
> if I say so myself. But from the knees down— Well, I rolled
> up his pants and put his feet in a basin of hot water, with an
> open box of Epsom salts near by. When I'd finished, I hung a
> cloth over the canvas to protect it while it was drying (and
> to hide it until I was safely out of uniform), and stored it in
> a locker.
>
> Not long after V-J Day, the office notified me to pick up
> my art gear and go on home. I looked in the locker for Ad-
> miral King. He was gone! The chief said, "Yep, your picture
> went to the Navy Archives in Washington, with our other
> originals."
>
> That's what it was, all right: an original. I wish I knew
> whatever became of it.

I wish I did too. Most of all, I wish that the ferocious Admiral
King had seen it—though not before John had become a civilian
again.

John also told me that just after the war, he and Ford had
done a book together, *The Horse of Another Color*—about a
small horse that was a Negro.

"Henry Holt published it," John said, "and sold thirteen copies. Instead of our book's being the laughingstock of the publishing business, *we* were. But I still treasure a line of Ford's about a stuffy mare: 'She was all dressed up like a plush Mrs. Astor.'"

APPENDIX IV

Ford's inscription in my copy of *The Gazelle's Ears*:

Slowly the sun sank behind Tarnation Ridge, and the distant hills were the color of burnished metal—of gold! Across the sagebrush the shadows lengthened, and into the twilight rode the man named Larrabee.

"I must be gittin' on," he sighed. "I'm the quaint character who wanders in an' out of these Western yarns, an' I reckon I'm needed in the next chapter."

And in my copy of *Never Say Diet*:

This rare presentation copy, first edition, to be left beside the telephone for making notes.

(signed) Hilaire Belloc, as told to Corey Ford.

SIDNEY JOSEPH PERELMAN

1904-1979

A Bird's-eye View of Sidney

S. J. Perelman stalks big game

I'VE been a Perelmaniac for sixty years, since back when I was heeling* the *Princeton Tiger* and clipping "exchanges" from other college humorous magazines, including the Dartmouth *Brown Jug.* I soon noticed that most of the *Jug*'s material seemed to have been written or illustrated by one S. J. Perelman. Even then his style of drawing was as individual as, say, that of Otho Cushing (who did those Greek gods and goddesses in the old *Life*) or of T. S. Sullivant (who did those wonderful ramshackle animals there). Perelman's prose style was no less unique. He himself has described it as "haut Melangesic—a mixture of all the sludge I read as a child, all the clichés, liberal doses of Yiddish, criminal slang, and some of what I was taught in a Providence, Rhode Island, school by impatient teachers." The result was a vocabulary as rich as a mince pie, as colorful as a pousse-café and as jeweled as a Fabergé Easter egg. In the very first paragraph of

* "Heeling" is the arcane Ivy League term meaning to compete for a position.

one of his "brocades" or "*feuilletons*," as he called them, you find yourself tripping over exotica like this:

> As recently as 1918, it was possible for a housewife . . . to march into a store with a five-cent piece, purchase a firkin of cocoa butter, a good secondhand copy of Bowditch, a hundredweight of quahogs, a shagreen spectacle case and sufficient nainsook for a corset cover and emerge with enough left over to buy a balcony admission to *The Masqueraders* with Guy Bates Post, and a box of maxixe cherries.

(Perelman published many lines—such as these—that might puzzle your schoolgirl daughter, but none that might embarrass you to explain to her.)

I ask indulgence here while I make a short, necessary detour:

As do most young editor-writers, I worked on half a dozen publications before I settled down: the Richmond *News Leader*, the *East African Standard*, the Chicago *Journal*, *Fortune*, *Time*, *The New Yorker*, *Town and Country*, and finally *The Saturday Evening Post* (as associate editor). *Town and Country* was sorely understaffed in those days, the early 1930s; I, as managing editor, was charged with recruiting an assistant, but I had no idea where to find one. I had known E. B. White slightly at *The New Yorker* and I greatly admired him, so I turned to him for help. He recommended a fellow alumnus of Cornell, Gustave S. Lobrano.

I asked, "What editorial experience has he had?"

"None, so far as I know."

"What's he doing now?"

"He's with a travel agency up in Albany."

It seemed a spur-track preparation for work on a slick magazine—on *any* magazine—but my confidence in Andy White's* judgment told me to take a chance. Lord, how it paid off!

---

* Andrew White was Cornell's first president; since then any undergraduate named White has automatically been nicknamed "Andy."

Gus Lobrano proved to be mild, soft-eyed, and soft-voiced, with a gourmet's taste in prose and a lively, gentle wit. Among Andy White's collected letters (which were edited by Gus's daughter) is one describing a trip that he and Gus took to Boston. As they strolled through Louisburg Square, Andy explained that this was Boston's social navel, "the hub of the Hub," the radiant heart of the lotus. Gus asked reverently, "Be all right if I smoke?"

He and Virginia Faulkner, the novelist, also newly hired, shared a cramped cubby in *Town and Country*'s offices. Miss Faulkner endeared herself to us at once by posting a sign outside its one door:

PLEASE USE

OTHER DOOR

The three of us had a happy time together, and the magazine flourished. But in 1937 I was invited to join the *Post*, and I accepted. Virginia resigned presently to write *A House Is Not a Home*, her best-selling "auto"-biography of Polly Adler, the famous New York madam; and Andy White again showed his judgment by bringing Gus over to *The New Yorker*. It was his spiritual home, as he soon proved by being promoted to its "jesus," the staff's traditional name for their managing editor. The stone that I had nearly rejected had become the head of the corner.

The *Post*'s offices were in Philadelphia, but my transfer there didn't mean that I no longer saw Gus. My job took me back to New York two days a week, to seine publishers and literary agents for material, so Gus and I met for lunch from time to time. To one of these lunches—at the Algonquin, *New Yorker* editors' favorite restaurant—he brought Sid Perelman. End of detour.

I hadn't known until then that the Perelmans had a farm in Pennsylvania, in Bucks County. (It became the scene of Sid's sourly hilarious *Acres and Pains*.) We ourselves moved to Bucks a few years later, just before the war, to Doylestown, not far from the Perelmans' town, Erwinna; and when I got home again, in 1945, Sid and Laura were among the first people we saw. (Every time I heard someone mention Erwinna, I had to bite my tongue to keep from adding "—and new champeen!" So much for *my* wit.)

Sid was in New York or Hollywood during much of the early postwar period, but when he and Laura were back in residence, we managed to dine together every few weeks. Just before one of our dinners, someone happened to tell me that a local grocery stocked preparations for tinting milk shakes, sherbets, the icing on cakes, and so on. They came in a variety of colors, had no odor or taste, and were government-certified to be harmless. I toyed with the idea of serving the Perelmans crimson biscuits, but plumped for a packet of the purple; and that evening I dropped a pinch into the first shaker of martinis.

Sid blanched when he saw his glass. "What witches' broth is *that?*"

I said, "It won't hurt you, honor bright. Try it!"

He took a cautious sip, then another. "Not bad! Not bad at all! What do you call it, and how do you make it?"

I said, "It's called the Elinor Glyn. I promised Elinor I wouldn't give away the secret formula."

Bucks County abounded in antique shops, especially around New Hope. In one of them I found an old stovepipe hat. It happened to fit me, so I laid out a quarter and hung it on the hat rack in our front hall. A soon as Sid saw it, his eyes lit up. He looked at the hat, then at me. "Are you a quick study, cobber?" he asked anxiously. "No-o-o-o, I expect not. Anyhow, it's too big a role for a kid like you. . . . But what am I going to do? Henry Irving has called in sick—probably shacked up with Mrs. Siddons, if the truth be told—so there's no help for it. The show must go on!"

"*What* role?" I asked. "*What* show?"

He brushed me aside. "Haven't time to tell you now, my bush-league Barrymore! It's already late, and the audience are beginning to stamp their feet. I've got to get into costume." While he was jabbering, he'd been chewing a stick of gum supplied by one of our children; another had brought him an umbrella, and he had borrowed a shawl from my wife. He beckoned to me: "You! Roll up your pants to the knee, suck your thumb, and try to look your mental age—not a day over seven. *That* part should be easy!"—with a Groucho Marx leer. "Here are your lines; pay attention!" He whispered them to me. "Got 'em? Good!" Then—seated in a straight chair, stovepipe hat on head, shawl around shoulders, chewing-gum wart on cheek, and hands folded over the crook of the umbrella—he called, "Quiet, everybody! The curtain is going up!" and signaled me to make my entrance.

ME (small boy's voice): How do, Mr. Lincoln!

SID (deep, slow voice): Good evening, my little man! How are you, this fine evening?

ME: Very well, thank you, Mr. Lincoln.

SID: That's nice. Tell me, my little man: what is your name?

ME: My name is Booth, Mr. Lincoln—John Wilkes Booth.

(Lincoln screeches. Business of hat leaping into the air. Lincoln grabs for it and belabors Booth with the umbrella. Curtain.)

Sid and I played our act, with or without audience, every time he and Laura came to our house, until I moved to Washington in 1949, and our indispensable prop, the stovepipe hat, was lost.

(I thought of our "Lincoln and Booth" when I read in *Remembering James Agee* that he too had an act—"Lee and Grant at Appomattox":

" 'Mah sword, suh!' with an elaborate bow.

" 'Drink to that!' replies Grant sliding out of his chair onto the floor.")

There were other routines that also gave Sid and me childish pleasure—for instance, the venerable Teacher-Willie series:

TEACHER: Willie, can you name a large city in Alaska?

WILLIE: No'm.

TEACHER: Correct!

And

TEACHER: Willie, what is notable about the capital of Alaska, Juneau?

WILLIE: No, I don't.

And "No News, or What Killed the Dog," and such classic monologues as "Ben Bernie's Polish trumpeter," and Fred Allen's account of playing a theater in "the tall celery."

Sid was "a son of the morning," by anyone's standards; in the *Guide Michelin*'s phrase, he was "worth the detour"; to borrow the boast of a famous sauce, he was "original and genuine," and further like it, he might even have been "made from the recipe of a nobleman in the county."

I owe much to Sid, and not only the "yacks, boffolas and downunders" that his company and his writings gave me over the years. This Perelman of great price was unique, a nonesuch. Who else would "search in every nook of granny," or name a Greek character "Manuel Dexterides," or go to the Corn Exchange Bank "to exchange some corn"? I also owe him my introduction to an assortment of authors whom almost certainly I would not have encountered otherwise: Joseph Shearing, for instance, and Flann O'Brien, and especially Professor David W. Maurer, whose *The Big Con* inspired Sid's play *The Night Before Christmas* (and Robert Redford's movie *The Sting*). Increasing my debt, he generously gave me first editions of many of his own books (I wish I had a copy of his *Selections from George Ade*, but despite his frequent promises to sit down to the editing, he didn't do it.) I have never hesitated to ask an author to sign a book for me. Some quail and go blank. Not Sid; the juices of his humor were always on tap. He'd grab a pen and go to it. Here are some inscriptions from my Perelman shelf:

In *Look Who's Talking*:

Whip up the droshky, driver, and let's slip over the hard crust to Port Arthur! Your friend and mine, Sid.

(He always wrote "Sid" with a circle over the "i" instead of a dot.)

In *Keep It Crisp*:

This disheartening example of what happens when movable type becomes available to every upstart.

In *The Dream Department*:

In memory of days in the green room with Della Fox and Ada Rehan, from his old sporting pal, Sid.

In *Chicken Inspector No. 23*:

This nosegay of henbane and nux vomica, to frighten the spiders out of his revolving bookcase.

In *Dawn Ginsbergh's Revenge*:

In memory of sun-drenched days and patchouli-scented nights along Route 232.

In *Strictly From Hunger*:

To Joe, whose mouth is a scarlet wound and whose country estate, "Boiling Diapers," is chic to the Nth degree.

In *Westward Ha!*:

This pathetic nosegay of old baggage labels, receipted hotel bills, and battered claim checks, in the hope that it will protect him from the Evil Eye afloat or ashore.

In *The Swiss Family Perelman*:

To Joe, the thought of whom sustained this cut-rate

Marco Polo from the opium hells of Macao to the shores of Twenty-One.

And finally, for a radical change of mood, in *Parlor, Bedlam and Bath*, by "S. J. Perelman and Q. J. Reynolds" (Quentin Reynolds):
This is without any doubt the worst book ever written.
I wrote one-half of it. Sid.

In addition to the Perelman *oeuvre* complete, I have kept a lot of oddments he gave me:

A postcard view of the Trevi Fountain in Rome, bringing the news that he was there "working on the new Esther Williams swimming picture, *Three Groins in the Fountain*."

Another postcard, from Zanzibar, eerily menacing: "ZANZI-BAR spelled backward is RABIZNAZ. There is no biznaz like rabiznaz."

The yellowing original of an old line drawing for *Judge*, or perhaps for *College Humor*, showing a furious character clubbing another over the head with a xylophone. The legend: "I'll give you something to marimba me by!"

A Christmas card wishing me "Seasonable seizures of happiness, from Laura and Sid."

But the plum of my collection, the pearl of my Perelmaniana, is a photograph of Sid—not a mere snapshot, a *studio* photograph:

He is seated, left profile to the camera. A palm frond sticks up from the back of his coat collar. It is camouflage, you realize, when you observe that he is squinting—eye steely, jaw firm—along the barrel of an air pistol at a toy stork perched on an artificial rose. Inscription: "This happened to me about four days' march out of Nairobi, and I can tell you it was a narrow squeak." I never remembered to ask him if he had ever seen a wide squeak.

Sid died in his sleep in October 1979, and—as *The New Yorker*'s obituary said—"the town grew suddenly sombre." For many of us, it has remained so.

APPENDIX

George and Bea Kaufman had a number of us over for lunch one Sunday at their place in Bucks, Barleysheaf Farm. The Harts were there, and Harpo Marx and Oscar Hammerstein II. We seldom saw the reclusive Mr. Hammerstein, and George took the opportunity to express admiration of his lyrics. He said, "My favorites are the ones in *Oklahoma!*, especially the lines in 'Oh, What a Beautiful Mornin'—

> 'So high is the grass
> as an elephant's eye.'"

My wife was going up to New York later that afternoon; Harpo was too; so I drove them over to Trenton for their train. My wife told me later that just as they sat down in the diner for a cup of tea, the waiter brought the check for two elderly ladies at the table across the aisle. Harpo grabbed it, put it between two slices of bread, and ate it.

Moss Hart's brother Bernie was his stage manager. He was a pleasant fellow, but he was also the merciless perpetrator of "a perpetual and unremitting series of bad puns," in Moss's own words, which he would "launch and send racketing down the years." You couldn't say "Hello, Bernie!" without his twisting it into a pun of wretched sorts.

One dinner at the Harts' Fairview Farm, the other guests included Moss's collaborator, the sardonic, saturnine Kaufman, and Bernie, unfortunately at the top of his punning form. Halfway through the meal, George said, "Bernie, if you were to go out of the room, there would be thirteen of us left at the table. But I, for one, would be willing to take the chance."

Budd Schulberg, who wrote *What Makes Sammy Run* and *Moving Pictures* and the script for *On The Waterfront* and many other successes, lived among us in Bucks for a while. He, too, had a George-Washington-slept-here house, but he was better equipped to deal with its caprices and deficiencies than were most of us. He told me that when their plumbing went on strike for the third time in a week, he swore to his wife that he'd fix those damn pipes once and for all, or bust a gut trying: "I'm going down to the basement and I'm going to stay there until I've got this plumbing *licked*! Don't bother me and don't worry about me. Just bring me a sandwich every now and then."

Down he went. Hours passed. Finally he called upstairs, "See how things are now, darling!"

He could hear taps being turned on and off all over the house. Then his wife called back, "Fine, darling! Wonderful! . . . But there's just one thing: should the toilets be boiling?"

FINIS FARR

1904-1982

Man of Letters

Finis Farr   (MATTHEW DYER)

Finis Farr wrote a spy novel, a sociological history of Chicago, and seven authoritative biographies. He wrote features for newspapers and articles for the best magazines. He wrote scripts for radio and for movies. He never "gave us a slim sheaf of verse," but otherwise he covered the field of writing as widely as anyone I know, and as professionally.

His books were translated into Dutch, Spanish, German, French, and Japanese. His biography of Frank Lloyd Wright was serialized in *The Saturday Evening Post* and was chosen by the British Book Society. Boston University established a research collection of his manuscripts and notes.

And yet, when I think of Finis Farr—"Finis" rhymes with "highness"—I don't think of the distinguished, versatile litterateur, but of my merry friend of sixty years: the Finis Farr who answered my invitation to a New Year's Eve party with this tele-gram: DELIGHTED. I TAKE A SIZE 7¼ IN LAMPSHADES; the Finis who explained his bandaged foot with, "I tripped and broke my toe, running across the room to turn off Sammy Davis on the TV"; the Finis whose letters were headed "The Millionaires' Club," or "Fitrite Shoe Corp., complaint department," and were signed "Peiping Tom, the Chinese Voyeur," or "Unsaturated Fats, gangster," or "The Crisco Kid (he's always fried)," or "Rudyard Kaplan, author of *A Boys' Life of John Wilkes Booth*."

Finis was in the class of 1926 at Princeton, a year ahead of me. We met in my freshman year; but before we actually said how-do, I had come to know him through the droll, urbane paragraphs that our campus humor magazine, the *Tiger*, was printing over his name; and a vivid image of the author formed in my mind: a tall, slender, witty young "blood," elegantly dressed and coolly aloof, part Whistler, part "Saki," and part P. G. Wodehouse's Psmith.

I too began to write for the *Tiger*; I was introduced to Farr, and *pop*! went the image. He proved to be chubby and jolly. He could have been an anticipatory plagiarism from Tolkien's hob-bits. He had the hobbit's "good-natured face" and "deep, fruity laugh," the same "thick warm brown hair" growing low on his forehead, the same pug nose and (as I would learn) the same ability to "disappear quietly and quickly when large stupid folk came blundering along."

I liked him at once. His conversation was a joy: a ragout—a Farrago, you might say—of tidbits from Kipling, Conan Doyle, Gibbon, Surtees, the Bible, Wodehouse, and John Buchan, plus many I didn't recognize, and the whole spiced with cockney slang and Broadwayese. He seemed to have ransacked all English liter-ature, trash as well as treasures, and to have forgotten nothing he had ever read. He was a Bartlett in breeches; apt quotations leapt to his lips, often with a twist of his own. I remember his stopping by my room for a cocktail and remarking, "How beautifully Eddie Guest expresses it!—'It takes a heap o' liquor t' make a house a home.' " Now and then I'd find a note under my door:

ARBUTHNOT: The Near East is a tinderbox! Blenkiron.

Or,

WATSON: The game is afoot! Holmes.

He was book-besotted. Books were his dominant—almost his only—interest. He took no part in campus politics or soul saving or athletics. The proms had to do without his patronage; a friend who once had the rare privilege of seeing him dance said "he looked like a man with rheumatism setting up a deck chair." He was neither a joiner nor a competitor, though his contributions to the *Tiger* and the *Nassau Lit* soon won him election to their boards. As for recreation, the undergraduates' two most popular— gambling and forays to New York—didn't entice him at all. He drank moderately (and sometimes immoderately). Reading aside, his dearest pleasure was an evening spent with a circulating bottle and three or four cronies, swapping stories and talking about favorite books.

When the booze had "slipped its little hand" into Finis's (a line of Wodehouse's that he cherished), he would sometimes give us a dramatic monologue from his large repertory, or would improvise one. There'd be no formal announcement, but when he pulled his eyeglasses down to the end of his nose and began blinking weakly, we knew that we were in the presence of Schultz, the Mad Inventor:

"Zo!"—guttural accent—" 'Dreamer' Schultz you call me, and you make fun of my leetle machine!"—business of cradling an imaginary box in his arms and crooning over it. "Vell, I tell you zomezings: Edison vos a dreamer. Heinrich Ford vos a dreamer—" and so on. The "leetle machine" could be a "turbo-encabulator" or it could be a "dripless marshmallow mold." Financial backing would be supplied by E. Capitoline Hill, a

Philadelphia banker known as "de Volf of Valnut Street," and production would start "chust as soon as I iron out a gubble small bugs." (Schultz had a colleague in the automobile business: Caspar Fell, inventor of the Fell clutch.)

Sometimes Finis would be Ol' Doc Wonder, a tailgate quack, peddling Tone-All, a nostrum "compounded of swamp root, orris root, and King Solomon's seal, plus four secret conjur-yarbs, plucked from a suicide's grave by a blue-gum nigger at the dark of the moon. . . . Of *course* Tone-All will cure you, sir! You and your horse too. It's a matchless lenitive for every fleshly complaint from the epizootics to the fantods! It says so right here on the bottle. . . . Now, if you'll just press in closer, folks. . . . What, madam? . . . No, don't take off your shoe. Tone-All works right through the shoe."

Or we might have a piney-woods revivalist: "Ah'm jes' one of Jesus's bulldogs, a-snappin' at the heels of sin." Or a Western: "Howdy, strangers! My handle's Collins—'Tex' Collins, some calls me. I'm foreman over to the Lazy Ritz Bar Ranch, and this here's my faithful paint pony, Podnuh." If Tex felt sentimental, we'd have a rhapsody about the new schoolmarm, Prairie Rose, "as purty as a little red wagon," or about Mesquite Mary, a dance-hall hostess with a heart of gold. If the sheriff had deputized him, Tex would vow vengeance against "that rattlesnake, that cattle-rustlin' greaser varmint, Diego Valdez. Hup, Podnuh! We'll head him off at Forward Pass!"

We found the lines funny in themselves, and especially so when Finis spoke them. He was an actor manqué. His father was a Presbyterian minister, and I have noticed the affinity between the pulpit and the stage—how ministers' sons often become actors. (Walter Matthau and Sir Laurence Olivier spring to mind.) Finis was born on the last day of 1904 in Lebanon, Tennessee. Farrs abound in that part of the South, he told me, but he never considered himself a southerner. Indeed, the only time I ever heard

him acknowledge any association with the South was when, in response to some Georgia chawbacon's ridicule of the name "Finis,"
he remarked mildly that Jefferson Davis's middle name was Finis,
and if it was good enough for Mr. Davis . . . Still, the heavy-
handed jocosity that his unusual name invited—"Finny-as," "Fy-
neece," and the like—was a frequent irritation. Then came the
morning when he handed a credit card to a pretty salesgirl. She
read his name aloud, "Finis Farr," and exclaimed, "Why, that's
music!"

He said, "I smiled all the rest of the day."

He looked on Cincinnati as his hometown. He spent his
childhood and his young manhood there and attended Cincinnati
schools, except for a term at Castle Heights Military Academy,
back in Lebanon. I asked what he had learned at Castle Heights.
He said he'd learned that if you painted the inside of a milk bottle white, you could keep your corn whiskey in it, with no one the
wiser.

Princeton gave him an A.B. in 1926, and he went straight back
to Cincinnati, to work as a reporter for the *Post*. It was the first of
a number and variety of jobs that he held during the next ten
years, in different fields and different cities: newspaperman, copy
writer at an advertising agency, men's fashion reporter, script-
writer for radio. In those years, I myself was also shuttling from
job to job, until I fetched up in 1937, working on the *Post*, and
living in a Philadelphia suburb with my three young children. I
hadn't seen much of Finis until then, though we had exchanged
letters every month or so, but now he began to come down from
New York to keep me company on weekends.

One of his radio successes was a series called "Mr. District Attorney." It ran at 6 p.m., when I was usually commuting, so I
seldom had a chance to hear it; but I remember one episode
clearly. Finis had wired me CATCH TONIGHTS ACT—something
he had never done before. I went home early, gathered the chil-

dren at my knee—their little faces shining through the milk and orts of their supper—and we tuned in.

Well, a venal bookmaker kidnaps the daughter of State U's football coach on the eve of the Big Game, and threatens to kill her if State doesn't lose by at least ten points. The girl is rescued in the nick of time, and the miscreant is laid by the heels and duly haled before the bar of justice. I was wondering why Finis had urged me to listen to this claptrap when here came Mr. District Attorney's rich, throbbing voice:

"In my long years as a tribune of the people, the scum of the underworld has passed before me, but none so slimy, so rotten, so contemptible as *you*, Joe the Rat Bryan!"

There was more, but I couldn't hear it through the chorus of "What did he say, Daddy? Daddy, why did Mr. Farr call you a rat? Who won the game, Daddy?"

One Saturday Finis and I were invited to dinner by George and Bee Kaufman, whose Barleysheaf Farm was only a few miles away. On our way home, Finis said, "You could ride the steam cars from hell to breakfast and not find a nicer spread than that, huh? And it all came from George's just putting one witty little word after another, and then teaching some actors how to speak them. What's Kaufman got that Bryan and Farr haven't got?— No, don't answer that." Long pause. "What say we give it a try?"

We started work next morning, and eight weekends later our show was finished: a comedy (I insist) called *We Were Here First*. Our agent sent the script to Mike Todd, and Todd actually produced it, at the Cleveland Playhouse, where it ran for a whole week before the stretcher-bearers carried it away. No matter. We'd had the fun of writing it, and the great Kaufman told us, "If I'd known you boys could handle dialogue like that, I'd have saved you from wasting it on that plot."

Finis and I disagreed on the ideal literary agent. He said that the best was none at all, and quoted a line of Claudio's in *Much*

Ado: "Let every eye negotiate for itself, and trust no agent." Second best, he said, would be part Billy Rose, part Mike Todd, and part Harlem mugger. This combination not being available, we settled for Mark Hanna. Born in the Bronx, he had lived in Bombay and Hong Kong; and he spoke a baffling amalgam of Yiddish, Broadway slang, and "elegant" English, with a sprinkling of Chinese, like this: "Peradventure this *meshugge* has been on his hip with a pipe of *yen hok*, because when the *momzeh* stands up and starts giving me this *megillah*, he falls flat on his *tochis*, and your Uncle Mark laughs until he nearly splits his lacy pantseroo" (nut . . . opium . . . tiresome harangue . . . on his ass).

Mark was a good agent, aggressive, hardworking, and honest (Helen Hayes was a client of his), but he had two weaknesses: his threshold of boredom was well below ground level; and he was a mysophobe—a speck of dirt, ash, or lint made him quiver like Mr. Coffee Nerves. I mention Mark and his weaknesses only because Farr played on them cruelly, and I, to my shame, was his confederate.

The news that Mark had sold *We Were Here First* required a celebration. I suggested it to Finis, who said, "Splendid! Moreover, it will give me a chance to heal the breach between us."

"Between you and Mark? I don't believe it! What happened?"

Finis said smugly, "I declined to give him the address of my glovemaker."

We called at Mark's office, and Finis led off: Would he dine as our guest on the following Tuesday? We were grateful to him and wanted to put on a really good show—the best of everything. When Mark had committed himself, Finis set the hook: "We thought we'd start the party at the Princeton Club, early. Tuesday will be a special afternoon there. Coach Charlie Caldwell is going to run the movies of the 1921 Princeton-Brown game. He'll begin by following the Princeton left halfback through every play, showing what he did and then telling us what he *should* have done. Then he'll run the film again, following the fullback. Then the *right* halfback, the quarterback and every member of the line, end to end—and *all in slow motion*! It'll be *something*, I promise you! And listen to this: *free beer*! As much as you can drink!"

Mark had already begun to twitch and wriggle and clear his throat, but Finis wouldn't be interrupted: "Some of the old Cleveland gang, classmates of mine, are coming on just for that afternoon, and they'll join us for dinner. We know you'll all get along like a house afire. Frankie Foster alone will give you a million laughs with his imitation of a guy doing birdcalls. Frankie tries to pick a fight with cops when he gets a few jolts under his belt, but don't you worry: we'll watch out for him.

"After the movie—that's only the *beginning* of our party for you! We'll take a taxi up to Mother Schwartz's deli on Amsterdam Avenue and buy a bucket of her coleslaw. It's the best in town— the wonderful *runny* kind. Oh, one other thing while I think of it: Frankie likes to ride on the roof of the taxi. You'll have to hold onto him while Joe and I are inside getting the coleslaw.

"So now we're all set. We'll go back to your apartment—"

Mark's face was like a TV screen. What he was visualizing played across it clearly and unmistakably: three hours of suffocating boredom at the Princeton Club, followed by a long ride in a taxi full of drunken, quarrelsome strangers, and ending up with an invasion of his immaculate apartment with "the runny kind" of coleslaw dripping over his precious rugs and upholstery. . . . He was teetering on the edge of hysteria when Finis relented, confessed all, and promised that our dinner would be at the best Chinese restaurant in New York.

The children and I sometimes played slapjack or idiots' delight after supper, with the expectable result that every deck of cards in the house soon became grimy and gappy. I was about to throw

away the worst of them when Finis asked to salvage the aces. He
stripped out half a dozen, clipped them together against a tree, and
fired a .22 bullet through their exact center. I had no idea what
he was up to until he showed me this note:

Mr. Frank Sullivan,   Natchez-Under-the-Hill
135 Lincoln Avenue,   July 22, 1867
Saratoga Springs, NY

Sir:

A few of us boys was having a little game of draw poker here
last night when a stranger passed a light remark about your
sister, Miss Ella Mae Lou.

When the resurrection men laid him out, they found this
card in the upper left-hand pocket of his weskit.

Happy to have been of service, Sir.

(Signed) BEAUREGARD FARR,
Colonel, CSA (Ret.)

Copies, with the other aces, went to Nunnally Johnson, Lucius
Beebe, Stanley Walker, Frank Norris, and Corey Ford.

One Sunday morning we drove over to Atlantic City, on a sudden yearning for steamer clams and lobster at Hackney's, where
the waitresses were massive, motherly women in white uniforms
so starched that they crackled. We gorged. Waddling back down
the Boardwalk, we came to a small shop with a large sign: GIFTS.

"Bear with me a moment," Finis said, ducking in. I followed.
The proprietor came forward. "Yes, gentlemen?"
Finis said, "I've come for mine."
"I don't understand, sir. You've come for your *what*?"
"For my gift. Your sign says this is a gift shop."

"Yes, but we don't *give* things away! We sell them."

"You *sell* them?" Incredulity mixed with indignation. "Then your sign ought to say 'sales.' This is arrant misrepresentation! It's a come-on, a trap for us poor tourists, and I'll see that the Better Business Bureau hears about it at *once*! Good day, sirrah!"

"But—"

"Good *day,* sirrah!"

Outside, he said, "I've always wanted to call somebody 'sirrah.' Be all right if I call you 'sirrah' every now and then?—say on Arbor Day and Millard Fillmore's birthday?"

Another stroll with Finis, this time in New York, took us up Fifth Avenue. I'd been telling him about Gus Lobrano's unfinished epic, "How Twenty-third Street Got Its Name."

Finis asked, "Know how *this* street got its name? Ever hear of Amos Fifth? I thought not. How fleeting is fame! Forgotten already, and yet a century ago 'Amos Fifth' was on every tongue. It was he, my boy, who negotiated the merger of those two giant banks, the Occasional Fidelity and the Grudging Trust. But first let me tell you how his career started. Pay attention—there's a lesson for all of us here. Amos Fifth was a visionary. He foresaw the construction of our subway system. He foresaw further that people running for a train would be jostled, and would drop their change through the gratings in the sidewalks. So what did Amos do? He began manufacturing magnets! And *why* did he manufacture magnets? Simple: Tie one to a length of string, lower it through a grating, and haul in the change. In a matter of weeks the demand for magnets had nearly swamped the fledgling company. The press was hailing Amos as 'the Magnet Magnate,' and before much longer, a grateful city had named its most splendid thoroughfare in his honor. Hats off to Amos Fifth, say I!"

Finis babbled on, amusing himself, not caring in the least if I was listening: "—and now, to our left, the Public Library, commemorating John Q. Public, the little man beloved of political cartoonists. A few blocks north, Central Park, once the private estate of Commodore Central, who bequeathed it to the city on condition that it bear his name *in perpetuo*—"

Still another of our strolls was along Park Avenue. A man's hat shop stood at the southeast corner of 47th Street, and as we passed it, I asked Finis if he knew there was a Knox College in Kentucky and a Stetson College in Florida, and I wondered if they were rivals.

Finis said, "*Of course* they are! Don't you ever read the sports pages? They meet every November in the Bowler Bowl, and I can tell you it's filled to the brim. As the Sweat Band strikes up a tune from *Panama Hattie*, President Homburg of Knox walks out to midfield with his lovely daughter Fedora, and shakes hands with President Sombrero of Stetson. The whistle shrills. The game is on—the game that caps the season, that *crowns* it, you might even say. I tell you, it's the berets! Shall I continue?"

"Pray do," I said. "But first, let us step into the Waldorf Bar here, where the acoustics are better."

"A burnt string would pull me," Finis said.

He hit a bad patch in 1938 when he hired on as a contributing editor at *Time*. The managing editor was a bully, and Finis's nerves became raw and more raw. One day after lunch, he was sitting on a sunny bench in Bryant Park, lamenting the need to go back to the torture chamber, when he suddenly said to himself, "I've got the answer!" It was "*Don't* go back!" and he didn't.

His friend Frank Norris persuaded him to come to the "March of Time" radio program as producing editor, and he stayed there until 1940, when he went to a Cincinnati newspaper as supervisor of its forthcoming centennial issue. His collaborator was the foreman of the composing room, an elderly, taciturn Scot. They worked together for half a year, Finis wrote me; then, finally, the last form was locked, the presses rolled, and the first copies came up. He leafed through one with satisfaction, even pride, while the Scot looked over his shoulder.

"Weel, Muster Farr," he said, "there she is! Ye ken, Ah've been in this beezniss a lang, lang time. Ah've wurrrked wi' some o' th' grrreatest newspapermen iver: Dana, Pulitzer, Watterson, an' th' like. Ah've seen 'em come an' Ah've seen 'em go. But Ah've niver seen a paper like this afore: fifteen sections, runnin' to thrrree hunner an' eighteen pages! Ye've done it all yersel, Muster Farr, an' let me tell you, a dom puir job it is!"

Hurt? Humiliated? Not Finis! He recognized at once that here was a formula capable of infinite application, and for the next few months, each of his letters to me was a fresh variation on the theme.

Sample: The star of a Broadway drama is taken ill on opening night. Understudy is thrust onstage. Her great chance! She gives her all! After the third-act curtain, she rushes to her dressing room, too drained of emotion to face the audience again, to face *anyone*. She waits until the huge theater is dark and empty, except for the stage-doorman, kindly old Pop. He touches her arm as she tries to steal out.

"Missy," he says gently, "I watched you tonight. Y' know, Missy, I've been with show business a long, long time. I've seen 'em come and I've seen 'em go: Cornell, Hayes, Eagels, Nazimova, Le Gallienne, Fontanne. . . . Wonderful actresses, wonderful women! And I want to tell you sump'n. Missy: Don't wait for the reviews! Don't even wait to pack! Take a taxi down to Penn Station *now* and hop the first rattler home to Cedar Rapids!"

Another sample: Dugout at Château-Thierry. Young second lieutenant, shaking with fatigue and nerves. Grizzled sergeant enters: "Sir, I've been in this man's army a long, long time. We was watchin' you out there today. Fresh from the Point, ain't you, sir?

Your first action? Well, sir, the men have asked me to be their spokesman, like, and they want me to tell you that of all the yellow—"

The newly ordained priest conducts his first service, in the presence of his bishop. The young intern performs his first major operation, while the great surgeon watches. There were others. The cast and dialogue were always Finis's alone. My only contributions were trivial, such as reminding him that tradition required the stage-doorman to be named "Pop," and the sergeant to be grizzled.

The surprise reverse, the "switcheroo," always had an appeal for Finis. When I was a freshman, he wrote a piece for the *Tiger* that began, "His suit was soiled and threadbare, but it had obviously been made by a bad tailor." A line like that was as rare in the college magazines of our day as would have been verses like Dorothy Parker's or drawings like H. M. Bateman's.—Which recalls an evening when Finis and I and "Red" Newsom, the chairman of the *Tiger*, were laying out the next issue. Finis handed me a piece of verse: "Read this. Keats might have written it."

I read it. It was dreadful. I said, "*Keats?*"

"Yeah. Charlie Keats. Chump I once met in Youngstown."

Long afterwards, I reminded Finis of the bad-tailor line. He said, "I should have explained that the guy was a hobo-Brummell."

Those were happy years, the late 1930s and 1940–41. Finis was making a name in radio; at the same time, it was getting about town that he was a witty dog, good company, soft-spoken, never sour, and definitely worth one's attention. He was also building up a nice stake. Thitherto, he said, "My money pocket could have been used as an echo chamber at NBC," but now headwaiters were beginning to ask, "Your usual table, Mr. Farr?" and Mr. Farr lapped it up.

Then came the attack on Pearl Harbor. Finis phoned me a day or so later. His opening remark gave me my first laugh since that terrible Sunday broadcast. He said, "I don't know about you, but this war couldn't have come at a more inconvenient time for me!" Possibly emboldened by his term at Castle Heights, he enlisted in the infantry as a private, in the Volunteer Officers Candidate program, and was eventually commissioned second lieutenant. He wrote me that he couldn't remember the name of the general who had addressed the graduating class, but he would never forget his closing remarks: "Men, each of you has the baton of a marshal of France in his knapsack. The marshal wants them back. MPs will now pass among you—"

His first tour of duty was in Washington, in the office of the Army's Chief of Staff, where he was appointed aide to General Hugh Drum.

> About all I have to do [he wrote me] is keep track of the general's engagements, but there are pitfalls. Yesterday morning, for instance, I told him, "Sir, the Army's Historical Section has arranged for you to have an official photograph taken at fifteen hundred hours today."
>
> He grunted, "Who's going to do it?"
>
> I said, "A fine photographer, sir: Hal Phyfe, of New York. He specializes in portraits and he's very good."
>
> The General began twiddling a pencil, faster and faster. Plainly something irritated him. Suddenly he broke the pencil in half and threw it across his office.
>
> "Farr," he growled, "even though you obviously have no respect for me as a man, pray try to show some for the uniform I have the honor to wear! Phyfe-Drum . . . . Phyfe-Drum . . . . Phyfe-Drum . . . . *Pah!*"

In November 1943, Finis was sent to the China-Burma-India theater on special assignment to General Joe Stilwell. He flew out in an LB-30, Washington to Karachi, via Natal, Accra, Khartoum, Cairo, and way stations. It must have been quite a flight:

The Atlantic leg was a piece of cake [he wrote], but then things got sticky. With Accra only a couple of hours behind us, one of our engines quit, then a second, and when the third began to cough, the pilot called back, "I've got to set her down!" All I could see below was jungle, but somehow he found an open patch and slipped her in. The landing was slam-bang, and my teeth were still rattling when we heard this hellish yelling. I peered out. My God, we were surrounded by hundreds of black fellows, all brandishing spears and trying to climb onto our wings! The worst of it was, I recognized them as Wabungi, the fiercest tribe in all Central Africa. The situation was damned ugly, I can tell you!

Our pilot had been stunned by the landing, and it turned out that I was S.O.P. [Senior Officer Present]. Fortunately, I happened to know a few words of Wabunga. I told the other men that I'd see what I could do to pacify these savages, and very gingerly I opened the door of the plane. The instant I appeared, the whole lot of them gave a terrific shout and went flat on their faces, and just lay there, trembling!

I picked out the *ngapo*—chief—by his headdress and beckoned to him. He crawled up to me, and we began to palaver. Well, it seems that the Wabungi have a tribal legend which says that a great metal bird would alight among them, and a white god—

Damn Farr! Anybody with an IQ above a turnip's would have been tipped off by "a few words of Wabunga," but I, poor gullible fool!—I swallowed this folderol right up to the "great metal bird."

When I mustered the strength to read on, I saw that the letter ended, "My right has collapsed. My left is a shambles. My center is in retreat. I shall surrender.

"F.F. (Ferdinand Foch)."

I didn't see Finis at all during the war; the Army kept him in Asia, and the Navy kept me in the Pacific; but from time to time I'd get a V-mail letter from him, such as

Major Reno:
    You stay here in the draw. I'll ride ahead and check out that Indian encampment.

Custer

Or,

Cavendish & Fotheringay
Natty gents' clothing

Mr. Bryan:
    Your collar button is ready.
Mort Goldblatt, prop.

—all very entertaining, though not very newsy; and it wasn't until long after V-J Day, when I read about Finis in the *Princeton Alumni Weekly*, that I learned what an un-cushy war he had had. The worst of it was his three campaigns in Burma, and the worst part of the three was operating with the Burmese guerrillas behind the Japanese lines. He had made captain by then. His main job, which he shared with Bert Parks (later the TV master of ceremonies), was producing programs for the U.S. Armed Forces Radio Network and dropping supplies from DC-3s. His admiration and affection for these old planes he put into a letter to Bill Buckley years later:

    ... How well I remember the Dakotas (as the British called them) in China, Burma and India. I have lashed myself to the fuselage and tossed out supplies over jungle outposts while the faithful airplane almost stopped, turned on its side, and waited patiently for us to shove the bamboo baskets across the deck, and out. Then the pilot poured on the coal, and she lunged up and banked for another pass over the target. What an aircraft!

And what a change for a puffy, pudgy, forty-year-old writer who had previously got his only exercise when he threw away a dead match! Parks told me it was Finis's duty to choose the missions and assign the men to fly them: "He always assigned himself to the hairiest. He'd say to me, 'You're married and you're only a kid'—hell, I was twenty-eight!—'don't stick your neck out. I'll take this one.'

"We'd sit around the fire at night, and Finis would fantasize about the great bartenders he had known, at 21 and Toots Shor's and the Stork—how they had 'an eye for measurements like a pharmacist's' and 'clean, deft hands like a surgeon's'—how they filled your glass not quite to the brim, and set it down in front of you with a dry bottom, so that it wouldn't drip on you when you raised it to your lips. It was a topic that brought to his face a look of rapturous reverie. There's no other way to describe it!"

General Hegenberger gave both Finis and Parks a commendation that spoke of "numerous combat missions . . . outstanding courage . . ." and General Wedemeyer backed it up with a Bronze Star.

Finis came home, after twenty-five months overseas, and notified me that he was in circulation again:

Honorable discharge in one pocket and a fat roll of C-notes in another, I celebrated my return to civilian life by taking myself to dinner in the Oak Room [at the Plaza Hotel, in New York]—a bangup dinner, with champagne wine for the host of honor and whiskey punch for the onlookers. Our old friend Carlo [the headwaiter] made a great fuss over me, so much so that when the booze had slipped its little hand into mine [Wodehouse's line again], I slipped fifty bucks into Carlo's.

The warm glow persisting into the next evening, I decided to go back, confident of Carlo's devout attentions. No Carlo. I asked for him and was told, "Carlo? He gone! Las' night his las' night here. He retire. He gone back to Napoli."

Finis never had much to say about his experiences in the war—he was too afraid of becoming a war-bore—and the little he did say was usually self-mocking. When he proposed our first postwar meeting, a dinner, his letter ended, "Save plenty of time for me to tell you about the Burma campaigns. Faces in the campfire. Stout chaps! Brave as lions! Few came through, more's the pity ... And I mustn't forget the singular incident at Taipha Ga, spring of '44, or was it '45?"

Soon after he was separated from the Army, he was married. Soon after that, he was separated from his wife. I never heard him mention her again.

He batted around awhile, roweled by postwar restlessness, and unable or unwilling to accept an office schedule. Being lashed to a desk was less exciting than being lashed to the fuselage of a DC-3, and in-and-out baskets lacked the interest of baskets of supplies. He contributed to magazines, became editorial director of the Mutual Broadcasting System, and joined Paramont Pictures as a staff writer. "I'm rolling in the stuff," he reported. "Way back in 1942, I had the forethought to copyright the line, 'Well, fellows, this is it!' and every war-movie or war-play since then has had to pay me a royalty." But the government wasn't through with him yet, nor with me. In 1949 I was tapped by the Central Intelligence Agency and instructed to staff a "section."

My dozen-odd recruits included Finis; Hugh Troy, a brilliant writer and artist (and practical joker); and Boris, a Russian. (All three are dead now, so there is no harm in identifying them.) Boris was almost as brilliant as Hugh, but he had the disposition of a Tasmanian devil. Finis limped into my office one morning and explained, "I passed too close to Boris's desk. He sprang the full length of his chain and sank his fangs into my ankle." Among our colleagues (in another section, I remember with thanks) were G—— and H——, both of them so abrasive that they inspired Finis to the formulation of "Farr's Prescription": "If you want to like G——, go and talk with H——. If you want to like H——, go and talk with G——." Finis was a patient man, and I know of only one other person who provoked him to an admission of distaste: a pompous journalist whom he enduringly dubbed "a mastodon's ass."

Memories of Finis are still bright among those of us who worked with him in Washington. One wrote me that when the Agency began requiring candidates to take a psychiatric test, and Finis's opinion of the innovation was requested, he replied:

> I have spent many hours in Third Avenue saloons. Accordingly, I would place the candidate in front of a one-way pane of glass, with three seasoned Irish bartenders on the other side. Then I'd ask them for a yes-or-no answer to one question: "Would you give this man a drink on credit?"

Howard Hunt, whose association with CIA is now public knowledge, treasures a remark from those days. Finis had invited the Hunts to dinner at a steak house. A block short of it, a fireman halted their taxi, and they saw that the restaurant was in flames. Finis asked Dorothy Hunt, "How do you like your restaurants—rare, medium, or well-done?"

His resignation from CIA in 1959 was followed by "a fallow interval"—his words—"i.e., a stretch of months in which I suffered from Farr's disease. You never heard of it? It's characterized by extreme lassitude. There are no symptoms, the patient being too indolent to show any." But in 1960 what he called "the spider's filament that I have for will power" was suddenly transmuted into high-tensile steel. He began doing research for a biography of Frank Lloyd Wright, and thereupon embarked on a period of such frenzied production that when it closed, in 1978, he had turned out six other biographies (of Jack Johnson, Margaret Mitchell, Franklin D. Roosevelt, John O'Hara, Westbrook Pegler, and Eddie Rickenbacker); plus a spy tale, *The Elephant Valley*; and *Chicago*, a panoramic 428-page history that reads like a novel. One of these biographies—I won't say which—led to "Farr's Law": "The more eminent the man, the more insufferable his widow." Another was shamelessly plagiarized for the stage; Finis sued and was given a generous settlement.

About halfway into his crushing schedule, he wrote me, "If you'd like a view of me at this moment, think of the central figure in the Laocoön group." Again, "I'm struggling to finish the Pegler book, convinced at last that I'm in the wrong business." And again, "Have you noticed that the older, fatter, weaker and more slothful we grow, wise Mother Nature takes care that our workload grows in proportion? This is her plan for the continuation of the race, and a hell of a plan it is!"

One would think that the research demanded by all these books, and then the writing, would have occupied every minute of Finis's day, yet he found time to double the output of his letters. Every week now brought me at least two, and one week brought five— three in a single day. Many were, of course, Finis's wonderful nonsense: "I have at last hit on the perfect title for my Chicago book: *Encyc. Brit., Vol. 14, HUS to ITA*." Or "When Dr. DeBakey operates on the Duke of Windsor's heart, I trust that he will also reduce the size of the knot in the Duke's necktie. It has become dangerously enlarged." Or:

> I ran into B——— [an alcoholic classmate of mine] in the Princeton Club yesterday. He was suffering from a bad case of martini-poisoning. Worse, someone had made him up

with Max Factor's Number 14, "Brink of Apoplexy." I'm afraid he has reached the stage where loosening the necktie and shoelaces constitutes undressing.

But letters like these—chatter and jokes—were exceptions. Most of them pursued a definite theme, sometimes for weeks, sometimes even for months. One such theme was the imbecilic communications that authors receive.

Here's something the great Duke of Wellington wrote: "It is quite curious with what a number of Insane Persons I am in relation. Mad retired Officers, Mad Women..." And here's something from my mail this morning: "There is a tradition in our family that while passing through Quincy, Ill., in 1908, my mother's uncle talked with a man named Mitchell or Miller in the baggage room of the MK & T station. Could he have been any kin to Margaret Mitchell of Atlanta? Please reply at once." I note that these letters are always written on ruled tablets.

Irritation made Finis drop this theme after a few weeks, and irritation made him take up another: careless writing, murky writing, vogue words, and redundancies. I've culled these examples from several dozen like them:

Security guards: what other kind are there? The same for *legal counsel. Complete stop*: what is an incomplete stop, a skid? People are *harkening back* too much. *Charisma* is something Teddy Kennedy puts on his hair. I once heard the winner of a backgammon tournament say that he had had *"fantastic dice."* That would be dice with the faces of little men on them, I suppose? Which makes you madder, a letter beginning "Dear J. Bryan, III" or "Dear Joe Bryan"? Such a witless salutation *always* precedes a gross imposition. I read that Evelyn Waugh detested this form of address. I agree. Do you?

As soon as I replied that yes, I did agree, the letters that had begun "Dear All-time Gridiron Great," "Fellow knight o' the pen," and the like, stopped abruptly; now all began "Dear Joe Bryan," though they continued to end with an exhortation: "Don't get hoited!" "*A basso il fascismo!*" "Defy the foul fiend!" or "Keep kissable!" Also, the signatures were as delirious as ever: "Ralph Waldorf Emerson," "Pollyadler, the Glad Girl," "Devil Anse Hatfield," "Mr. Thirsty Fibre," "Taiwan On, the Chinese Lush," "Horatio Alger Hiss, author of the *Little Liar* series," "Willa Kafka," or simply "Spunky Farr."

Bill Buckley has said that Finis possessed "a limpid and subtle prose style." Sloppy writing infuriated him. A biography of one of his idols, Kipling, in which the author referred to "the Great Trunk Road" instead of the Grand Trunk Road—*twice on the same bloody page!*"—made him leap and howl; and when he read in another Kipling biography that Kipling himself had been guilty of the phrase "32 knots in the hour," Finis's wound was almost mortal.

Balm and solace were usually close at hand. Finis loved to drink. Let him get comfortably braced against the mahogany or perched on a padded bar stool, and he would "leap for the rumjug, like a bullfrog for a red rag." Yet in our whole long, joyful companionship, I never saw him sloppy or noisy. Tiddly, yes, but never out of control. Moreover, he was tolerant of those whose heads and stomachs did not enjoy the staunch equilibrium of his own. One such, a classmate, tried to keep pace with him in their sophomore year. They had "cocktails" (raw applejack) in the host's room—indeed, several cocktails—then went to a tea-roomy, chintzy, candle-in-a-Chianti-bottle restaurant just off Nassau Street. The first course was cantaloupe. The host never made it to the second. He slid under the table and "lay like a warrior taking his rest," snoring and blowing small, sticky bubbles. The proprietress heard the crash and rushed up, distraught. "The poor gentleman has fainted!" she cried. "I'll call a doctor!"

Finis said gravely, "Calm yourself, madam. There is no emergency. The gentleman merely ate his melon too close to the rind."

During Prohibition, Finis gave most of his drinking custom to Dan Moriarty's; and after repeal, to the Players and, in later years, to the Racquet & Tennis Club. He was sure of finding a crony at one or another: at Dan's, Frank Sullivan, Henry Redmond, Noel Busch, or Mike Romanoff; at the Players, Corey Ford or Frank Norris; and at the Racquet, John McClain, Azzy Guirey, Bobby Grant, Jack Durant, or Garry Stephenson.

His cronies particularly enjoyed having someone who hadn't met Finis join their table, then watching the newcomer's expression as Finis eased into one of his come-to-Jesus drivels:

". . . When you know me better, sir—and that will be soon, I *most sincerely* hope and trust—you'll find that I'm somewhat different from these good fellows here, valiant soldiers of the Cross though I am confident that they are. Christians to a man! Whereas I—alas!—frail of flesh and spirit, am selfish and self-indulgent. You see, sir, all I do is just go around helping people. It's my hobby, you might say. To put it another way, I get *my* happiness out of making *others* happy. I don't want them to thank me. I ought to thank *them*, for giving me a chance to help them, to share with them some of the rich blessings that our bountiful Father has heaped on my undeserving head. So if I can ever help *you*, my dear new friend, please do me a favor and call on me. I beg you to do so! Meanwhile, I ask your permission to remember you in my orisons."

Two minutes of this bosh was all that most strangers could stand, especially if, at Finis's mention of orisons, he put his hand on their shoulder and rolled his eyes upward in ecstatic, if rather rancid, piety.

The Racquet—or "the Fortress," as he called it—was his favorite refuge. It did no drop-in trade, so there were no incursions by bellicose rowdies. It offered "peace, perfect peace, with loved ones far away." Its high-ceilinged bar was like a cathedral; it discouraged raucousness, even exuberance. Here Finis would hole up on an afternoon, "Farr from the madding crowd's ignoble strife," he liked to say, "Farr from sorrow, Farr from sin . . . By the way, don't confuse the madding crowd with the Owney Madden crowd. Different mob altogether."

The barmen at the Racquet were veteran professionals; a member could be certain that his quirks, once learned, would never be forgotten. Finis had quirks aplenty. For instance, it enraged him to order a martini and be asked, "Straight up, sir, or on the rocks?"

"Straight up?" Next they'd be calling the noble martini a "Silver Bullet" or a "Crystal Yum-yum" or "Razor-Blade Soup" or some other nickname fancied by the smart-asses!

"Normal!" he would snarl.

He rated the Scotch and soda as the king of drinks and the dry martini as the queen. His accolade for the martini was "the Breakfast of Champions!" He wrote me once from Dallas, "Why is it that every time I pass the corner of Olive and Bryan Streets, my thoughts turn to gin and vermouth? Deuced odd, eh?" Martinis and Scotch were his standard, conventional tipples, but the pace and rhythm of his consumption was wildly unorthodox. If he and I happened to meet on one of his martini days, he'd have made scarcely a dent in his first by the time I'd finished mine. When I was halfway through my second, I'd still be a whole drink ahead of him. But as I worked into my third, Finis would be on his *fourth*, and from there in he operated on the principle of the Automatic Stoker.

Another of his quirks was to invite you to meet him, never in "the bar" at the Racquet, but always in "the North Room," and never to offer you "a drink," but always "an aperitif" or "a cordial" or "some refreshment." He was not attitudinizing: Finis was as unpretentious as a homemade loaf of bread; the harmless little Edwardian niceties gave him satisfaction. He had his own corner in the North Room. From it he watched with interest and impatience the construction of Lever House, just across 53rd Street. I saw him gazing at it one afternoon and asked why he found it so absorbing.

He said, "They'll finish the damn thing pretty soon and start assigning the offices. Some poor, harried bastard will draw the one just opposite us. I'll be able to look through his window from here and read his name on the door, and I'll find out his phone number, and when I catch him with his feet on the desk, I'll give him a little ring: 'Takin' it easy, are you, buddy boy?'—soft, sinister voice. 'Too nice a day to work, eh? Much better just to sit back and read *Playboy*?'

"He'll panic and yell, 'Who is this?'

"Then I'll chuckle like Sidney Greenstreet in *The Maltese Falcon* and repeat, 'Who is this? Why, this is *management*, buddy boy. That's all: just *management*! And management is telling you that if you take your feet off that desk, it won't fly out the window. And if you *don't* take your goddam feet off it, *you'll* be flying out the door!' "

Lever House was finished and the offices were occupied, but—alas for Finis's plot!—the North Room gave no view of the windows and doors.

Somewhere in the mid-70s Finis hit on a theme that kept us happy and busy for the next four years. This was the Spurious Lincoln Anecdote. It began starkly enough, with Lincoln being quoted as saying, "Stanton, you remind me of a proverb I used to hear from the country folks back home: 'A shoat'll never root

under a fence unless he wants to get something on the other side.' "
The goal was, as you see, pure pointlessness.

Finis drew the guidelines: "It's a two-part form: one, there must be a definite situation; two, Lincoln must remark on it, and —note this!—not only must the remark be utterly devoid of sense in itself, but it must have *no* bearing on the situation *whatsoever*." Our technique improved as we worked. We mustered a cast of characters that included Nicolay and Hay, Welles, Seward, Stanton, Hooker, and Herndon. We chose as our stock properties shoats, britches, rail fences, and hound dogs. We agreed that Lincoln always had to *drawl*, and that every S.L.A. had to end "—but a twinkle in the Great Emancipator's eye took all the sting from his remark." (Our original ending was "—until he noticed that Lincoln had put his hand over his mouth to conceal a smile," but we scrapped it for the twinkle.)

Here are a few specimens of our work:

Secretary Welles proudly laid the plans for the *Monitor* on the President's desk. Lincoln skimmed over them, shoved them aside, and drawled, "Gideon, did I ever tell you about the old farmer back home who had a hound dog that couldn't count above ten? Well, they tried and tried to teach it, but ten was the best it could do. At last the old fellow said, 'I reckon this here dog jes' ain't much good at arithmetic!' " Welles flushed, but a twinkle in the Great Emancipator's eye etc.

One morning when Lincoln was a small-town lawyer, a knotty legal problem arose, and his partner, William Herndon, was impatient to dispose of it. Lincoln leaned back in his chair, put his big feet up on the desk, and drawled, "Whoa there, Billy! *Whoa* there! Nobody wins in a race between a shoat and a bedbug!" Young Herndon expostulated, "But Mr. Lincoln—!" And then he saw the twinkle that etc.

News had come that Joe Hooker, with 80,000 men, was ready to engage Longstreet at Fredericksburg, but had no way of crossing the Rappahannock River. Seward was using the delay to undermine Stanton. Lincoln stood up, his face more deeply lined than ever, and looked down on Seward from his great height. "Mister Secretary," he drawled, "back where I come from, the country folks have a saying, 'If you want to keep a hound dog from standing on his head, tie his tail to an anvil.' " Seward was notoriously hot-tempered; he might have taken offense at the homely parable but for the twinkle etc.

Finis and I got a lot of fun out of our S.L.A.'s. Years after we'd dropped them for new themes, one would occur to us—say, Lincoln's analogy between a politician and a three-legged shoat—and we'd add it to the collection. But gradually we found ourselves turning from S.L.A.'s to P.P.'s—"Plantation Proverbs." The step was short, easy, and natural. As before, Finis was the pioneer in this virgin territory. I can't remember the first of his P.P.'s, or how he came to compose it; but I remember how some of them ran:

Don't fuss wid de jay-bird effen you meets him on de Big Road. *He* know whah he gwine!

Chop down de peach tree, 'gator do de cakewalk; chop down de pear tree, hant come in de do'.

Br'er Chinch-bug, he mouty proud of he new weskit, but Br'er Mushrat, he got mo' sense den buy he clo'se at *dat* sto'.

Finis pictured his humble philosopher as "Uncle 'Lige," a venerable Negro who pauses in the careful loading of his stub pipe to shake his woolly head, shoot a keen glance from under his shaggy gray eyebrows, and utter some pithy, pregnant observation, such as "One 'tater bug, bad luck! Two 'tater bugs, wuss luck!" Our Afro-aphorist (as we thought of him), quickly became Finis's pet, his obsession. He did no other work of any sort while he refined, honed, and polished his P.P.'s.

> It's like carrying *pi* to forty decimal places [he wrote]. I draw nearer, ever nearer, to the perfect imbecility, but it continues to elude me. Every one of our P.P.'s is a *not quite*. Always I have this terrible, frustrating sense that some hint of rationality has crept in. But don't despair! This evening I'll brew strong Turkish coffee, set out a packet of shag for my blackened briar, turn up the student lamp and concentrate in the clouds of aromatic smoke until the early hours.
>
> P.S. I'm considering bringing in Miz Boll-weevil and Br'er Mud-turkle as pinch-hitters.
>
> P.P.S. I think our best so far is "De yearthquake allus mean hard times a-comin' for po' folks."
>
> P.P.P.S. Or maybe, "Effen you wants Misto' Catfish, 'taint no use a-s'archin' in de corncrib or de cotton-patch." . . . No, that makes sense! And so I press on toward my goal, toiling, rejoicing, sorrowing.

But in 1978, Finis's "fans," as he called them—"that is, the butcher, the baker and the candlestick maker, not to mention the landlord, the tailor and the grocer"—became clamorous; he had to get back to work, and fast. He said, "I was suspended over the gumbo by a very fine thread." We had always assumed that though Finis was in no hurry to play go-for-broke against Mr. Rockefeller, at least he wasn't hurting. Perhaps he misled us by his frequent annoucements of grandiose, nonsensical schemes that would make him rich "beyond the dreams of avarice—you remember Dick Avarice, don't you? Class of Twenty-four."

One such was to persuade the Rhode Island State Legislature to pass a Comparison Tax and give him a percentage of the proceeds. "Here's how it will work: somebody wants to convey an idea of the size of Zanzibar, for instance. Naturally, he says, 'It's about three times as big as Rhode Island.' Okay, our inspectors clamp down on him, he pays the tax, and I get my cut. I can't understand why nobody thought of it before."

Pending action by Rhode Island, Finis resigned from his clubs in New York and moved to Portland, Maine, where his sister and her family lived. He rented an apartment, reluctantly turned his back on Lincoln, Br'er Chinch-bug and his other *dramatorum personae*, and settled down to write the book that had long been closest to his heart: a social history of the 1930s.

After a year's research, he produced a 30,000-word "treatment," and his agent, Roberta Pryor (Mark Hanna had died), began shopping it around. The second editor who read it was enthusiastic. He called Finis in, and their consultation ended with Finis's agreement to rewrite the treatment from a slightly different viewpoint. He set to work again, stimulated by the editor's encouraging letters. The revision took five months. Ms. Pryor sent it in and was told that the editor had just moved to a new publisher, one who, it developed, had no interest in such a book.

Finis wrote me:

> 12 Jan 81
> Picture Window Drive,
> Sunken Heights, Maine.
>
> ... I was sitting here munching on a box of Lowney's chocolates, and humming the latest song-hit, "Henry's Made a Lady out of Lizzie," when the postman brought me the news that my book had been rejected. It's a good thing that I not only am independently wealthy, but have a steady market for my stuff at *McClure's*, *Ainslee's*, *The Literary Digest*, and *Everybody's* ...
>
> P.S. What do you bet that the Sioux City Hilton doesn't have a "Sitting Bull Cocktail Lounge," and that the restrooms aren't labeled SQUAWS and BRAVES?

By May, two more editors had turned down his book; and by June, a fifth. He wrote me:

Roberta [Pryor] assures me that all the rejections are "respectful." I'd rather have an impudent acceptance. She's now trying still another editor. Know what I want?—*all* I want? It's to quit work, take three drinks a day, have the complete works of Trollope on my bed-table, and be granted leisure for writing foolish letters to my friends. Pipe when so disposed c/o *Billboard*, Cincy.

—*One-Eyed Jacques,*
riverboat gambler

Toward the end of December, he wrote me:

Having cabled my Christmas greeting to the Pontiff and denounced all caitiffs, I was taking my mastiff to visit the bailiff, when I noticed a strange vehicle in my backyard— a chariot with wings, if you can imagine such a thing. Puzzling, eh? Well, may your ship o' dreams find the port o' happiness!

It was the last letter I ever had from him. Two days after the New Year, his brother-in-law telephoned me: Finis had died of a heart attack. As soon as the news reached Roberta, she rang up the editor who had been sitting on the 1930s ms. since June. Before she could speak, he said cheerily, "Great that you should call me at this moment! I was about to call *you*, to tell you that we're taking the Farr book."

Bill Buckley's obituary of Finis in *National Review* spoke of him as "a dear man and steady friend . . . a happy patriot, one of the disappearing band of conversationalists and writers of letters." All true. Further to Bill's last phrase, Roberta wrote me, "How dismal my mail is now, without Finis's jokes, his charming bits of esoterica, his stories and his erudition!"

Her mail and mine.

HUGH TROY

1906-1964

The Master Flabbergaster

Hugh Troy and his briard, Kimberly

Sit, gods, upon your thrones,
and smile at Troy!
—*Troilus and Cressida*

I once saw Professor Einstein, from a distance; and I once met Walt Disney; but the only authentic genius I ever *knew* was Hugh Troy. He was rated one of the ten best mural painters in the country; he wrote and illustrated three delightful books for children (the New York *Herald-Tribune* praised his *Five Golden Wrens* as "the best children's book of 1943"); but his genius lay in neither of these directions. Painting and writing were merely his diversions; his profession was practical joking, and at this he was supreme. Hugh Troy was not just "one of the ten best" or "the best of nineteen-something"; he was *the* best—the *very* best—for all time. Harpo Marx called him "the most eminent practitioner of the art." Tom Wolfe said he was "a Leonardo, the free-style practical-joke champion." The Washington *Post* said simply that he was "the master." I say "Amen!"

A.J.A. Symons spoke of "that vexing form of illiteracy, the practical joke." Ordinarily, I'd agree. I'd sooner boast of knowing a rock star than a practical joker; and rather than invite one home for dinner, I'd invite Typhoid Mary or a poltergeist or even a male tennis champion. But I'm proud to remember that Hugh Troy and I were close friends for thirty years, and that during the four of them when we worked in the same office, there was a beaten path between his house and mine.

Hugh was special, unique. What set him apart was that he spoke a language completely different from the exploding cigar, the dribble glass, the snatched-back chair, and the vulgarities that bridegrooms sometimes suffer at the hands of their ushers. His jokes never hurt anyone. His object never was to embarrass you, much less cause you pain or fright; it was to bewilder you, flabbergast you. The response he sought wasn't "Ouch!" but a dumbfounded "Hey, what goes *on* here?"

That's just what he got from some weekend guests of mine. Over cocktails, one of them remarked to me, "We haven't seen your bird yet."

"What bird? There's no bird here."

"No? Then why all that stuff in our medicine cabinet?"

I went to the guest bathroom. The standard supplies were there—aspirin, Kleenex, nailbrush, Bromo, and the rest—but they had been supplemented by two packages of Ajax Nesting Hair, one of No-Nits Plumage Powder, and a can of Supershell Eggshell Conditioner. I could imagine my guests' wild speculations:

"What do you suppose he *does* with that nesting hair? No, I'd rather not think about it!"

"And the eggshell conditioner: brush his teeth with it? Maybe he—"

Hugh's hand, of course. I suddenly remembered a recent evening when he had dropped in for a drink. I'd been called to the phone and held there, and Hugh had wandered upstairs. Now, when I confronted him, he said, "I like setting little time bombs and wondering who'll find them."

He told me about a small general store near his house when he lived in Garrison, New York. The proprietor happened to mention that he'd be closed the following Friday and Saturday while he took inventory. Hugh immediately drove to a neighboring town, to a similar store, and bought twenty dollars' worth of miscellaneous staples—light bulbs, paper towels, flyswatters, mousetraps, screw drivers—and smuggled them onto the shelves of his local store. "Shop-stuffing," he called it. "Makes a nice change from shoplifting, don't you think?"

Another of his time bombs, one that now—alas!—will never explode, was the mural he painted for the Bowery Savings Bank, in a branch that was razed some years ago. The scene was South Street in downtown Manhattan in the heyday of the clipper ships, which the artist showed moored side by side, with their bowsprits overhanging the street. The ship in the foreground was a brave sight, full-dressed with signal flags. Their message, composed by Hugh but prudently not submitted for his employers' approval, was KEEP YOUR MONEY IN YOUR MATTRESS.

Hugh also helped paint and letter the huge globe of the world in the lobby of the *Daily News* building, on East 42d Street. Proof of his work lies near the globe's South Pole, where you can find the "Troy Islands," an otherwise nonexistent archipelago.

Hugh was born on April 28, 1906, in Ithaca, New York, where his father was professor of dairy chemistry at Cornell. In childhood, three questions goaded his imagination: What is "pinking"? (He had seen a sign in a dressmaker's window, "Pinking Done Here.") Where is the Donzerley Light? (Our national anthem asks if you can see by it.) And what is the Great White Also? (His natural history book said that "Among the largest animals on our continent are the black bear, the brown bear and the great

white also.") The Also haunted his dreams. Long after he had
identified it, he was ashamed of his timidity until he read that
Theodore Roosevelt had had a similar bogey: the zeal, which he
had encountered in Psalm 69:9: "The zeal of thine house hath
eaten me up." Still more confusion was generated in young Troy's
mind by this verse in a hymn: "Jesus is sneaking through Hum-
boldt Park." His grandmother clarified it for him: "Jesus is
seeking the humble heart."

No indication of genius appeared until the boy reached fourteen, but the prank that then led off his record was a manifest
promise of the *chef-d'oeuvres* to come, although it displayed a
quiet purity and simplicity that would not always mark his later
handiwork.

The Christmas Eve service at a church in Ithaca was almost
over when Hugh entered, brushing snow from his overcoat as he
tiptoed up the center aisle to a front pew. The congregation
buzzed with surprise; the night sky had been clear when they came
in. They were even more surprised to find it clear when, presently,
they went out. Hugh's "snow" was borax.

His next prank grew from his sister's mockery of some verses
he had written. Hugh indignantly offered to bet her three treats to
the movies that he could write verses good enough to be printed
in *The New York Times*. She took the bet. Forthwith, "Miss Julia
Annsbury, Auburn, N.Y." (young Hugh) wrote to enquire of
the *Times*'s Sunday book review section if anyone could help her
identify a poem about "a gypsy lass struck ill on the trail and left
behind by her heartless tribe." Miss Annsbury's letter ended, "It
has obsessed me since childhood, and I beg your readers' help."

Some weeks passed. Then, "Why, yes," replied "Poetry Lover,
Rahway, N.J." (Hugh again), "I happen to remember the poem
that Miss Annsbury seeks. It is the beautiful 'Curse of the Gypsy
Mandolin,' by the poet laureate of Ithaca, N.Y., Hugh Troy, and
if memory serves, the final stanza goes like this:

"So we leave her,
So we leave her,
    Far from where her swarthy kindred roam,
In the scarlet fever
In the scarlet fever
    In the scarlet fever convalescent home."

Hugh entered the Cornell School of Architecture with the class of 1926, but transferred to Fine Arts and dropped back to '27. No use. He was too firmly committed to practical joking to find the necessary time for his studies, and when he left, he was unable to take with him the academic degree he had hoped for. What he did take was a reputation that had already overflowed the banks of Lake Cayuga and was trickling down to every campus in the Ivy League. Except Jack Slagle, the Princeton football star, Rudy Vallee, the Yale crooner, and Lucius Beebe, the Harvard bon vivant, the most celebrated undergraduate of his day was Hugh Troy of Cornell. He was already Shakespeare's "Troy . . . bright with fame."

"Hugh Troy? Sure! It was Troy who conned Ithaca into believing that a rhinoceros had fallen through the ice and drowned in the city water supply."

"Hugh Troy? Isn't he the fellow who faked the crash of a goodwill flight from Amsterdam, Holland, to Amsterdam, New York?"

"Hugh Troy? They tell me he borrowed some professor's overshoes and painted human feet on them, complete with bunions, corns, cracked toenails and the rest, then covered them with lampblack, which washed off in the first puddle."

Your ear caught snatches like this wherever college men gathered. The latest Troy story was an infallible icebreaker. Together they were the currency of intercollegiate conversation. So I knew Hugh's name and some of his more spectacular pranks long before we met.

Most certainly I hadn't expected a leprechaun or a pixie, but neither had I expected the creature that now faced me—one that stood six-six and weighed 225 pounds (a useful size for a practical joker, if one of his jokes backfires). He was too loose-hung for his gait to be called "walking"; he *shambled* and *lumbered.* He could have skied on his enormous bargelike shoes. His shirttail usually hung out. His friend H. Allen Smith said that Hugh was "a gentle giant" and wrote that "when he entered a room, he seemed to bring with him at least four frisky Saint Bernard dogs, all dressed in his clothes and all laughing and playing the piano and winding up clockwork toys." Another of his friends, Stephen Potter, the *Gamesmanship* man, described him as "tenderly shining, like some eolithic dawn, softly mad, insinuatingly looming." *Tenderly* and *shining* and *softly* are lovely words, woven of gauze and gossamer, but I wonder if they are *quite* appropriate to someone who, as a university senior, had published a parody newspaper featuring an article with this headline:

PRESIDENT BREAKS WIND FOR
NEW AERONAUTICAL COLLEGE

When Hugh and I met, he had been in New York for a year or two. He had come straight from Cornell to the studio of Ezra Winter, the muralist, as his assistant and apprentice. Commissions were plentiful. He did murals for banks, restaurants, nightclubs, private houses, the lobbies of theaters, and the foyers of hotels. They ranged as widely in size as in subject. One, for a Park Avenue bathroom, was a small panel of pink pigs, dancing (he also decorated Bernard Baruch's bathroom). Another, done for the Café Lounge at the Savoy Plaza Hotel, showed elegant gentlemen and ladies in antebellum costumes, and covered 1,500 square feet.

He was wise and lucky to have fattened his savings account this early, because the lean years of 1929–32 were close ahead. Many of his fellow artists not only were out of work, but were out of food and shelter. Hugh had rented a third-floor walk-up, one large room and bath, at 16 Minetta Lane in the Village. Here he spread mattresses and springs on the floor to make a harem-type bed, seven feet wide by fourteen long (the famous sailmaker, Ratsey, stitched the sheets for it), and his grateful friends moved in.

One of them said, "I became an involuntary witness to Hugh's generosity. No one ever knew how many meals he bought for us. He just quietly gave. But my fondest memories center around his wonderfully gentle and kind disposition. In the years I knew him, from the twenties into the thirties, I never heard him utter an un-kind remark about anyone." I myself would add, "Nor utter a word of blasphemy or obscenity."

Despite the demands of hospitality and of his hobby, painting, he found the courage and resolution not to neglect his profession, practical joking. Some of "Troy's proud glories" were created during this period—excavating Fifth Avenue, for instance; per-fecting a portable fireplug of balsa wood, to assure himself a parking space in front of his apartment; releasing dozens of huge moths (*Samia cecropia*) in a movie house, where they instantly flew into the beam from the projector; and, most notably, "steal-ing" a bench from Central Park. The press picked up many of these stories; by now they are too well-known to need repeating here. But others that Hugh told me—

Correction: Instead of "Hugh told me," make it "I dragged from him." He never volunteered an account of his pranks, but if I had happened to hear about one new to me and asked for details, he would furnish them, often in such hilarious abundance that I had to take notes on the spot, for fear of forgetting something precious. Even so, my notes often failed me. The stories came so thick and fast, my pencil couldn't keep pace, and I didn't dare slow Hugh down for fear of breaking the flow. For instance, one of my notes says only:

Baldwin's Fish Market—Cohen's Grocery.
>"Roe, Roe!
>Shadroe!
>Beat Cohen's!
>Let's go!"

If the anecdote hadn't been funny, I wouldn't have bothered to jot down these key phrases; but what are they the keys to? I have forgotten.

Fortunately my notes on the Subway Series are more nearly complete. Soon after Hugh's arrival in town, he discovered the subway system's potential for pranks, and it immediately became one of his playgrounds. If, he found, you put a token in a turnstile slot but didn't enter (thereby not turning the stile forward), it couldn't be turned backward to permit exit. The beauty of the game was that it was self-fueling: people trying to leave the platform were locked in, because everyone trying to enter put a token on top of the one waiting to drop. Hugh reckoned that he could paralyze the whole Times Square station for $1.90.

The game could be played at any station, but Times Square had a feature that invited another of Hugh's games, one that let him exploit his height. Above some of the turnstiles were I-beams low enough for him just to reach their ledges. Once he realized this, the script wrote itself:

Go to the station at a dead hour and stash a token on a ledge. Come back at rush hour, get in front of your turnstile, and pretend to search your pockets while an impatient file builds up behind you. Snap your fingers, as if at a sudden recollection, reach up to the ledge, retrieve your token, deposit it, and pass on through. (A ledge just out of normal reach on the south side of St. Thomas's Church, at Fifth Avenue and 54th Street, served as another of Hugh's caches. So did the Second **O** in the big aluminum sign of Hanscom's Bake Shop nearby.)

Hugh had a large repertory of subway games. I remember the
Artificial Leg, clad in a woman's stocking and slipper, which he
would smuggle into the car under his overcoat and teasingly expose when he took his seat. I remember his feigned absorption in
a Chinese newspaper, to the puzzlement of his fellow passengers.
Granted, any merry-andrew could have done as much, but only
a Hugh Troy—I submit—would polish his prank to the point of
producing a red crayon and, with loud, attention-attracting
chuckles, circling items here and there. And I remember the Sore-
Tooth Drama, which was inspired by his dentist's showing him
a box of extractions, cleaned and sterilized. Hugh begged one,
painted its roots with mercurochrome, and put it in his mouth.
Then, in the subway, he clutched his jaw and began moaning,
louder and louder. When he had drawn the sympathetic looks of
the other passengers, he gave a final moan, "wrenched out" the
property tooth, and flung it on the floor, "bloody" roots and all.

Hugh's favorite subway game required an accomplice with a
handkerchief in his breast pocket. He and Hugh would enter a
car from opposite ends and slowly make their way toward each
other. When they met face to face, Hugh would try to stifle a
sneeze, but couldn't. Just before it exploded, he'd pluck out "the
stranger's" handkerchief, sneeze into it thunderously, and tuck it
back, with "Thank you, sir!"

"Not at all," the other would say. "Any time." Friendly nods,
and they would separate.

Hugh seldom made use of accomplices. The only other instance
I recall was when he persuaded his cook's teen-age daughter to
enroll in a short-story class taught by a friend of his. Hugh paid
her tuition and wrote all her stories, to the end that week after
week the bewildered instructor found himself reading accounts of
certain naughty episodes in his own career, ostensibly imagined
by a young black girl. Names and places were slightly changed,
but the intimate details matched the facts. Hugh told me he could

have kept it up for weeks, if he hadn't carelessly sent in a story containing an incident that only he and the instructor could have known about.

By now, the late 1930s, Hugh's genius was reaching full flower. He had outgrown his primitive pranks in the subway, and was ready to begin staging his masterpieces. One of the first was the Episode of the Phantom Passenger:

A friend of his, Harry ————, had played him a Trojan trick. He had invited Hugh to dinner and asked him to escort a certain young lady, a newcomer to town. When Hugh went to fetch her, she proved to be a circus midget, thirty-nine inches tall—precisely one-half Hugh's own height. Other jackanapes could have warned Harry that he was playing a very, very dangerous game, as they had discovered for themselves, and painfully; but several months passed without reprisal, and Harry began to boast that the score was Self, 1; Troy, 0. Then word reached Hugh that Harry was planning to sail for Europe, on the SS *Goliath*. Hugh happened to know the president of the line, and called on him with two requests. First, could he arrange for Harry to be alone in a double stateroom? Answer: It's off-season, the ship is not nearly full; no problem. Second, might Hugh have access to the stateroom on the morning before the midnight sailing? Answer: Nothing easier.

So foolhardy Harry, bulging with farewell champagne, wove his way to his stateroom, and what met his horrified and unfocused eyes?

Item: On one of the berths, a cheap, tattered straw suitcase with a broken handle.

Item: Tumbled beside it in an unsavory and insanitary heap, a suit of soiled underclothing, a sleazy shirt, and a pair of raucous socks, frayed at toes and heels.

Item: Hanging from the rim of the basin, a used cornplaster.

Item: In the toothbrush holder, a brush of a color suggesting that it had cleaned a farmer's boots.

Item: Stuck in the frame of the mirror, two obscene photographs.

Harry was a young man of delicate sensitivities. He reeled at the thought of sharing his stateroom with this—this *animal* for seven days and nights. Well, damned if he'd share it that first night! He went to the smoking lounge and slept on a sofa, twitching and moaning. Next morning he steeled himself for the encounter and returned to the stateroom. No roommate. Gingerly he picked up the tattered straw suitcase, to stow it far from his offended sight. Under it was a note:

BON VOYAGE!

HUGH

Hugh's counter to Harry's brash challenge employed merely the power of suggestion. His counter to the Truculent Cop was more direct and more vigorous:

In the 1930s, before you could drive through the Holland Tunnel, you had to stop at a toll booth, buy a ticket, and surrender it to a cop at the entrance, fifty yards farther along. One summer Hugh commuted through the tunnel every weekend, on his way to the Jersey shore, and every weekend, he found the same cop on duty at the Manhattan entrance. A big man, florid and burly and surly, he snatched the tickets with what seemed unnecessary vehemence. Hugh was slow to wrath, but his patience wasn't limitless, and when it had been exhausted, he took steps.

His first step was to buy a plaster cast of a left hand, life-size. (Artists' supply shops carry them.) Next, he worked a glove over it. Lastly, he glued a big hunk of ground beef to the wrist end. Now he was ready. He bought his ticket, drove a few yards, and pulled his car to the side, pretending to have engine trouble, while he used a quick-drying cement to fasten the ticket between the thumb and forefinger of the glove. After dawdling as long as he dared, to let the cement set, he took the wrist end in his left hand, pulled his coat cuff down over it, and drove up to the cop, who snatched the ticket as usual. With it came the hand, its wrist trailing horrid shreds of raw red flesh. Hugh saw this much. He saw the cop blanch and clap his hand—his *own* hand—to his mouth. Here, Hugh thought it wise to drive on.

The villain-victim in a third story of reprisal was a woman in Queens—a woman quite unknown to Hugh, who rang his number several times a day, day after day, insisting that he call to the telephone some man also unknown to him. Hugh, exasperated, finally asked her name, so that he could deliver the message when her friend arrived. The poor silly woman gave it, and a sharp ear could have heard the trap snap about her ankle.

Forthwith Hugh opened a campaign to "make her turkey-conscious." Neither I nor Allen Smith, nor any of the other Schliemanns who have dug into Troy, was ever able to discover why he chose turkeys as the instruments of his wrath; but Hugh swore a mighty oath that turkeys would soon "dominate her wretched life," and according to Allen's account in the New York *World-Telegram*, this is how he set about it:

> Mr. Troy began by buying a carton of Thanksgiving Day greeting cards, all with pictures of turkeys, and mailed them to the pest so that she'd receive one in every delivery. He sent her pamphlets from the Department of Agriculture on how to raise turkeys. He bought her a roasting pan, with directions for cooking a turkey. He subscribed her to poultry journals, and answered their advertisements in her name, and filled in entry blanks for poultry shows. Once a week he telegraphed her simply "Gobble! Gobble! Gobble!"

I showed a clipping of Allen's story to Hugh, and asked if anything important had been omitted. Hugh said, "Well, I don't know how 'important' it is, but I also had department stores mail her samples of Turkish coffee and Turkey-red carpeting, and

American Express prepared an itinerary for her tour of Turkey, and on Christmas I saw to it that she got a half-pound box of Turkish Delight, compliments of the Turkish ambassador. There was more, but I've forgotten it."

"How did the campaign end?"

"I had mercy on her eventually and laid off. But not before she'd changed her address three times, trying to dodge the bombardment."

No, for all his mildness and gentleness, Hugh was not a person to suffer affront gladly, to be imposed upon scot-free. *Nemo Hugh impune lacessit.* You could be certain of retaliation, though never of the form it would take. Observe that the ploy of the Truculent Cop came to a climax as sharp and sudden as a pistol shot; and that the Phantom Passenger was slower-paced and subtle—it had to sink in; and that the Plague of Turkeys was slowest of all—it was cumulative; weeks, even months, elapsed before its full effect was felt. Troy had more pitches than Sandy Koufax. These were only three: fireball, change-up, floater. Another of them I can't label. It was something like Christy Mathewson's "fadeaway," something like a spitter, and something like Frank Merriwell's famous "upshoot." Here it is in action:

Back in 1936, the *Official Postal Guide* printed a ruling that the owner of a rural mailbox must have his name "inscribed upon it in neat black letters one inch in height." Soon after the ruling went into effect, Hugh spent a weekend with friends on a farm in Pennsylvania. The sight of him at breakfast in his paint-speckled overalls (he was going to do a sketch in the orchard) reminded his host of the new ruling, and he asked Hugh to letter his mailbox. Sure, Hugh said. He shambled down to the lane entrance and was lettering away, chewing on a blade of grass, when a glossy car stopped and a glossy man called out, "Hey, bub! Whatcha charge for that?"

Hugh immediately became a yokel handyman. "'Pends," he said. "Letters *so* big"—gesture—"fetch six cent apiece. I also got a eight-cent letter. Fancier. I call 'er 'Little Beaut.'"

The glossy man flicked him a visiting card. "Like to do my box this afternoon? Just up the road, second house on the right."

"Plain letters or Little Beaut?"

The glossy man grinned. "I'll take a chance on Little Beaut."

"Okee-be-be-dokie," Hugh said, then added quickly, "Hold yer hosses a minute, mister!" He studied the card, pausing to scratch his head and stare at the sky while his lips and fingers did counting exercises. Finally he had it worked out. "Comes to a dollar thutty-six. Call 'er a dollar thutty-five even. Oke?"

"I'll see if I can scrape up that much." The car moved on up the road.

That afternoon the glossy man and his guests were sitting on his terrace when a handsome new station wagon drew up at the mailbox below. A chauffeur in whipcord and leggings set up two beach chairs, while a butler spread a luncheon cloth and anchored it with an ice bucket. Now came a second station wagon, identical, bringing two incandescently beautiful girls, along with Hugh, still in his speckled overalls, still chewing grass. The girls took seats and accepted glasses of champagne, and ooooh-ed and aaaah-ed in rapturous admiration as Hugh did his lettering. Up on the terrace sat Mr. Glossy, slack-jawed.

The job finished, Hugh shambled up to him and announced, "Thet'll be one thutty-five, mister. . . . Thanks. Pretty little place you've got here. Everybody's pretty well forgotten about that poisoned well by now. . . . Well, don't take no wooden nickels! Haw!" The chauffeur and butler packed up, and the station wagons drove off, leaving the terrace to God knows what feverish conclusions.

That's a nice story as it stands, I think: amusing, complete,

well-rounded. But I also think it could have been conceived and
carried through by almost any impish fellow, whereas I said that
Hugh Troy was a *genius*. This postscript helps prove it:

A few weeks later, the glossy man found a note in his neatly
lettered mailbox. It said:

> The Museum of Modern Art is preparing an exhibit of
> the mailboxes I have done, and since I consider yours the
> finest example of my Blue Phase, I hope you will lend it.
>
> *Hugh Troy*

MOMA had been an unwitting party to a Troy prank once before, in 1935, when it held the first American exhibition of Van
Gogh's work. Hugh carved a chunk of dried beef into the likeness of a human left ear and mounted it in a shadow box, which
he smuggled into the exhibition and covertly affixed to a wall.
Next to it he put a placard:

> This is the ear
> that Vincent Van Gogh
> cut off and sent to his
> mistress, a prostitute,
> December 24, 1888.

There were 127 items on display. Hugh's could hardly be seen
for the crowd around it—until MOMA's authorities indignantly
took it away.

One more story of "vengeance" belongs here, even though it is
incomplete. I don't know how the late Otto Kahn offended Hugh,
but I am told that Hugh was seen patrolling the sidewalk in front
of the Kahn mansion on Fifth Avenue, handing out cards that
read:

> OTTO KAHN
> Pants to Match your Coat

"Handing out cards" recalls a prank of Hugh's that I had almost forgotten. No, "prank" is the wrong word; "act" is closer, because this once there was nothing mischievous about what he did—quite the contrary. The date is 1930, when construction began at Rockefeller Center, and hoardings went up around the excavation. Hugh suggested to Mr. Rockefeller that portholes be cut in them, so that passersby could watch the work. Mr. Rockefeller liked the idea; the portholes were cut; people waited in line for a turn at them; and Mr. Rockefeller's biographer, Raymond Fosdick, hailed them as "a benefaction to mankind." Hugh followed up by printing cards that he handed out to the spectators, appointing them members of "the Sidewalk Superintendents Club" (a phrase of his own minting). Rockefeller liked that too; he even handed out some of the cards in person.

How did Hugh manage to accomplish as much as he did? In addition to his painting and his joking—each a full-time job in itself, you'd have thought—and pursuing his mysterious feud with Mr. Kahn, and serving Mr. Rockefeller as counselor-without-portfolio, and contributing to *The New Yorker, Esquire,* and the old *Life,* he wrote and illustrated those three charming books for children:

Maud for a Day (1940), in which a mule kicks a field goal for the Army team to win the Navy game, and is rewarded with a commission as Brigadier Mascot; *The Chippendale Dam* (1941), in which two pet beavers, Boulder and Croton, save a widow's house from watery ruin by building a dam with her furniture; and his best, *Five Golden Wrens* (1943), in which the birds nest in the King's crown and wake him every morning with songs so sweet that his melancholia vanishes, and happiness is restored to his kingdom. The Oxford University Press published all three.

The success of these books surprised no one who had ever seen Hugh in the company of children. One of his young friends wrote of him years later, "He was a warm, endearing man who responded to children with a childlike quality of his own." Another said, "He taught me to wet my finger and play a tune on the rim of a wine glass." And another, "Every child should have an Uncle Hugh." If Hugh had heard that remark, he might have chosen it for his epitaph.

By the time *Wrens* appeared, in 1943, two other interests were engaging his attention: one was a wife; the other, the Army Air Force. His wife was Patricia Carey, a handsome, merry girl, a graduate of Cornell and an alumna of the Sorbonne. They had only a few months together before Hugh was drafted. I won't follow his basic training; I'll pick him up in August 1943, at the Army Air Base in Richmond, Virginia, where he was a lieutenant in B Company of an engineer outfit—a lieutenant who had become thoroughly browned off at the landslide of paperwork that fell on his desk every day. A good half of it was utterly futile, he told me; he had to draw graphs and furnish statistics of no conceivable use to anyone; he was learning nothing and getting nowhere, and his contribution to the war effort was a big fat zero. He hesitated to protest to his C.O., who was not a sympathetic type. Hugh had discovered this when he was ordered to letter signs for the barracks washrooms:

DO NOT THROW BUTTS

IN THE URINALS

"Sir," Hugh said, deadpan, "I respectfully submit that the wording should be changed to '*into* the urinals.' As it is now, we are implying that the smoker is standing in the urinal when he throws away his butt, whereas 'into—' "

The C.O. snarled, "I'm not implying any damn fool such thing, lieutenant! Go do it like I told you!"

It was with misgivings, therefore, that Hugh made his pitch about the paperwork. The C.O. lived by the book. When he had heard Hugh out, he said, "If Washington wants you to do this paperwork, you'll do it. Yours not to reason why, as Shakespeare says. Surely you don't suggest that a mere lieutenant knows better than the chief of staff of the Army of the United States?" The operative word was "mere." It cocked a trigger that a gnat's weight—or a fly's, as it happened—could trip.

That afternoon, Troy was inspecting a mess hall. Although it was now midsummer, fly screens had not yet been issued; so the mess sergeant had hung up half a dozen of those sticky-paper spirals. Troy saw them, and the trigger tripped. Back in his office, he drew up a form:

FLY REPORT

B Company Mess hall, date _____

Fly-strip #1:

    Flies this week _____

    Flies last week _____

    Gain/loss (strike out one) _____

    Average flies per week _____

Fly-strip #2:

    Flies this week _____

    Etc.

---

and so on, for all six strips. Then he ran off a sheaf of copies, filled in random figures on the top one, worked out the totals and the averages, and sent the form forward, keeping a carbon for his files. His plan was to let the weekly carbons pile up for a month, then spread them in front of the C.O.: "See, sir, I told you nobody reads our flapdoodle!"

The month ended without an echo, and Troy was gathering his carbons for the confrontation when a distraught lieutenant burst

into his office: "You Troy? Thank God I caught you! I'm from A
Company. Listen, what's all this about some 'fly report' I'm supposed to turn in? The Old Man just got a rocket from Washington, asking why his fly reports weren't complete, and he's chewing
out every adjutant on the base. I wouldn't know a fly report if it
pinned a medal on me, but my clerk says he heard your clerk mention 'em. Brief me, will you?"

Hugh reeled. With a feeling that he had sown the wind and
was about to reap the whirlwind, he brought out one of his forms
and explained how to complete it.

"Gotcha!" the lieutenant said. "Thanks!—But wait! Hold on
a minute! There's one thing here I don't dig. You say 'flies this
week' and 'flies last week.' When you check your spirals, how do
you tell last week's flies from this week's?"

A genius capable of the grand conception of the Fly Report was
easily capable of working out its details. "A very good question!"
Hugh assured him. "You're the first who's had the vision to ask it.
The answer is"—and it came to him at that instant—"I have a
sergeant follow me around with a matchstick and a saucer of ketchup, and as I count each fly, he daubs it. No sweat at all! Some
sergeants prefer mustard as a dauber, but we here in B Company
find that ketchup has a certain quality that mustard lacks."

The lieutenant glowed. "How could the Nips and the Nazis ever
hope to lick a country that can dream up a system like that? Well,
I've got the pitch now. Thanks a million, chum! If it hadn't been
for you, my wife would be addressing my letters 'Pfc.' "

He rushed out, almost colliding with a C Company officer, entering with one from D Company. It developed that they had to
turn in some fly reports—or else; and what in the name of Robert
E. Napoleon was a "fly report"? Hugh sighed and reached into
his drawer for more forms.

Soon afterwards, he was transferred from the engineers to a
photo-interpreter school, and he never learned whether his whirl-

wind had harmlessly spent itself or had cut a swath of devastation. But he liked to think that somewhere in the Pentagon there was a Fly Report section, where its C.O., a bird colonel, spent half his time writing petitions in triplicate for "personnel increments," so that he could discharge his duties with the thoroughness their importance deserved.

We cut now to Guam in June 1945. A day or two earlier, Captain Troy had reported to the 21st Bomber Command, 20th Air Force, as chief of its Photo Interpretation Unit. He was sitting in the Air-Sea Rescue Officer's tent, waiting for him to turn up, when a lieutenant from Communications came in and handed him a dispatch, assuming that Hugh himself was the ASRO. Hugh glanced at it, saw that it was in code, and pretended to study it. In a moment, "Damn the Navy!" he burst out. "Damn 'em! *Damn* 'em!"

The lieutenant asked, "What's the trouble, sir?"

Hugh showed him the dispatch. "See what it says here? One of our B-24s had to ditch at—" He mumbled random numbers as his finger moved across the groups—"forty-eight, sixteen south, one fifty-two, seventeen east, which would put them at—let's see"— he seemed to be working out the position mentally—"yes, roughly sixty miles southwest of Rakanitzu Jima." (Recognize the technique? It was the Chinese newspaper in the subway.)

He "read" on: "The radioman had time to send out a Mayday before they ditched, and all eleven of the crew got into their rafts safely. A picket destroyer eventually came alongside, but as she was taking our boys aboard, her medical officer told her skipper that one of them had measles. The skipper said his ship was more valuable to the war effort than any B-24 crew—he couldn't risk being quarantined, so he ordered them all back into their rafts, and shoved off and left them. How do you like *that*? Just *left* 'em, adrift in the Pacific Ocean! *That's* why I say 'Damn the Navy!' Our 'sister service,' eh? Nuts!"

The lieutenant said, "I call that shameful, sir! Absolutely shocking! I sure hope it doesn't get into the papers. . . . But look here, sir: How's about we send a Cat [*Catalina*, the PBY, a seaplane] after those boys? A Cat can stagger along with an overload like that, and this way only its crew, just three men, would be quarantined. How's about it, sir?"

Hugh jumped up and grasped his hand. "You'll get a commendation for this!" he said throatily. "I'll see to it myself!"

It was a superb piece of improvisation, and the line "See what it says here?" shows Hugh's genius at its brightest and best. But the story left me unsatisfied, for a reason it took me years to identify. At last it came to me: what did the dispatch *really* say? Did it, by a wild coincidence, deal with an air-sea rescue? The next time I saw Hugh I asked if he had ever bothered to find out. He laughed. "Yes. I had to. It was something about how much black pepper should be issued to our mess per month. But I still don't know why it was delivered to Air-Sea Rescue."

General Curtis LeMay, commanding the 20th Air Force, was a strapping, scowling hulk, with a cigar locked in his heavy jaws. He was a first-class officer and airman, but not a clubbable type, not given to giggling at quips and pranks, not a man to be approached with a jaunty "Say, General, did you hear the one about the iceman and the young bride?"

Hugh had been warned about LeMay's dourness and resisted any temptation to test it—for about the first four weeks. Then circumstances overwhelmed him.

His job required him to examine the aerial photos that flowed through his office from the various commands in the forward area—Army, Navy, Air Force—to evaluate them and prepare a digest for presentation to LeMay at 0800 every day. The digest was Top Secret, limited to only three copies: one for LeMay, one for MacArthur, one for Nimitz.

The services worked together happily and efficiently, Hugh said. The only irritant was the Navy men's insistence on writing their reports in Navy terminology: "port, starboard, bow, stern, and all that salty nonsense." Still, he indulged their whim until July 29, when he began to receive photos of their air-strike against the Kure Naval Base, on Japan's Inland Sea. Among the ships most heavily hit was the battleship *Haruna*. It was Hugh who looked through the photos and appraised the damage, but it was his personal hobgoblin who wrote the report, thus:

> This big steamboat is tipping way to the left. One of its chimneys has been knocked down and is hanging over the edge. The floor is badly rumpled up in back. The walls are full of holes. The boxes that hold the cannons are every whichway. The front flagpole is broken off. Most of the windows have been busted out. It will be months before they can fix this boat to run again.

Hugh told me that he slid his report onto LeMay's desk and tried to sidle out. No luck. LeMay picked it up at once, and the very first sentence touched off a roar: "Troy! Come back here!"

Hugh stood there, sweating, while LeMay read to the end and flung the paper down. "God Almighty!" he said in a whisper. Then, back to his roar, "What the hell do you think you're doing?—trying to get me court-martialed or what? *Answer* me, goddammit!"

Hugh said meekly, "Sir, no, sir! But that Navy jive—I just got fed up with it, sir! If plain English is good enough for the rest of us, I don't see—" He fell silent.

LeMay swallowed hard and chewed his lip and swallowed hard again. Finally he managed to say, "You've got a point. There are times when I feel that way myself. . . . Okay, take your report back and write it up properly!"

"Yes, sir." Hugh was at the door when LeMay called him back: "One other thing"—now he was bellowing—"DON'T YOU EVER TRY TO PULL A TRICK LIKE THIS ON ME AGAIN!"

"No, *sir!*"

The war ended two weeks later, and Hugh came home. He and Pat found a house at Garrison, New York, on the east bank of the Hudson. What Hugh called their "abandoned eagle's nest" offered a beautiful view, but it had one severe drawback: it was directly across the river from the Military Academy, and when reveille roused the cadets at six in the morning, it also roused the Troys. Having risen reluctantly to the bugle, Hugh rose joyously to the challenge. He rigged a loudspeaker and an amplifier and at *five* a.m., he turned on a recording of reveille, full blast.

"Men poured out of the barracks," he reported, "rubbing their eyes and buttoning up, until an officer herded them back. The Academy got my message. After that they toned their bugles down."

I didn't see Hugh in his Garrison years. His beat was far from mine, which was now Washington. I had been brought there in 1949 by the Central Intelligence Agency, and charged with staffing its Political and Psychological Warfare section. Finis Farr, Howard Hunt, and a number of other brilliant idea-men signed up, and in 1951 I persuaded Hugh to join us. I was confident that our section offered an ideal field for exercising his unique combination of talents.

He spent eight years with the Agency. What he accomplished officially still carries a SECRET stamp; but what he accomplished unofficially is discussed freely and with laughter whenever his former colleagues meet. The most famous of all his pranks (possibly excepting the "stolen" park bench) belongs to this period. It "broke" in an advertisement that Hugh placed in the Washington *Post*:

Too busy to paint?   Call on:

THE GHOST PAINTERS

1410 35th St., NW   Phone MI-2574

WE PAINT IT—YOU SIGN IT!

Primitive (Grandma Moses Type),

Impressionist, Modern, Cubist,

Persian, Abstract

Why Not Give an Exhibition?

I'm not going to describe the monstrous beanstalk that instantly sprang from this small seed.* It is enough to say that Hugh's telephone and doorbell went mad, and that reporters and the wire services spread the story so widely that the *Times* of London picked it up and ran an editorial branding ghost-painting as "another of the many ills that beset American society."

Hugh was delighted, of course. Nothing made him happier than having one of his jokes taken solemnly, unless it was being preternaturally solemn himself about something basically silly. A case in point was his response to a new directive that required any CIA employee who had conversation with a newspaperman to report it at once, in writing and in full, *no matter how sterile the topics had seemed.*

One of Hugh's next-door neighbors was a newspaper publisher. They often left their houses at the same time in the morning, met on the sidewalk, and exchanged greetings, with perhaps a comment on the weather. This Hugh duly reported, with mounting impatience at the purposeless waste of time. Did the Fly Reports now recur to him? They may have, because he resorted to the same tactic of compliance to an absurd extreme:

7:00 p.m. Was having dinner with my wife when interrupted by low rap on front door. [The "low" rap is a beautiful

---

* A full account of this and many other pranks of Hugh's can be found in *Laugh with Hugh Troy,* by his cousin Con Troy; Trojan Books, 1330 Cleveland Ave., Wymomissing, PA. 19610; $13.95; abundantly illustrated.

Troy touch.] Investigated. Opened door and at first saw no one. Then looked down and saw Leroy, last name not available, a representative of *The Washington Post*. Conversation ran as follows:

"Hello, Leroy. How are you?"

"Fine, Mr. Troy. How are you?"

"Fine, Leroy. What's the bad news?"

"Same old bad news, Mr. Troy. I come for the money."

"How much do I owe you, Leroy?"

"Two weeks, Mr. Troy."

"Here you are, Leroy."

"Thank you, Mr. Troy."

Conversation terminated. Subject Leroy disappeared down street.

I had resigned from CIA when this happened, so I can't vouch for the story that Hugh's outraged superior hand-carried the report all the way up to the Director, fuming and demanding disciplinary measures. The Director read it (the story goes) and laughed until he fell out of his chair. But I was still on hand when a piece of Hugh's nonsense infected our whole section and brought production to a temporary halt. Years before, he had written me on a letterhead of his own design:

SHIRLEY, GOODNESS & MURPHY
Private Detectives
"We follow you all the days of your life."

Something now brought this wonderful title to mind. I mentioned it in the office, and everyone immediately took up the game. That first flurry of enthusiasm produced the Office Clock-Watcher, Willys Scarlett O'Dea; the Agency Chaplain, Rev. Evans A. Bove; the Fattest Girl in Town, Ella van Dass, and a pair of lawyers, Abe S. Karpis and Duke S. Teacomb, with their secretary, Effie Davids. Then we turned to law firms; Taggart, Taggart, Byrne & Bright was one, and Finis Farr added another: Myers, Terhune, De Holgaard & Bonjavue. The word was getting around. The mail brought a gem from John Falter, who'd heard about the game from Corey Ford, who'd heard about it Lord knows where; John's gem was a brokerage firm: Howard, Jalecki, Polk & De Puss. We tried to put together a theatrical stock company and came up with the leading lady, Nathalie Kladd; the villain, Curtius Foyle Duganne; the character man, Seth M. Ortlebard; the juvenile, Gellish Lofter; and the soubrette, Ginny Breth; but we never found a satisfactory ingenue. Hugh's final contribution was the Pullman Porter, "Smokey" Carr-Ford, his wife, Dinah Carr-Ford, and her friend, Polly Carter de Reah.

When the game had burnt itself out, and the office got back to work, we agreed that Hugh's original* private detective agency was still the cleverest title of the lot, and that a close second was:

AUBER & WEIR

Landscape Architects
Tarns and Woodlands a Specialty

Hugh left CIA in 1960. I still saw him and Pat from time to time, though not so often as I'd have liked. One evening he rang me up. "I'm alone," he said, "and you know how people hate to drink alone. Something shameful about it. —No, I'm not coming to your place and I'm not inviting you over here. I just want to tell you that I've got the drinking-alone problem licked. You take your first drink and when you're ready for your second, you dial a certain number—I've got to clear this with the phone company, but say it's Adams 0001. A man's voice says, 'A bird can't fly on one wing! Here's how!' You finish your second and when you're

---

* By "original," I don't mean to suggest that the name game originated with Hugh. Joyce's *Ulysses* (1922) speaks of "Lord Winterbottom, a cold stern man," and I daresay still earlier examples can be found.

ready for your third, you dial Adams 0002, and another man's voice says, 'Nothing more useless than a two-legged stool! Good health!' And so on until you've had your fourth drink, or maybe your fifth or sixth. You dial again and this time you hear a barbershop quartette singing 'Sweet Adeline,' only they're leaving the second-tenor part open for you."

Hugh was alone much of the time now. He was in and out of hospitals, suffering from a terrible depression. He neglected his work, ignored his mail, and discouraged his friends from calling. Allen Smith became so worried that he flew to Washington, and the two of us went to Hugh's apartment. We rang his bell and knocked. No answer. We could hear him stumbling around inside so we called, "Hugh, it's Allen and Joe. Let us in, will you?" We rang and knocked again. Finally a thick voice said, "Please go away."

In a few days I received this note:

July One, '64

So damn sorry I couldn't see you when you were here. It was one of those situations when I couldn't see anybody, even the doctor.

I hope you and Allen will forgive me and will accept my thanks for coming.

Much love
Hugh

I had to go abroad for several weeks. When I returned, I was told Hugh had died. I repeat: he was a genius.

APPENDIX

I am treating this story as an appendix because Hugh was not the star. He was responsible for what happened, but he didn't *contrive* it. He—enough: if I explain any further, I'll kill the point.

The scene is Guam again. The war was over by now, and the men were impatient for Uncle Sugar and their discharges—not only impatient, but "island happy," restless and edgy. One night at the Officers' Club, Hugh asked if anyone could suggest a fresh form of entertainment as a safety valve.

A SeaBee captain said, "Why don't you get Mrs. Johnson's hula troupe? They're a smash hit wherever they put on their show."

Hugh didn't ask for details, except Mrs. Johnson's address. He borrowed a jeep and bolted there at once. She proved to be a native Guamanian, dignified and well-educated, the widow of a Marine corporal who had died in a prison camp. Hugh told her that her troupe had been recommended and asked if they were available for that Saturday evening.

Mrs. Johnson said, "Yes, we're free then. It happens we've just had a cancellation. How many girls do you want?"

"How many have you got?"

"Forty, give or take a couple."

The only "theater" at Hugh's disposal was the small, narrow mess hall. He pictured it jammed with forty writhing girls and a hundred and twenty roaring soldiers. "I'm afraid we haven't room for that many," he said. "About fifteen is all we can handle."

Mrs. Johnson said, "That's all right. Will my girls be allowed to dance with the men afterwards? The last camp we went to, the chaplains said no, and the girls were furious."

"Don't worry about that, Mrs. Johnson. By the way, how much do you charge for a performance?"

"Charge? Nothing. The girls like to have a good time."

Hugh went back to camp, wondering if he had a tiger by the tail. With some misgivings, he posted this notice on the bulletin board:

---

15 BEAUTIFUL GIRLS 15

The World-Renowned Johnson Hula Dancers Have Consented to Give an Exhibition in Our Mess Hall this Saturday at 1900 Hours

15 BEAUTIFUL GIRLS 15

They GYRATE!

They OSCILLATE! !

And they WRIGGLE! ! !

(HOW They WRIGGLE! !)

One night only

15 BEAUTIFUL GIRLS 15

Guamanians are an extremely handsome people, with pale, copper-colored skin, so Hugh had no qualms about billing the girls as "beautiful," sight unseen. Then he posted a second notice:

THE CHAPLAINS REJECT

ANY RESPONSIBILITY

FOR THIS PERFORMANCE

Saturday morning, he detailed four men to knock together a stage of sorts at one end of the mess hall, and to rig a draw curtain all the way across it. That afternoon, two six-by-six personnel carriers were sent to pick up Mrs. Johnson and the troupe. Long before they were due to return, the mess hall was packed, and the men were whistling, hooting, stamping, and wolf-calling. When Hugh heard the carriers grind up the hill, he went outside to meet them. The drivers had been grinning and licking their lips when they left; now they seemed strangely quiet. Mrs. Johnson climbed down, followed by her troupe. The eldest of the fifteen girls, Hugh learned later, was just eleven years old.

The rest of this story is exactly as Hugh told it to me:

"Children! I couldn't believe it! Three or four of them were little boys, spotless clothes, hair neatly brushed, giggling with excitement. The little girls were—well, they were modest and demure, cuter than buttons. The whole lot, boys and girls, were absolutely adorable. I shepherded them backstage, and Mrs. Johnson gave me the program. I glanced at it, then stepped between the curtains and announced, 'The first number will be a solo by Señorita Rosa Batanga. A big hand for Rosa!'

"Here she came, cradling a doll almost as big as herself. (She couldn't have been a day over six years old.) The noise from the audience rose about twenty decibels. The men thought it was a joke or something. Then, as Rosa started to sing, the noise died away until there was absolute, pin-drop silence. Her song was 'Rock-a-bye, Baby,' and she sang it in a whispering little voice as she rocked the doll. When she finished, the silence held for a few seconds before the men began to clap their hands raw. You'd have thought it was V-J Day over again, from the shouting and cheering.

"The second number was another solo—correction: a duet— 'Little Sir Echo,' sung by Antonia Solan onstage, and one of the boys—can't remember his name—Ramon something—in the wings. Antonia wore a pale blue dress with crisp pleats. She'd sing 'Little Sir Echo, how *do* you do?' and Ramon would sing back, 'Hello! Hello! Hello!' His voice was so high and thin, you could hardly hear it above the chirping of the crickets, but the pair of them were another smash. They must have taken twenty bows.

"The third number was a hula, by four more girls. Their costumes were bodices and 'hula skirts,' made of strips of cellophane, and—as the Lord is my judge!—white long johns. You'd have busted out laughing if the children hadn't been so serious, so wrapped up in their performance. There were half a dozen more numbers—songs and dances—and then came the finale: Ramon, the boy who had been Little Sir Echo, came out and recited the Gettysburg Address, with gestures. I had a lump in my throat the size of a coconut.

"The instant Ramon was through, every man jack in the audience broke for the stage, half of them crying. It was a stampede! They swept up the children and carried them back to their seats and perched them on their knees, hugging them and patting them. Many of them brought out snapshots of their own children, and introduced them: 'Here's my Sue-Ellen. She's just about your age. I wish you could meet each other. I know you'd get along fine!' The men without snapshots just handed out Hershey bars and smiled a lot and cried a little. Everybody was on an emotional jag. Everybody went soft. Nobody thought of dancing. They all just sat there and made a fuss over the children until Mrs. Johnson said, 'Bedtime!' and took them home.

"Next morning, one of the chaplains told me what a wonderful evening it had been—'and frankly, what a *surprise*!' I didn't see any reason to tell him that he was no more surprised than I was."

GEORGE BOND

1909-1973

The Abominable Bond

George Bond, in civvies but still aboard ship

Scene 1: Brisbane, Australia, December 1942–June 1943.

ON Christmas Eve 1942, I, a lowly lieutenant in the U.S. Naval Reserve, reported for duty as ACIO, staff COMAIRSO-WESPAC. Reinflated, this comes to Air Combat Intelligence Officer on the staff of the Commander of U.S. Naval Aircraft, Southwest Pacific Forces. Our headquarters were in Brisbane, a dull city with little memorable about it; but during my six months there, I met a man who not only was far from dull, but was unforgettable. He was Lieutenant (j.g.) George H. Bond, Jr., USNR, an ACIO like myself; and he was unforgettable for having been the most impertinent, disrespectful scamp I ever laid eyes on, in or out of the service. Most of my witnesses are gone now, but time was when I could have mustered a dozen to testify that Bond was a rascal, a knave, and—this is the odd part—a good friend and a witty, delightful companion.

I met him soon after I arrived. Two of the clubs in town, the Brisbane and the Queensland, were offering guest cards to American officers, so I went to the Brisbane one idle day for lunch and there, to my surprise and pleasure, I bumped into a fellow Richmonder, my favorite bridge partner, "Kip" Chase. Our greetings were echoes: "Hey, how did *you* get here?" Kip was wearing the bars of an Army captain, plus enough other insignia to qualify as a one-man scrap drive. I pointed toward them: "All that tinware come with your soldier suit?"

Kip said no, it meant that he was an aide—to General Kenney, no less, commanding the Fifth Air Force. They were based at Port Moresby, up in New Guinea—"the septic tank of the Pacific," Kip called it—but luckily the general had to spend a good deal of time here in Brisbane, conferring with "El Supremo," General Mac-Arthur. My day brightened: I could see some grand slams ahead. I was telling Kip about my assignment when I heard behind me a loud, hoarse voice:

"Starve the bardies and stone the crows if it's not Chaplain Case!—Sorry: *Cap*-tain *Chase.* Why aren't you in New Guinea, Chase? Don't tell me the Japs are closing in on Moresby! I see the picture now: the Army is leading the retreat as usual, leaving our heroic Navy to hold the line."

Kip laughed. "Hello, George! Joe, this is George Bond, widely known as 'Tojo's Secret Weapon.' "

I turned and got my first sight of Lieutenant (j.g.) Bond. He was some years younger than I, which put him in his early thirties, but his cropped hair was already pepper-and-salt; I would come to believe that deviltry had grayed it. He was "bright-eyed and bushy-tailed," in a catch phrase of the period. His expression matched his rasping voice: it exuded impudence and brashness spiked with a lordly scorn. On the spot I made a bet with myself: that he wore his Navy cap not "squared," but cockily atilt. I won.

I could have bet also that when he talked to me, he would peck at me with his forefinger. He did so now. "You a college man, Brown?"

Kip said, "The lieutenant's name is not Brown; it's Bryan. Make a note of that. And until you get another half-stripe, you better call him '*Mister* Bryan, *sir*.' "

Bond ignored him and repeated, with another peck, "You a college man?"

I felt a prickle of irritation, but I wasn't going to let this bumptious j.g. see it. I said, "Princeton."

"Ah," he said, "that's almost the same thing, isn't it? Nothing to be ashamed of. On the contrary! Uncle Bull told me that Princeton men make first-rate troops. Give 'em white officers, and they'll go anywhere."

Before I could stop myself, I said, "Uncle Bull?"

"Halsey. He's not really my uncle, but he asked me to call him that, so I humor him. Part of my contribution to the war effort."

Kip said, "What was your college, George? Colgate, wasn't it?"

Bond clapped his right hand over his heart and gazed toward heaven. "Williams!" he said fervently.

This was my chance. "A natural mistake, Kip. I have the same trouble, telling those shaving-soap colleges apart." Whistler or George Kaufman or Dorothy Parker could have done better, I admit, but because this would be one of my very few scores against Bond, I quote it.

Bond laughed. "Good on yer, cobber! That's a fair crusher! You and I are going to rub along fine, pro-*vided* you mind your manners." He prodded me again. "Well, I've got to get back to the store. Ta-ta, mates." He slapped his cap on, cocked it over his left ear, and sauntered off.

Kip said, "Sassy, ain't he?"

"Very, but funny. What does he do to earn his pay?"

"He's on the staff of COMSOWESPAC, one of you Air Combat Intelligence Officers."

"Is that Aussie slang part of his job?"

"You'll understand when you meet his roommate. Porter Sulver, also a SOWESPAC ACIO. Sulver's a Trade School boy—"

"A what?" I was new in the Navy then.

"Do we Army types have to educate you swabbies in your own jive? A Trade School boy is one who went to the United States Naval Academy, a.k.a. Annapolis, or the Trade School, or if you want to be not only derisive, but offensive, the Factory."

"Thank you," I said humbly. "Thank you, you brass-trimmed GI."

Kip went on, "Sulver resigned from the Navy soon after graduation—'swallowed the anchor,' as he likes to put it—and rejoined right after Pearl Harbor. He hasn't been to sea since his midshipman cruise, but he talks saltier than Nimitz, King, and Halsey rolled into one. He and Bond are billeted in an old hotel down the street—it's typically Aussie; twelve bedrooms and four bars—and Sulver insists on calling their room a 'compartment' and the ceiling the 'overhead' and the floor the 'deck,' and so on, until Bond is ready to climb the wall—the 'bulkhead,' Sulver would say. So Bond's taken up Aussie-talk, complete with accent, in revenge and self-protection. By the way, do you know what a bison is?" (This, I would learn, is the standard question asked of all new arrivals in Australia.)

"A bison? Sure: it's a buffalo."

"Not down here it ain't! A bison is a plyce where Austrylians bythe their fyces."

I met Sulver a few days later. I was having lunch alone at the Brisbane Club—I never got used to the overdone steak with a fried egg on top, but the toheroa soup was a delight—when I heard a familiar loud, hoarse voice, and here came Bond, steering a Navy two-striper toward my table. "Don't get up for *me*," Bond said (I'd made no motion of the sort). "Let me introduce Lieutenant Tuna, the chicken of the sea."

The lieutenant scowled. "Belay that, Bond!" He turned to me. "My name is Sulver, Porter Sulver. Glad to have you aboard." When we shook hands, I noticed the Annapolis class ring on his other hand, "the Nugget on the knuckle."

He was a handsome man; his tan gabardine uniform fit beautifully; his buttons shone; his shoulder boards had just the right camber. Bond saw my open admiration and remarked, "No wonder my choom here is known far and wide as 'Sterling'; just as I'm known as 'Gilt.' Sterling Sulver and Gilt-edged Bond. Get it? Haw!"

"Pay no attention," Sulver told me. "Bond rattles on like an ammo hoist."

Bond groaned. "'Ammo hoist'! Will you listen to this overdressed fraud? 'Ammo hoist,' I ask you! I've wrung more salt water out of my pants than he ever sailed over! Know why this Stork Club commando joined the Navy? Because every occasion is black-tie. Sea boots by Peal, wings by Cartier: that's Sulver! He's eating his heart out for a ribbon to put on his blouse"—Bond pecked at the spot—"but the only one he'll ever get will come from a typewriter. 'Ammo hoist'! Why, you pool-parlor paratrooper—"

Sulver broke in, "Two-block your tie, j.g.! You can at least try to look like an officer."

So it would go, day in, day out, with Bond pecking and yapping at Sulver, and Sulver standing on his superior rank. Their exchanges may sound acrimonious, but they weren't at all. Bond and Sulver bickered merely as a form of exercise and as a relief from the boredom that pervaded our commands. It was a boredom that made you numb and kept you so. As for the war, Australia was the end of the line, with Brisbane at a comfortable distance from the combat zone. Except that the city's signposts were turned askew to foil an invader, and except for certain shortages—whiskey, vermouth, gasoline, cigarettes, golf balls—the war impinged on us scarcely at all.

COMAIRSOWESPAC, for all the might and majesty of his title, commanded nothing but one workhorse DC-3 in Brisbane and a few patrol planes, PBYs, at Perth, on the other side of the continent. The only attention any of them needed was mechanical, not strategic. An hour or two in the morning was enough for clearing my desk, and I was usually free for the afternoon. Bond's and Sulver's duties at COMSOWESPAC were even less onerous. The local golf clubs were as hospitable as the city clubs; Sulver didn't play, but Bond and I were able to get in a round once or twice a week. He'd pick me up in the ancient red sports car he had rented, and we'd clatter off to the Virginia Club or Indooroopily ("Sounds like throw-up," Bond said vulgarly). We weren't very serious about the game (or about much else), and it was pleasant to hack around in January's summer sunshine.

The serenity was too good to last. AIRSOWESPAC's Operations Officer was Commander Kent, USN, an Annapolis man and, like most of them, suspicious of us Reserves and—well, *distant*. One morning I was astonished to have him invite me to play golf next day. I already had a match, with Bond, but I told Kent we'd be glad for him to join us. I was a bit apprehensive about sponsoring the unpredictable Bond to the hard-lining Kent, especially after, on our way to the club, Kent happened to mention the Black Dragon Society, a secret, supermilitaristic clique in Japan, and Bond, assuming a transparently specious air of innocence, asked, "Anything like the Green Bowler Society, sir?" The Green Bowler was rumored to be a secret, superselect clique at the Naval Academy.

Kent glared at him and grunted, "I wouldn't know about that, and I strongly suggest that you pursue your interest in the matter no further."

Still, lunch at the Indooroopily Clubhouse passed quietly enough, with sandwiches and bottles of Tasmanian beer, though when we changed in the locker room, I was dismayed to see Bond pull on a T-shirt emblazoned

PARK FALLS, WIS.
"Home of the Fighting Muskie"

Kent looked pained, but said nothing, and the game began. It went slowly. If we lost a ball, there was no question of making only a perfunctory search; replacements couldn't be bought or borrowed. We waved the next match through and searched on. Thus we had finished only five holes when our lunchtime beer became insistent. Kent was the first to acknowledge it. He said, "I wish there was a head around here somewhere, but I don't even see a bush. Looks like it's ladies' day, too."

I said, "Hold everything, Commander. The next hole is blind. If you hit a straight ball, it'll be out of sight except from dead behind—dead *astern*, I mean—and Bond and I'll screen you while you do your business."

Kent accepted that. He had to. He drove nicely, walked—almost trotted—up to his ball, and had unzipped for action when Bond said doubtfully, "We-l-l-l-l, I don't know, Commander. You *may* be able to reach the green with that, but me, I'm going to use a four-iron."

Silence fell and time stood still while Commander Kent's complexion darkened to a thunder-cloud purple. Plainly he was debating whether to stalk off the course or promise Bond a court-martial or behead him on the spot. He ended by doing none of these. He laughed! It was a choked, grudged laugh at first, but it worked up to a full-throated guffaw, with me joining in from sheer relief.

When control was restored, Kent wiped his streaming eyes.

"Bond," he said, "you're the by-goddest j.g. in the whole U.S. Navy! If I had one wish, it'd be that you were in the Nip navy, preferably as some admiral's chief of staff. All right: carry on. Who's away?"

The next Bond-Kent rencontre took place a week later, at the bridge table. Kent had asked me to find a partner to make a fourth with him and our admiral. My usual partner, Kip Chase, had flown back to New Guinea with General Kenney—although Bond professed to believe that their real destination was safely in the opposite direction, and he saw Kip off at the airport with pleas to name a sled dog in his honor.

"Why not?" Kip yelled back. "Like you, they're sons of—" The revving engines drowned out the rest.

I didn't know many officers that early in my tour of duty, so—again apprehensively—I brought along Bond. We cut, and Kent dealt. As the bidding started, the admiral called, "Wait a minute! Full astern! I've only got twelve cards."

Bond instantly threw in his hand (I daresay a poor one), crying, "Misdeal! Misdeal!" and turned a reproachful look on Commander Kent. "Surely, sir, you know that every admiral is entitled to a quarter-deck!" Somehow he managed to suggest that Kent had short-carded the admiral deliberately, for some fell purpose.

The admiral laughed. "The boy's right, Kent. I'm entitled to a full quarter-deck and I want all that's coming to me. Thirteen cards," he added, in case anyone still missed the point. "Tell me, son," he said to Bond, "what year were you at the Academy?"

His bland assumptions (a) that there was only one academy, and (b) that Bond had of course attended it, were more than Bond's irrepressible impudence could accept in silence. His answer is branded on my memory: "What academy is that, Admiral?"

The Admiral puffed up like an angry turkey-gobbler and stammered, " 'What acad—' Why, I never—"

I cleared my throat vehemently enough to have dislodged my

tonsils, if I'd had any left, and made a noisy, clumsy business of
scrabbling the cards together, and reminding Commander Kent,
"Still your deal, sir! Still your deal!"

The game resumed. It was a set game; Bond and I were partners
throughout. Once when I was playing a hand, he cried, "Give 'em
a whiff of grape, Bryan!" and once when he was overtrumped, he
fell back in his chair, moaning, "Kiss me, Hardy!"; but on the
whole he behaved himself better than I had dared hope.

The cards ran evenly; the pairs were evenly matched; and halfway into the fifth and last rubber, the score stood at two-all, game-
all, with Bond playing four spades, which Commander Kent had
doubled. Kent took the first three tricks, but after that the hand
was a lay-down, and there was absolutely no excuse for Bond to
welcome Kent's next lead with, "That's the one that gives it to
us!" and to cackle as he spread his cards. Kent could have retorted that *any* lead would have given it to us, but he was too
furious to see this. He just glowered.

I said that boredom besieged us. Indeed, it threatened to become
so overwhelming that in a desperate attempt to hold it at bay, half
a dozen of us, including Commander Kent and myself, decided to
swear off drinking and smoking for Lent. The day before Ash
Wednesday, Bond and Sulver and I were lunching together when
Kent passed our table. Bond greeted him jovially. "Ah, there,
Commander! Lent begins tomorrow. What are you going to give
up, your ship?"

Kent did not reply. Bond himself was giving up nothing. He
said he'd conduct the fight against boredom in a positive and
vigorous way, by starting a mustache and watching it grow.

Giving up cigarettes was torture, but giving up booze was
comparatively easy. I didn't much enjoy the local beer anyhow,
and the local gin was a watery sixty-proof, sweetish to boot.
Besides, vermouth was not to be had; we had learned to make
do with dry sherry or beer stirred flat, but the combination

was still an insult to the noble martinis of fast-fading memory.

It took about two weeks for the pangs of the double withdrawal, cold turkey, to reach their almost intolerable worst. One evening around then, Bond joined me at the AIRSOWESPAC mess. We all sat at one big oval table, the admiral at the head, the rest of us anywhere. Bond, as it happened, found himself across from Commander Kent, who was grousing as usual about the idiocy of his pledge, and was trying to find a loophole through which he could reach a drink. Our flight surgeon, sitting next to him, was topping off his meal with a crème de menthe in a small coffee cup, and Kent argued that there was no valid reason why he shouldn't have one too, since it wasn't really alcoholic. His clincher was, "I *know* it's not! I've seen women drink it."

Our hoots of derision at the flimsiness of this evidence only made him bristle. "I can prove it!" he shouted. "Give me the rest of your cup, Doc!"

Doc slid it over, and Kent began looking for a match. Nobody at the table had one—we were nonsmokers, remember—so he went out to the kitchen. (All right, Sulver: the *galley*.) Bond, as I said, hadn't taken the pledge. Now he whipped out a cigarette lighter, one with a transparent reservoir. I'd seen it before. When I commented on its unusual design, he had remarked offhandedly, "Used to be Admiral King's. Ernie insisted I take it. Souvenir of a favor I'd done him." Now he unscrewed its cap, emptied it into Kent's cup, and pocketed it again. The whole job took only a few seconds. Back came Kent, with a match. He struck it and dropped it in. . . .

I think he was about to say, "See? What did I tell you!" but he had got no further than "See—" when there was a flash, and a soft *boom*! and a cloud of black smoke boiled up. Somebody yelled, "General quarters! General quarters!" Somebody else yelled, "Set Condition Modified Affirm!" The admiral guffawed. Doc demanded that Kent buy him a replacement drink. And in the uproar and confusion, Bond sneaked out.

He dodged Kent for the next week or so, but his impudence still ran at full throttle. Early one evening for instance, he and I walked through the Botanic Garden on our way to dinner at the Queensland Club. Two American Army officers came toward us. They were close enough for us to see that they were colonels when one of them cursed and snatched off his cap: a disrespectful bird had bombed it. As we passed, Bond remarked casually and clearly, "They sing for the Navy."

He was warming up for what followed. At the club, a rather drunken commander in the Royal Navy joined us, uninvited, and immediately let us know that he had been serving in the *Prince of Wales* or the *Repulse* (I forget which) when the Japs sank them in Sunda Strait, a few days after Pearl Harbor. Now, more than a year later, his terrifying experience was still fresh in his mind, and he gave us an account of it—a tedious and interminable account. I don't know how he succeeded in transmitting such vivid material into stodge, but he did, and as he droned on and on, Bond became restless, especially when the commander told the details twice over:

"Do you know, those Jap blighters strafed us in the water? Right there in the water! Swimmers and men in rafts alike. Up and down their planes went, up and down, strafing us with their little thirteen-point-seven machine guns. Up and down. Up and down. Up and down . . ."

When he paused to take another drink, Bond broke in, "Tell us, sir, how about you? Were you saved?"

"Oh yes, I was saved." Then it dawned on him. "*Of course* I was saved!" He struggled to his feet and lurched from the room.

I said, "Not funny, Bond. You should be ashamed!" But he never was.

One of Bond's tricks was to drop his voice almost to inaudibility, leading you to cup your ear and ask, "*What did you say?*"—

whereupon he, oozing sympathy, would tell you, "Oh, am I on your bad side? Sorry!" and he'd take a chair on your other side.

"You know," he'd go on, "I'm quite deaf myself, in my right ear." If you were foolish enough to enquire how, in that case, he was accepted by the Navy, he'd put on a noble look—part Casabianca, part Nathan Hale—and murmur modestly, "Waivers. My country needed me, so I brought pressure to bear on the examiners."

The fact is, Bond was no more deaf than a barn owl, not in either ear. He feigned deafness for one purpose only: so that he could walk on your right. I'd better explain that. The Navy's Emily Price Post was Captain Leland P. Lovette, and the etiquette chapters in his book, *Naval Customs, Traditions and Usage*, lay it down that "If walking with a senior, the position of honor is to the right." So Bond always maneuvered to be there, both for his own self-esteem and to suggest that the senior knew no better. Many a morning I saw him and his roommate, poor Sulver, leave their hotel for their office, with Bond on the left where he belonged; and before they'd gone twenty yards, he'd have bobbed up on the right.

COMSOWESPAC occupied the upper floors—"decks," in Sulverese—of a bank building on Queen Elizabeth Street. The first time Bond and Sulver took me there, Bond ushered me into the elevator and pointed to a familiar logo on the controls: OTIS. "As you see, this is an O-T-one-S," he explained, "the new Optional Turboplane, Mark I, by Sikorsky." He held the door while several more officers crowded in: all seniors, Americans and Aussies, airmen, with wings and ribbons. Bond included them in his audience. "There's absolutely no cause for apprehension, gentlemen. I've had a hundred and forty hours of stick-time in this crate. Besides, she almost flies herself. Fasten your shoulder harnesses, please. Aerology has warned us that there may be a turbulence ahead." He swung the handle, and we started upward. "Notice the smooth-

ness of our VTO. For the benefit of any nonflyers with us today"—
he fixed a contemptuous look on Sulver—"that means 'Vertical
Take-Off.' "

The officers laughed, but Sulver went pink with mortification. I
was afraid that turbulence was indeed ahead, for when we reached
their floor and got off, Sulver said, "Damn it all, Bond—!" But
Bond was already introducing me to their staff: "Ensign Benson
. . . Yeoman Bowman . . . Chief O'Keefe . . . Meet Lieutenant
Bryan. He's the genius who coined the fighting slogan, 'Back the
Attack from the Sack!' and was the natural model for the poster."

The staff seemed to enjoy Bond's foolery, and I admit that it
added savor to the slow, dull round of my days in Brisbane,
though perhaps not to Sulver's. Bond pestered him like a swarm
of gnats, calling him "John Paul Jones" and loudly accusing him
of every crime from barratry and bottomry to malingering and arrant cowardice. "*Lieutenant* Sulver?" Bond would sneer. "You
fellows low-rate him! He's actually a commander, a three-striper:
two on his cuff and one down his back."

Sulver might have retorted that he'd seen every bit as much
combat as Bond had—i.e., none—but he was too nice a man to
enter mud-slinging contests, whereas Bond reveled in them. His
Satan-sent talent for insult, surged to the fore whenever Sulver
mentioned Annapolis. Sulver once suggested, half-jokingly, that a
senior officer such as himself, "especially a graduate of the United
States Naval Academy," deserved more respect from a lubber like
Bond.

Bond pounced on that one. "Sulver, we'd be willing to forget
this bar sinister across your academic career, if you'd only stop
dragging it in front of us, like a dog with a dead skunk."

Bond would discourse for hours about the scars that an Annapolis education—"I use the term loosely"—left on "a clean,
innocent lad like John Paul here. Would you believe that he still

stores his gear the way that his Annapolis nanny taught him? Shoes with their toes at the front edge of the shelf; hankies folded so that no free corner shows; gloves laid with their wrist ends out; books 'sized off' on his desk, the tallest at the left. He still does it! John Paul *still* does it! He inspects himself in the mirror every day and marks himself 'four-oh,' as he calls it. Nanny taught him neatness, I'll grant that, though I'd hardly give him more than two-oh in toilet training."

Sulver cried in anguish, "*Really*, Bond! You have no more sense of decency than—"

Bond ranted on, "Know what he says he misses more than any-thing else? A *ge*-dunk, whatever the hell that is! Can you imagine a grown man pining for something called a *ge*-dunk? I wouldn't put it past Sulver for a *ge*-dunk to be a kids' mess, like a chocolate sundae!"—which is exactly what it is in Annapolis slang, as Bond very well knew. He also well knew that Sulver's Annapolis stiff-ness and air of superiority aside, he was a thoroughly good sort. So was Bond, for that. There was never any malice in his gibes; they didn't sting. He climbed Sulver because he was there. I never understood why Sulver put up with it. He was easily embarrassed and he hated being made conspicuous, and Bond exploited these weaknesses to the utmost. Why didn't Sulver strike off this "bond of iniquity"? There was much that he could have done to protect himself. As a lieutenant, he could have put the j.g. in hack, "con-fined him to quarters and to his job space"—or he could at least have *threatened* to; and Bond didn't know enough about Navy regulations not to have been intimidated. But Sulver held off, and Bond's deviltry suffered no check. "Deviltry" is right; Bond was a true "son of Belial, flown with insolence."

I remember an evening in the bar at the submariners' base. One of the officers asked Sulver if he knew when General MacArthur would be back from Port Moresby.

"Negative," Sulver said. "I haven't been told."

Bond overheard them and whispered loudly to another officer, "They keep things from him! They have to! Security risk!"

Far worse was his behavior one day at lunch at the Brisbane Club, when Sulver mentioned his fear that he had contracted trench mouth.

"Trench mouth? *Trench mouth?*" Bond repeated it in a voice that stilled every knife and fork within earshot. "Don't try to tell us you caught it from a toilet seat!"

His inexcusable vulgarity ran even to a chant he had picked up, probably from a West Pointer or a Naval Reservist:

"Annapolis! Annapolis! Rah-rah-rah!
Three dits, four dits, two dits, dah!"

(I forbear to decode.) Sulver's most casual reference to "the Academy" or, worse, to "Crabtown" would touch off the chant; and when he once declared (rather pompously) that "Annapolis men are the backbone of the Navy," Bond answered with a particularly raucous horselaugh: "Too right, cobber! And we all know which end of the backbone!"

Lent had dragged to an end; Bond's moustache had come to full flower (though it looked more like a dirty nailbrush), and numbness settled over us again. Suddenly I had a flash: Australia is famous for its parrots and cockatoos; why not buy a young parrot and pass the time by trying to teach him some ambiguous remarks? Forthwith, after foolhardy consultation with Bond, I put this want ad in the daily *Courier-Mail*:

Wanted: King parrot or
cut-throat. Must talk. BOX W 76.

I had been told that these two breeds were the most loquacious. I've forgotten what a king parrot looks like, but a cut-throat was a beautiful green except for a wide scarlet slash under his chin.

Several days passed before I had an answer. Here it is, verbatim:

Box W 76: I seen your ad about wanting a cut-throat. Well, I know plenty people who will be glad to accommodate you, ear to ear. Haw! Seriously, pal, I'm what you need. But first, what's this "must talk" stuff? Do you want a parrot or a stool-pigeon? If you got folding crackers, lay 'em on the line, and I'll blow my top. But no dough, no dice!

This here letter is being written by a certain little secretary bird who goes with the deal. I will entertain your proposition (along with the above-mentioned lady) in room 8 at the Grand Central Hotel any evening after 6.

—*Claude Parrot.*

Bond, of course. Eventually I bought a young cut-throat, but he was not a success. It was his molting season, and he spent it glumly plucking out his feathers, without even a croak or a whistle. Time may have brought a jet of witty apropos to his tongue, but I wasn't there to hear them. On June 23 our Communications Officer brought me a flimsy: ". . . . HERDET PROREP COMBATDIV 8" (. . . hereby detached. Proceed and report to Commander Battleship Division 8).

Bond and Sulver came down to the airport with me. Their farewells were in perfect character. Sulver said, "I'm happy to have been shipmates with you." Shipmates in an office building! Bond said, "I'm going to write ACI headquarters they were wrong. You *have* got some ability. [Loud aside] I love an uphill fight!"

Scene 2: Pearl Harbor, eighteen months later.

I was carrying my new orders to COMSOPAC for endorsement when I heard a familiar phlegmy voice: "Stone the crows! It's Left'nant Commander Bryan! I'd know that ragged haircut and rumpled uniform anywhere!"

Lieutenant (s.g.) Bond and I needed only a few minutes to fill in the long gap. He was eastbound to Washington for duty in the Navy Department, and I was westbound to join the staff of a carrier admiral somewhere off Japan.

Bond was incredulous. "*You* on a carrier? Somebody's been giving you a lot of *hoomalimali*. [Hawaiian for "nonsense."] They must have— Let me see those orders of yours."

I handed them over. He mumbled a few lines, pecking with his forefinger. "Just as I thought! They left out a word. See where it reads 'Carrier Division Six'? What they meant to write was 'Carrier *Pigeon* Division Six.' That's it, obviously. They'll start you out on cleaning the coops, and if you show any aptitude, they may promote you to giving the pigeons a rubdown after their hops. I knew you'd find your right slot, cobber!"

Scene 3: Air Combat Intelligence Office, Navy Department, Washington, six months later.

After three months on the *Yorktown*, COMCARDIV 6's flagship, I was ordered to the ACI home office. Some twenty or thirty of us ACIOs—including, George Bond—shared a big room. The war was winding down. It was summertime, and the duty was easy. We had typists to handle the few reports we were told to write, and there was little else to do but drink coffee and tell lies about our heroic exploits in far places.

Bond was the same noisy, amusing nuisance as ever, unchanged except that he had added another half-stripe to his cuff and several new annoyances to his repertory. One was to make his way to the rear of the office, unseen, and yell, "At-ten-SHUN!" Everybody jumped up, only to find Bond lecturing a junior officer: "—to small details is the mark of the four-oh commander and leader. Never forget this, son!"

Another prank was leave memos on our desks: "Tuesday, 1115. Bryan: Admiral King did not call." Or "Thursday, 1625. Stone:

No message for you again today." Or "Monday, 1400. Barnes: Punctually at 0920 tomorrow, Admiral Nimitz does not want to see you." All these memos were addressed to us by name, followed by "p2c." Someone asked Bond, the obvious culprit, what the "p2c" stood for.

Bond said, "It's the new rating the Navy Department has authorized for people like you: 'person, second-class.' "

One of our typists was a nice, quiet young girl who came from the Pennsylvania coal-mining area, bringing with her a Polish name—Zwipticicj, Zbignifets, something of the sort—so unpronounceable that in the interests of office efficiency we asked her permission to call her simply "Miss Z." Permission granted. One day Miss Z came back from lunch with a new hat, an appalling concoction of flowers, felt, ribbons, feathers, fruit, silk, and straw that made Carmen Miranda's wildest headdress seem as austere as a black beret. We were invited to admire it, which we did; we told her how beautiful it was, and how chic and how becoming. When she had withdrawn, beaming, someone wondered what had possessed so demure a girl to buy such monstrous millinery.

Bond had the answer. He said, "It's the first hat Miss Z ever saw that didn't have a lamp on the front of it."

The word "monstrous" in conjunction with "Bond" calls up the image of Bond and the monster WAVE j.g. She was one of the biggest, most formidable, and most overwhelming women I ever saw, more like a tsunami than a mere wave. She could have been a mud wrestler in civilian life; and she was as brash as she was brawny, indifferent to seniority and rank. I don't remember what business she had with Bond, but it required her to consult him several times a week in our office. As soon as she showed up, all his bumptiousness drained out of him; he cowered and cringed; he didn't dare peck *her*. His desk was in the row ahead of mine and three to the right, so I had a clear view of him, though he couldn't see me without turning around.

One morning the WAVE was towering over him, plainly demanding faster action, and Bond had steeled himself to put up a show of resistance. He was leaning back in his chair, his feet on his desk, pretending to be cool, unflurried. This was my chance. I dialed his number, and when he answered, I said in a low voice, "Bond, your fly's open."

He dropped the phone and grabbed at the front of his trousers. It took him a moment to realize that all was in order. Then, furious, he wheeled on me and cried, "Goddam you, Bryan!"

The WAVE leaned over him like a toppling obelisk. "Mr. Bond," she bellowed, "I do not like blasphemy and obscene gestures, and I will request your admiral to protect me from your further insults! You have been warned! Good day!"

Bond babbled, "Bryan, you—! you—!"

By now the whole room was laughing at him. Sulver and I were avenged at last.

Scene 4: Private dining room in a New York hotel, March 1947.

We ACIOs were a close-knit lot, almost like a fraternity. (Many of the friendships we made during the war have lasted for these forty years.) So when it was proposed that we hold a reunion in March 1947, some sixty of us turned up, including Bond. I hadn't seen him since ACI disbanded, soon after the surrender, and I was eager to find out if he had changed. No, it soon appeared, he hadn't. I had hardly joined the crowd when that harsh voice rasped my ear: "Well, Bryan—your name *is* Bryan, isn't it? Yes, I see now. Yes." He stood back and began scrutinizing me from head to toe, as if for a captain's inspection. "You know, I *thought* you'd look like that in civilian clothes."

Porter Sulver (not his real name) was killed in the crash of an airliner in July 1954.

George Bond died after heart surgery in September 1973.

~AFTERWORD

Before I quote Cicero (I'm trying to break the habit) and say "Go forth, my little book!" I want to anticipate a question that some readers may ask: "What, if anything, did these fourteen people have in common?"

Well, let's see. Two of them never married; the other twelve were married a total of twenty-one times (Dottie Parker married the same man twice) and had seventeen children. Fred Allen didn't drink; Art Samuels, Marc Connelly, and Sid Perelman drank moderately; the rest fairly lapped up the stuff. Seven of the fourteen went to colleges, all Ivy League. Six couldn't drive a car (I'm sure this is significant, but I don't know of what). Corey Ford was handsome; Dottie Parker had been pretty. Allen was devoutly religious; Frank Sullivan was mildly so. Bob Benchley and Ford had elfin handwritings, and Allen's typing was unique in that he never used capital letters. Only Samuels was musical, and only George Bond, a lawyer, had no connection with writing-editing. All except Hugh Troy and Allen richly enjoyed ribald stories; neither of these two ever spoke a word of obscenity, blas-

phemy, or profanity in my hearing. Hugh was enormous; Don
Stewart was big; the others were of average size. It's an interesting
coincidence, I think, that two of them were born Sullivan (Fred
Allen was the other).

The whole fourteen have two things in common: all were
wonderful company; and all—all, *alas!*—are dead. God rest their
merry souls!

J. (for "Joseph") BRYAN, III, *was born in Richmond,*
Virginia, in 1904. He graduated from Princeton in
1927, traveled in Russia, Persia, and East Africa, and
returned home, briefly, to write editorials and features
for the Richmond News Leader. *He left Richmond*
again in 1932 to work on first the Chicago Journal,
then Time, Fortune, Parade *(Cleveland),* The New
Yorker, Town and Country *(as managing editor), and*
finally The Saturday Evening Post *(as associate editor).*
He resigned from the Post *in 1940 to become a free-*
lance and has been one ever since. His articles have
appeared in all the major American magazines; and
his latest book before this one, The Windsor Story
(written in collaboration with Charles J. V. Murphy),
was a main selection of the Book of the Month Club.
After serving in the Army (1st lieutenant), Navy
(lieutenant commander), and Air Force (colonel),
Bryan returned to Richmond for good in 1959, and
lives there in a house built by his great-great-great-
grandfather.